Workshop on Evaluation of Multi-Modal Generation (EvalMG 2025)

Abu Dhabi, United Arab Emirates
20 January 2025

ISBN: 979-8-3313-1365-4

Printed from e-media with permission by:

Curran Associates, Inc.
57 Morehouse Lane
Red Hook, NY 12571

Some format issues inherent in the e-media version may also appear in this print version.

Association for Computational Linguistics
209 N. Eighth Street
Stroudsburg, Pennsylvania 18360

Phone: 1-570-476-8006
Fax: 1-570-476-0860

acl@aclweb.org

Additional copies of this publication are available from:

Curran Associates, Inc.
57 Morehouse Lane
Red Hook, NY 12571 USA
Phone: 845-758-0400
Fax: 845-758-2633
Email: curran@proceedings.com
Web: www.proceedings.com

EvalMG 2025

The Workshop of Evaluation of Multi-Modal Generation

Proceedings of the The First Workshop of Evaluation of Multi-Modal Generation

January 20, 2025

Order copies of this and other ACL proceedings from:

Association for Computational Linguistics (ACL)
209 N. Eighth Street
Stroudsburg, PA 18360
USA
Tel: +1-570-476-8006
Fax: +1-570-476-0860
acl@aclweb.org

Messages from the Organizers

Multimodal generation techniques have heralded new possibilities in creative content generation. Yet, the evaluation of such multimodal outputs remains a largely uncharted area, with fundamental questions still unresolved. These include understanding the contributions of individual modalities, the utility of pre-trained large language models in multimodal contexts, and the metrics for assessing faithfulness and fairness in generated outputs.

The first EvalMG workshop seeks to address these gaps by convening leading minds from natural language processing, computer vision, and multimodal AI. Our objective is to spearhead the development of robust evaluation methodologies that will propel further research in multimodal generation.

We received 21 submissions for this workshop, out of which 7 were accepted, including 5 long papers and 2 short papers. We have invited 11 reviewers and each submission was rigorously reviewed by at least three reviewers. The meta-reviews and final decisions were collaboratively handled by the organizing team.

We extend our deepest gratitude to all contributors—authors, reviewers, and particularly The University of Adelaide, for their generous support of this workshop. Your collective efforts are instrumental in shaping the future of multimodal research.

Organizing Committee

- Wei Emma Zhang
- Xiang Dai
- Desmond Elliot
- Byron Fang
- Haojie Zhuang
- Mong Yuan Sim
- Weitong Chen

- Necva Bölücü
- Danae Sanchez Villegas
- Wenhao Liang
- Lipin Guo
- Ali Shakeri
- Yutong Qu

Table of Contents

A Dataset for Programming-based Instructional Video Classification and Question Answering
Sana Javaid Raja, Adeel Zafar and Aqsa Shoaib 1

CVT5: Using Compressed Video Encoder and UMT5 for Dense Video Captioning
Mohammad Javad Pirhadi, Motahhare Mirzaei and Sauleh Eetemadi 10

If I feel smart, I will do the right thing: Combining Complementary Multimodal Information in Visual Language Models
Yuyu Bai and Sandro Pezzelle 24

LLaVA-RE: Binary Image-Text Relevancy Evaluation with Multimodal Large Language Model
Tao Sun, Oliver Liu, JinJin Li and Lan Ma 40

Persian in a Court: Benchmarking VLMs In Persian Multi-Modal Tasks
Farhan Farsi, Shahriar Shariati Motlagh, Shayan Bali, Sadra Sabouri and Saeedeh Momtazi 52

TaiwanVQA: A Benchmark for Visual Question Answering for Taiwanese Daily Life
Hsin-Yi Hsieh, Shang Wei Liu, Chang Chih Meng, Shuo-Yueh Lin, Chen Chien-Hua, Hung-Ju Lin, Hen-Hsen Huang and I-Chen Wu 57

Guiding Vision-Language Model Selection for Visual Question-Answering Across Tasks, Domains, and Knowledge Types
Neelabh Sinha, Vinija Jain and Aman Chadha 76

A Dataset for Programming-based Instructional Video Classification and Question Answering

Sana Javaid Raja, Adeel Zafar, Aqsa Shoaib
Faculty of Computing, Riphah International University
Correspondence: sanajavaidraja@gmail.com, adeel.zafar@riphah.edu.pk

Abstract

This work aims to develop an understanding of the rapidly emerging field of VideoQA, particularly in the context of instructional programming videos. It also encourages the designing of a system that can produce visual answers to programming-based natural language questions. We introduce two datasets: CodeVidQA, with 2,104 question-answer pair with timestamps and links taken from programming videos extracted using Stack Overflow for Programming Visual Answer Localization task, and CodeVidCL with 4,291 videos (1751 programming, 2540 non-programming) for Programming Video Classification task. In addition, we proposed a framework that adapts BigBird and SVM for video classification techniques. The proposed approach achieves a significantly high accuracy of 99.61% for video classification.

1 Introduction

One of the most interesting trends on the internet is the availability of information in the form of videos. Similarly, instructional videos have become the usual way of teaching and learning how to solve certain problems. Programming-based instructional videos have emerged and effectively convey targeted information via instructional demonstrations and voice-overs. 80% of all of those videos are in English, 2% are in Spanish and 4% are in German (Kadriu et al., 2020).

Hence, the practice of self-learning has become more convenient, especially with the availability of massive open online courses (MOOCs) (Hill, 2014). Approximately 19% to 20% of a developer's time is dedicated to using the internet for purposes of searching information for development and programming. Although more programming tutorials are being produced and used, developers are sometimes hard-pressed to find good videos that give as much coverage to actual use cases as they do to the theory behind them. For example, developers looking for specific questions may scan through many videos to find one that they want. Moreover, during tutorial sessions, language barriers may impede the learner's comprehension of the subject, especially among those whose second language is English (Brandt et al., 2009).

Despite being widely believed as popular, Video Question Answering does not escape from inherently challenging hurdles. To answer questions, VideoQA models need adequate knowledge of the visual content so they can recognize visual objects and understand their semantic, spatial, temporal, and causal relations (Khurana and Deshpande, 2021). However, information on their effectiveness remains limited, often certainly, because of the absence of proper frameworks and datasets for evaluation. Uncovering the causes behind failure in VideoQA is a tough nut to crack, either posed by the dataset or the trained model (Khurana and Deshpande, 2021).

The contributions of this work are the new CodeVidQA dataset which contains 2,104 comprehensively annotated timestamped question-answer pairs curated from videos extracted from Stack Overflow and a new dataset, CodeVidCL consists of 4,291 programming and other related videos. We also suggest that the employment of BigBird and SVM models in the structure of the ensemble would increase the efficiency of VideoQA and the classification of programming videos.

The CodeVidQA dataset facilitates advancements in VideoQA systems by offering timestamped question-answers pairs for precise video-based educational content retrieval. Similarly, the CodeVidCL dataset supports the classification and analysis of programming tutorial videos, enhancing AI-driven educational applications. Both datasets are publicly available on GitHub, promoting acces-

Proceedings of the First Workshop of Evaluation of Multi-Modal Generation, pages 1–9
January 20, 2025.

sibility and further research in the domain[1].

2 Literature survey

2.1 Existing Datasets for VideoQA

One of the first novel datasets used for VideoQA is the YouTube2Text(Guadarrama et al., 2013) dataset, including 1,987 videos and 122,708 natural language descriptions. Other similar datasets include Movie QA (Lei et al., 2019), VideoQA (Mun et al., 2017), and TVQA+ (Kim et al., 2017) covering different types of videos.

Further, MarioQA (Calzolari et al., 2020) is based on a game, Pororo-QA (Gupta et al., 2023) is based on cartoon and life scenarios like LifeQA (Lei et al., 2018) and MedVidQA (Hamon et al., 2017).

2.2 Video Question Answering in Natural Language Processing

VideoQA is an extended problem in Natural Language Processing NLP in which question answering is performed through the contents of the video sequence. It is also divided into multi-choice QA, where models choose from the options available choices, and open-ended QA which involves generation, regression, or classification (Choi et al., 2021).

The main problem of VQA is manifested in the need to accurately identify the correct answers based on the comprehension of the context of the video. For example, the proposed models process keyframes by using attention mechanisms, or apply knowledge-guided methods for further complex queries. In particular, a Siamese Sampling and Reasoning (SiaSamRea) has been proven to achieve initial success across multiple benchmarks, improving the performance on MSRVTT-QA(Xu et al., 2017), MSVD-QA(Xu et al., 2017) and Activity Net-QA(Yu et al., 2019) datasets(Yu et al., 2024).

2.3 Need for Programming-based Instructional Video QA Dataset

Simply predicting natural language answers to most of the questions don't reflect real-world interaction as people want to follow visuals step by step along with textual answers. Therefore, recent developments in video question-answering systems on specific domains like medicine, movies and games, etc. there is need to design systems that are related to programming. Although there are datasets for entertainment, such as MovieQA (Lei et al., 2019), or TVQA (Tapaswi et al., 2016), there is a lack of datasets specifically on programming instruction.

2.4 Need for Programming-Based Instructional Video Classification Dataset

A large amount of programming instructional videos are used in the learning process to develop programming skills, but there is a lack of efficient methods for classifying them that need domain-specific datasets for the Programming Video Classification task. This paper establishes that there are several methods of classifying videos through the use of video transcripts and contextual features. Specifically, Kinetics (Lopez et al., 2007) which is related to human actions and COIN (Gupta et al., 2023) which consists of 11,827 instructional videos collect from 12 domains.

3 Material and Methods

3.1 CodeVidQA Creation

The selection of several videos is required to construct a high-quality programming instructional VideoQA dataset from several general programming languages and databases such as Java, Python, JavaScript, MySQL, Oracle, and MongoDB, can be selected.

Real-life questions, such as, "How can I use queues in Laravel?" Counterarguments to the above arguments can only be effected by practical implementation, as theoretical answers to the problems can hardly be comprehended. The dataset creation process is initiated by systematically pulling questions from the Stack Overflow website, where specific questions related to programming and non-programming instructional were identified. After that annotation was performed on programming instructional videos extracted from YouTube that results in the generation of question brackets together with timestamped answers by two programming experts.

Both programming experts have more than two years of experience in developing programs and possess proficient knowledge of more than one programming language. For annotation purposes, programming instructional questions were divided equally between both experts for the formulation of the resulting dataset. The following schematic outlines the key steps involved in the methodology for the CodeVidQA dataset. Each component illustrates the processes and relationships integral to the

[1]https://github.com/sanajavaid01/codevid-datasets

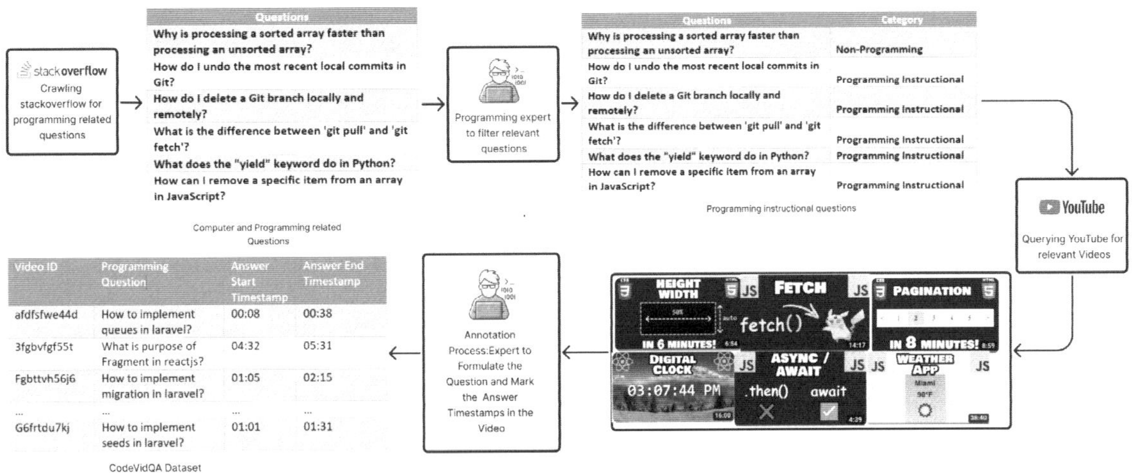

Figure 1: Schematic Overview of the Methodology for CodeVidQA Dataset

model development.

Step 1: Crawling Stack Overflow for programming questions.

Step 2: Filtering programming instructional and non-programming videos.

Step 3: Querying YouTube for relevant videos.

Step 4: Annotation Process: The expert formulates the question and marks the answer timestamps in the video.

Figure 1 shows the steps of workflow for creation of CodeVidQA Dataset.

3.1.1 Extracting Stack overflow questions

Dataset generation begins with the collection of programming-related questions from community question-answering (CQA) platforms such as Stack Overflow. As one of the largest CQA sites, Stack Overflow comprises millions of questions posted by developers.

We collected about 2,500 high-voted questions in different programming languages such as HTML, JavaScript, and Python using the Stack Overflow v2.3 API[2] without limiting by tags.Figure 2 shows the tag cloud of the tags against questions extracted from tack Overflow API. Most frequently occurring tags are JavaScript and Python which are shown in larger font depicting the large number of questions belong a specific language. These extracted questions act as topics for searching instructional videos.

[2]https://api.stackexchange.com/2.3/questions

Figure 2: Tag Cloud of frequently used tags against Stack Overflow questions

3.1.2 Identification of relevant programming-related questions

High-voted questions were collected from Stack Overflow using the API and then identified as either programming instructional or non-programming instructional. Questions like "Daylight saving time and time zone best practices" or "What is the difference between POST and PUT in HTTP?" are considered as non-instructional because they can be demonstrated through theory without any implementation. The task of categorization of the questions was done manually by the programming experts and they divided them into 1,946 'programming instructional' and 553 'non-programming instructional'. Figure 3 illustrates the distribution, questions with tags JavaScript and Python accounting for 16.9% and 14.3%, and the questions with tags Java and Git making up a part of 11% each.

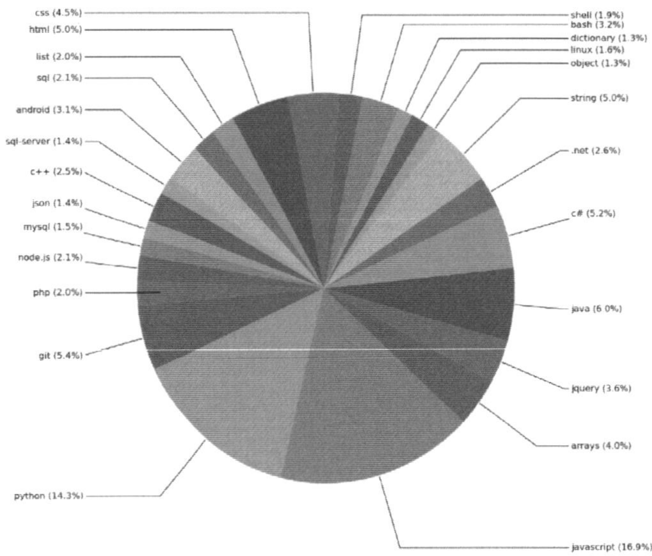

Figure 3: Distribution of the instructional programming questions category collected from Stack overflow

3.1.3 Searching YouTube Videos Relevant to Each Programming Instructional Question

The next important process in dataset construction is the process of collecting corresponding YouTube videos associated with a particular Stack Overflow question or topic. The following criteria were used for selecting videos:

i. There have to be at least a thousand subscribers of a channel from which the video will be selected.

ii. Videos should be in English since the majority of tutorials are in English (80%) then German (4%) and Spanish (2%) (Kadriu et al., 2020).

iii. Subtitles should be on and are in the English language.

iv. If a video does not contain a verbal explanation it is considered non-instructional.

v. The Integrated Development Environment(IDE) has to be used for the implementation should be observable.

For each question or topic, a YouTube search option is performed with the most relevant high-quality video. Selection is made on CONTENT only, PRESENTER's way of teaching and ANSWERS provided are all from the first page results.

3.1.4 Expert Annotation for Programming Instructional Videos

Programming experts need to identify videos as either "programming instructional" or "programming non-instructional" based on a YouTube search. This important step is necessary because:

- Retrieve videos from the search may contain theoretical communication rather than programming against a specific programming query.
- It is essential to ensure the reliability of programming videos as instructional.

To identify a programming video as instructional from the pool of YouTube videos, the following criteria should be met:

i) Programming instructional videos should demonstrate the implementation of a specific problem that is queried using YouTube search, yielding decent results for the problem.

ii) Programmers should clearly define each step of the implementation using an Integrated Development Environment (IDE) and provide reasoning for each step.

Programming instructional videos can be of any level of expertise. Most programmers begin the video with an introduction and end with concluding notes. Skip these sections while annotating videos. Only the segment of the video where the programmer provides proper steps for implementation considers the answer.

3.1.5 Formulating Instructional Questions and Visual Answers from Videos

After defining what programming instructional videos are, the following steps were followed to generate programming-related questions and mark their answers. A programming expert marked the starting and ending timestamps of the answer and formulated the question for annotated timestamps along with the identification of the programming language.Of course, the majority of questions were about implementation, But basic notes or explanations also apply to the videos, for instance, "How do I align an element to the center in the horizontal direction?"

For the majority of the cases, some questions were either different or were of the same timestamps whereby some of the tutorials provide around 15 questions. This approach serves to make questions diverse to accommodate how developers approach a problem only to find the same resulting answers or solutions.

3.1.6 Creating dataset having a question and respective answers

After formulating questions against timestamps, the programming expert has to add the video Id, question, starting timestamp, and ending timestamp along with the programming language of the video in an excel sheet. This resulted in the creation of 2,104 pairs of question and answers timestamps. The programming language feature will help the video question-answering system to search videos against a specific language if the user mentions that language in its query.

3.2 CodeVidCL Creation

A programming-based video (QA) system that aids visual answers to programming-related questions must be able to distinguish between "programming" and "non-programming" videos. For building these types of systems that can perform effectively on datasets CodeVidCL needs to be created that can train the system to differentiate between programming and non-programming videos.

In the first step, a video classifier will be trained that can be utilized to get a high-confidence video category. In the second step, programming experts validated the programming and non-programming video categories predicted by the classifier and then sampled those videos for the CodeVidCL dataset.

The following steps should be performed to achieve the proposed solution for the creation of CodeVidCL. Figure 4 shows the steps of workflow follow for the creation of CodeVidCL Dataset.

Step 1: Collecting programming and non-programming videos.

Step 2: Extracting subtitles of videos.

Step 3: Build an ensemble classifier based on Big Bird transformers.

Step 4: Get the high confidence of the video category.

Step 5: Validate predicted video categories and add them to the dataset.

3.2.1 Collecting programming and non-programming videos

To train the classifier, we need to collect programming and non-programming videos for the training dataset that can be input for fine-tuning in the classifier. We utilized 2,104 human-annotated programming videos from the CodeVidQA dataset and for non-programming videos, we sampled 3,795 videos from HowTo100M (Jang et al., 2017), which is a large-scale YouTube dataset based on instructional videos from various categories like food, art, craft, sports, cars and vehicles etc. There are total of 143 categories in HowTo100M data having 12,38,912 entries. Figure 5 shows number of entries against the top 20 categories. To remove the imbalance between programming and non-programming videos, the HowTo100M dataset was reduced to get the equally distributed entries against each category that resulted in 27 entries for each category except Diwali(26 entries), School Stuff(22 entries), Social Activism(15 entries)and National Days(6 entries) categories.

3.2.2 Extracting subtitles for all video

A total of 6,104 collected videos in previous are taken and pass to YouTube API to get subtitles. We use the YouTube-transcript-API[3] module of Python to get subtitles of video along with many words.

Most of the videos have to disable transcripts or use a language other than English for transcribing. This type of video is eliminated from the dataset based on the number of words. After doing all the data cleaning, add one more column in the Python dataframe with name category (programming, non-programming) and class (1, 0).Using a stratified

[3]https://pypi.org/project/youtube-transcript-api/

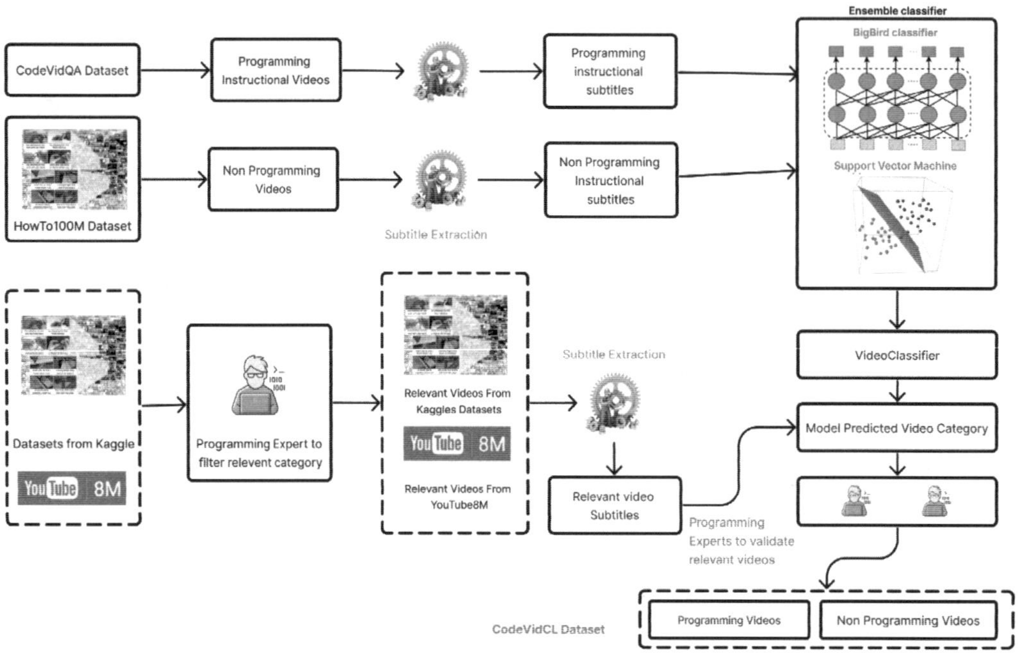

Figure 4: Diagrammatic Representation of the Methodology for CodeVidCL Dataset

Table 1: Performance metrics for different models

Models	Accuracy	Precision	Recall	F1 Score
BigBird (bigbird-roberta-large)	99.61%	99.05	99.01	99.50
SVM	99.80%	99.81	99.81	99.81

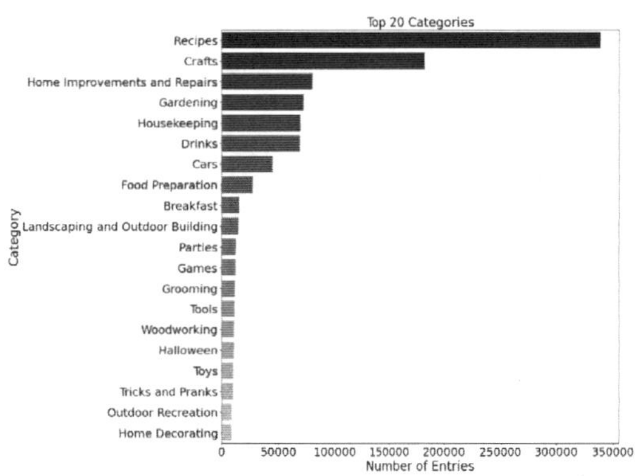

Figure 5: Number of Entries against top 20 Categories of HowTo100M

splitting, we utilized 20 % for testing, and 80 % of the videos in the collection for training purposes.

3.2.3 Building Video Classifier

In the next step, a classifier is trained on training dataset videos that are created in the previous step. The subtitles are first extracted here because they can be longer than 2000-3000 words. A classifier based on a transformer, the BigBird(Zaheer et al., 2020) model by Hugging Face [4] and SVM are trained. SVM was used as a statistical classifier that is effective for categorization tasks, especially when the data is structured and separable into distinct categories, which fits well for coarse-grained categorization.BigBird was chosen as a deep learning classifier due to its capability to handle long-range dependencies and accommodate long sequences like subtitles from videos. BigBird is suitable for capturing context from the sequential nature of subtitles, which is common in videos. The models above were combined in the ensemble classifier, and majority voting is apply in making the final forecasts. The subtitles were extremely lengthy and hence, it was crucial to work with large-grained categories such as programming and non-programming.

BigBird is designed for sequence processing and training on PyTorch. To combat class imbalance, class weights were modified, early stopping was

[4] https://huggingface.co/google/bigbird-roberta-large

used and a variable learning rate was implemented. Training settings were warm-up scheduler with 5 steps, weight decay of 0.0001, gradient accumulation with 4 steps and mixed precision activated by fp16. This model was trained for one epoch with a batch size of four and was evaluated every 20 steps.

Labels in the SVM were represented numerically, and the TF-IDF was used as features and balanced class to address the issue of imbalance. Predictive probabilities of the class distribution were computed and the final Classifier uses votes between BigBird and SVM predictions for accurate classification. This approach enhances the performance of these models making them a hybrid. Table 1, shows the accuracies of fine-tuned BigBird and SVM.

3.2.4 Identification of relevant video

We selected a subset of YouTube8M's(Abu-El-Haija et al., 2016) computer-related, non-programming videos as well as other Kaggle datasets that have been expertly categorized by programmers.

We built a subset from YouTube8M and different Kaggle datasets, such as YouTube data science[5] and YouTube programming videos from free code camp[6], TED-ED[7], and caption datasets[8], after training our ensemble model. 5,722 videos were produced overall from this procedure, of which 3,120 were classified as programming and 2,602 as non-programming.

3.2.5 Predicting Relevant Video Category Using Video Classifier

In this step, we utilized an ensemble setting for predicting videos with a high confidence vote on the category for the dataset gathered in the previous step. The ensemble classifier predicted 1,751 programming videos and 2,540 non-programming videos. To create a high-quality dataset, programming experts only chose those videos to which the classifier gives high confidence in the category.

3.2.6 Sampling High-Quality Video

In the last step, videos with a predicted category and high confidence are validated and chosen by programming experts to create a high-quality CodeVidCL dataset. This dataset contains the video title, video Id, video category, subtitle, and number of words in subtitles for each video.

4 Results & Analysis

4.1 CodeVidQA Analysis and Validation

When building CodeVidQA, we aim to compile reliable programming courses from YouTube only. This way we can say that a video is reliable if it has more than a thousand subscribers, from a reliable programming institute, from a famous programmer or famous programming platforms like W3Schools, Treehouse, etc. We collected 2,500 questions about programming from Stack Overflow, selecting only those that contain the instructions that can be illustrated in an IDE. Such theoretical questions as those which do not require an answer in instructional situations were not included. The second phase only included the instructional questions, therefore, we have 2,104 paired questions and visual answers obtained from 1, 363 instructional videos, making up 132 hours of video. Figure 7 and Figure 8 show the answer duration of videos in seconds and the distribution of question length in CodeVidQA dataset respectively. For Python alone, more than 400 pairs were produced and this was trailed by both JavaScript and Flutter. Figure 6 shows the number of question answers key pairs against programming language.

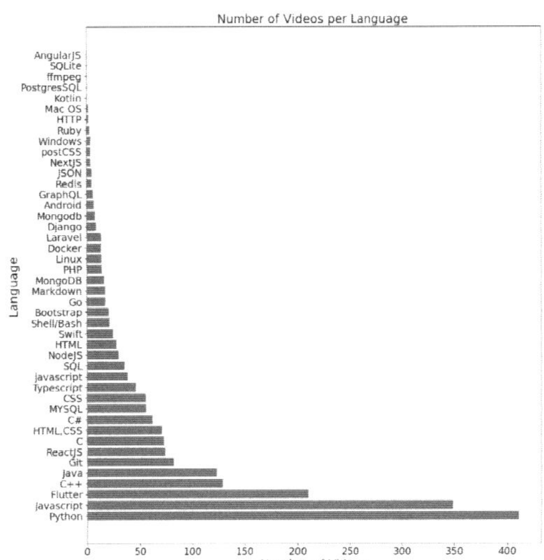

Figure 6: Number of videos against each programming language in CodeVidQA

For evaluation,100 questions are sampled that

[5]https://www.kaggle.com/datasets/sandhyakrishnan02/youtube-datascience-video-views

[6]https://www.kaggle.com/datasets/nuhmanpk/all-programming-tutorial-from-free-code-camp

[7]https://www.kaggle.com/datasets/hadilhagar/ted-ed-dataset-acquired-via-youtube-api

[8]https://www.kaggle.com/datasets/shivendrra/youtube-caption-dataset-for-finetuning-or-training

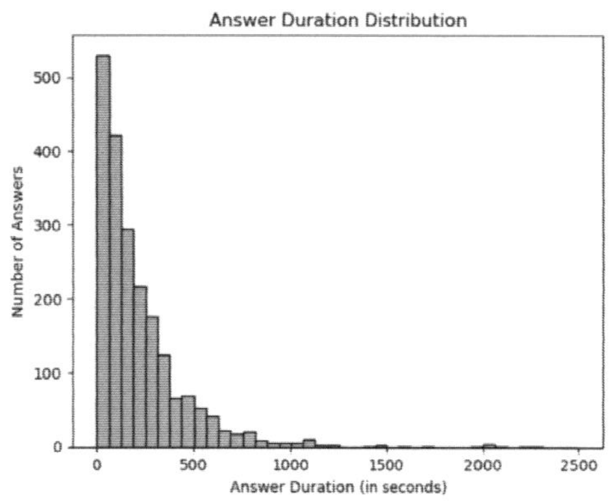

Figure 7: Answer Duration Distribution of CodeVidQA

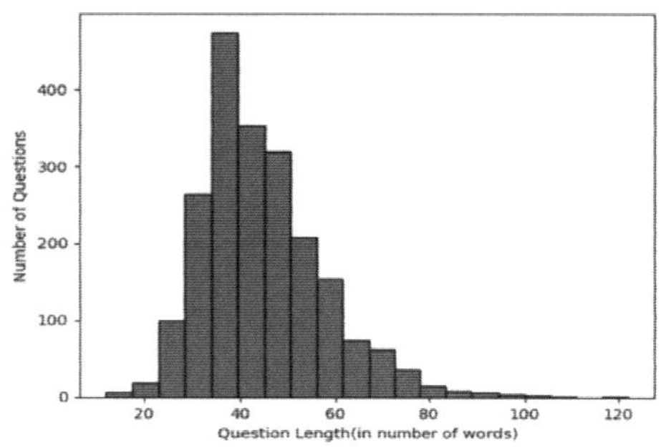

Figure 8: Question Length Distribution of CodeVidQA

are extracted from Stackoverflow and two programming experts categorize them as instructional or non-instructional. After categorizing those both programmers are in same agreement except for a few questions upon which theoretical and practical demonstration can be given. To validate the dataset, 50 videos are sampled and ask both programming experts to annotate answers along with the formulation of questions. Semantic similarity of formulated questions were assessed and the absolute differences between answers timestamped were calculated. The second assessment validates their agreement on proving the precise and valid answer timestamps from the videos. We found that both the annotators formulated 80 and 67 questions, and 54 out of them were semantically similar. The CodeVidQA dataset's quality is confirmed by these evaluations.

4.2 CodeVidCL Analysis and Validation

To construct the CodeVidCL dataset, we took a selection of human-annotated programming instructional videos from the CodeVidQA dataset and non-programming videos from HowTo100M dataset that is used as the training set for the CodeVidCL dataset. To generate a validation and test set, we sampled high-confidence videos that a video classifier had predicted. To further evaluate CodeVidCL dataset, we asked both the programming experts to look over the video category that the model had predicted on a dataset created from YouTube8M and different Kaggle datasets .

The experts asked to update the category and label videos as non-relevant if there is insufficient data to categorize them into any of the categories in case the video classifier incorrectly classifies them. The final CodeVidCL collection contains 4291 videos, 2540 of which are non -programming videos and the remaining ones are programming.

5 Conclusion

One of the most famous and actively developing methods of obtaining knowledge is the use of online instructional videos, especially in programming. Video Question Answering (VideoQA) is an essential research domain, that focuses on equipping AI with the ability to interpret and engage with visual information using natural language. However, VideoQA is significantly less investigated than Image-QA, which creates difficulties for models to understand the content of videos and to answer the queries. To fill these gaps, this research proposes two datasets, CodeVidQA and CodeVidCL for programming instructional video question answering and classification.

CodeVidQA contains 2,104 entries where each entry represents an expert-curated programming question-answers pair along with a video Id. Moreover, up to 99.61% accuracy has been achieved after the training of the BigBird model and SVM for the creation of the CodeVidCL dataset. These results not only prove the applicability of the proposed datasets but also open the research avenue for the enhancements of future VideoQA systems regarding the preciseness of response and richness of the learning experience in programming through videos.

6 Limitations

The existing dataset covers only a limited set of programming languages for video classification and question answering. A larger and more diverse dataset, such as CodeVidQA and CodeVidCL, which spans a broad range of programming topics, is needed. Additionally, result explainability is a significant factor, as current models do not identify the features that contribute to their predictions.

References

Sami Abu-El-Haija, Nisarg Kothari, Joonseok Lee, Paul Natsev, George Toderici, Balakrishnan Varadarajan, and Sudheendra Vijayanarasimhan. 2016. Youtube-8m: A large-scale video classification benchmark. *arXiv preprint arXiv:1609.08675*.

Joel Brandt, Philip J Guo, Joel Lewenstein, Mira Dontcheva, and Scott R Klemmer. 2009. Two studies of opportunistic programming: interleaving web foraging, learning, and writing code. In *Proceedings of the SIGCHI Conference on Human Factors in Computing Systems*, pages 1589–1598.

Nicoletta Calzolari, Frédéric Béchet, Philippe Blache, Khalid Choukri, Christopher Cieri, Thierry Declerck, Sara Goggi, Hitoshi Isahara, Bente Maegaard, Joseph Mariani, et al. 2020. Proceedings of the twelfth language resources and evaluation conference. In *Proceedings of the Twelfth Language Resources and Evaluation Conference*.

Seongho Choi, Kyoung-Woon On, Yu-Jung Heo, Ahjeong Seo, Youwon Jang, Minsu Lee, and Byoung-Tak Zhang. 2021. Dramaqa: Character-centered video story understanding with hierarchical qa. In *Proceedings of the AAAI Conference on Artificial Intelligence*, volume 35, pages 1166–1174.

Sergio Guadarrama, Niveda Krishnamoorthy, Girish Malkarnenkar, Subhashini Venugopalan, Raymond Mooney, Trevor Darrell, and Kate Saenko. 2013. Youtube2text: Recognizing and describing arbitrary activities using semantic hierarchies and zero-shot recognition. In *Proceedings of the 2013 IEEE International Conference on Computer Vision*, ICCV '13, page 2712–2719, USA. IEEE Computer Society.

Deepak Gupta, Kush Attal, and Dina Demner-Fushman. 2023. A dataset for medical instructional video classification and question answering. *Scientific Data*, 10(1):158.

Thierry Hamon, Natalia Grabar, and Fleur Mougin. 2017. Querying biomedical linked data with natural language questions. *Semantic Web*, 8(4):581–599.

Phil Hill. 2014. Online educational delivery models: A descriptive view.

Yunseok Jang, Yale Song, Youngjae Yu, Youngjin Kim, and Gunhee Kim. 2017. Tgif-qa: Toward spatio-temporal reasoning in visual question answering. In *Proceedings of the IEEE conference on computer vision and pattern recognition*, pages 2758–2766.

Arbana Kadriu, Lejla Abazi-Bexheti, Hyrije Abazi-Alili, and Veland Ramadani. 2020. Investigating trends in learning programming using youtube tutorials. *International Journal of Learning and Change*, 12(2):190–208.

Khushboo Khurana and Umesh Deshpande. 2021. Video question-answering techniques, benchmark datasets and evaluation metrics leveraging video captioning: a comprehensive survey. *IEEE Access*, 9:43799–43823.

Kyung-Min Kim, Min-Oh Heo, Seong-Ho Choi, and Byoung-Tak Zhang. 2017. Deepstory: Video story qa by deep embedded memory networks. *arXiv preprint arXiv:1707.00836*.

Jie Lei, Licheng Yu, Mohit Bansal, and Tamara L Berg. 2018. Tvqa: Localized, compositional video question answering. *arXiv preprint arXiv:1809.01696*.

Jie Lei, Licheng Yu, Tamara L Berg, and Mohit Bansal. 2019. Tvqa+: Spatio-temporal grounding for video question answering. *arXiv preprint arXiv:1904.11574*.

Vanessa Lopez, Victoria Uren, Enrico Motta, and Michele Pasin. 2007. Aqualog: An ontology-driven question answering system for organizational semantic intranets. *Journal of Web Semantics*, 5(2):72–105.

Jonghwan Mun, Paul Hongsuck Seo, Ilchae Jung, and Bohyung Han. 2017. Marioqa: Answering questions by watching gameplay videos. In *Proceedings of the IEEE International Conference on Computer Vision*, pages 2867–2875.

Makarand Tapaswi, Yukun Zhu, Rainer Stiefelhagen, Antonio Torralba, Raquel Urtasun, and Sanja Fidler. 2016. Movieqa: Understanding stories in movies through question-answering. In *Proceedings of the IEEE conference on computer vision and pattern recognition*, pages 4631–4640.

Dejing Xu, Zhou Zhao, Jun Xiao, Fei Wu, Hanwang Zhang, Xiangnan He, and Yueting Zhuang. 2017. Video question answering via gradually refined attention over appearance and motion. In *Proceedings of the 25th ACM international conference on Multimedia*, pages 1645–1653.

Weijiang Yu, Haoteng Zheng, Mengfei Li, Lei Ji, Lijun Wu, Nong Xiao, and Nan Duan. 2024. Learning from inside: self-driven siamese sampling and reasoning for video question answering. In *Proceedings of the 35th International Conference on Neural Information Processing Systems*, NIPS '21, Red Hook, NY, USA. Curran Associates Inc.

Zhou Yu, Dejing Xu, Jun Yu, Ting Yu, Zhou Zhao, Yueting Zhuang, and Dacheng Tao. 2019. Activitynet-qa: A dataset for understanding complex web videos via question answering. *Preprint*, arXiv:1906.02467.

Manzil Zaheer, Guru Guruganesh, Kumar Avinava Dubey, Joshua Ainslie, Chris Alberti, Santiago Ontanon, Philip Pham, Anirudh Ravula, Qifan Wang, Li Yang, et al. 2020. Big bird: Transformers for longer sequences. *Advances in neural information processing systems*, 33:17283–17297.

CVT5: Using Compressed Video Encoder and UMT5 for Dense Video Captioning

Mohammad Javad Pirhadi[1], Motahhare Mirzaei[1] and Sauleh Eetemadi[2]

[1]Iran University of Science and Technology, [2]University of Birmingham Dubai
mohammad_pirhadi@comp.iust.ac.ir, m_mirzaei96@comp.iust.ac.ir,
s.eetemadi@bham.ac.uk

Abstract

The dense video captioning task aims to detect all events occurring in a video and describe each event using natural language. Unlike most other video processing tasks, where it is typically assumed that videos contain only a single main event, this task deals with long, untrimmed videos. Consequently, the speed of processing videos in dense video captioning is a critical aspect of the system. To the best of our knowledge, all published work on this task uses RGB frames to encode input videos. In this work, we introduce the use of compressed videos for the first time in this task. Our experiments on the SoccerNet challenge demonstrate significant improvements in both processing speed and GPU memory footprint while achieving competitive results. Additionally, we leverage multilingual transcripts, which seems to be effective. The encoder in our proposed method achieves approximately $5.4\times$ higher speed and $5.1\times$ lower GPU memory usage during training, and $4.7\times$ higher speed and $7.8\times$ lower GPU memory usage during inference, compared to its RGB-based counterpart. The code is publicly available at https://github.com/mohammadjavadpirhadi/CVT5.

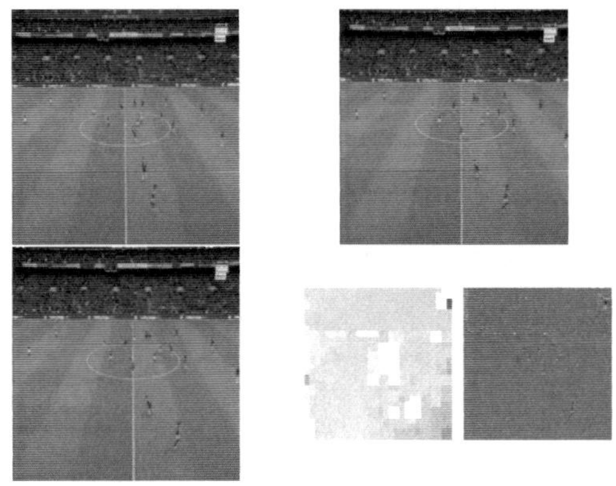

(a) (b)

Figure 1: Comparison between two consecutive RGB (left) and compressed frames (right). The upper frames are identical and are the first frame of a video. The lower frames are the second frames of the same video. In the compressed format, the left frame represents the motion vector, and the right frame represents the residual.

1 Introduction

In the video captioning task, the input video is typically assumed to be very short, containing only one main event. The desired output in this case is a textual description of that event. However, this assumption does not hold for most real-world scenarios, where input videos are long, and multiple events occur at different times. The dense video captioning task, first introduced by Krishna et al. (2017), aims to detect all events in a long, untrimmed video and generate a description for each event using natural language. This task is challenging because the model must not only recognize objects in the video but also understand the actions and interactions between them. Solving this task bridges the fields of computer vision and natural language processing, attracting increasing attention. Dense video captioning has potential applications for blind people, human-robot interaction, and more. However, the proposed methods must be fast and accurate, enabling the system to detect and describe events in a timely manner using reasonable computational resources.

To the best of our knowledge, all existing methods for dense video captioning use RGB frames to encode the input video. However, there is a significant amount of redundancy between consecutive RGB frames since most of the pixels remain unchanged. This redundancy demands considerable processing time and resources while providing minimal additional information. Video compression methods like H.264 significantly reduce the resources required for storage and transmission by keeping only a few frames intact and reconstructing

Proceedings of the First Workshop of Evaluation of Multi-Modal Generation, pages 10–23
January 20, 2025. ©2025 Association for Computational Linguistics

the others using motion vectors and residuals. For instance, consider a video corresponding to half of a match in the SoccerNet dataset (Mkhallati et al., 2023). With a frame rate of 2 frames per second (FPS) and a resolution of 224×224, the video consists of 5,400 frames, requiring over $775MB$ of storage without compression. However, compression reduces this size to approximately $78.5MB$ making it about $10\times$ smaller. Figure 1 illustrates the comparison between two consecutive frames when using RGB frames versus compressed ones.

To address these challenges, we propose an end-to-end CNN-Transformer model to generate dense captions using videos in the compressed domain. Compressed videos consist of I-frames, motion vectors, and residuals, with minimal redundancy between consecutive frames. As a result, our model processes videos more efficiently, requiring less time and fewer resources during both training and inference. Additionally, we extract and utilize multilingual transcripts of the input video, which, as our experiments show, positively impact the results.

The contributions of this paper are summarized as follows:

1. We propose an end-to-end CNN-Transformer model for solving the dense video captioning task.

2. We leverage multilingual transcripts of the videos.

3. Our experiments on the SoccerNet dataset demonstrate significant improvements in processing speed during both training ($5.4\times$) and inference ($4.7\times$), along with a substantial reduction in GPU memory usage during both training ($5.1\times$) and inference ($7.8\times$).

2 Related Work

2.1 Dense Video Captioning

Most previous work on dense video captioning follows a two-stage approach: first, event proposals are generated, and then captions are created for these events. E2vid (Huang et al., 2020) separately extracts text and video features and passes them to a decoder to generate captions. The video frame features are extracted using a pretrained vision model on each RGB frame individually, which are then passed through a transformer. This paper employs three different pretraining tasks: text, text-video, and segment alignment and ordering. Similarly, PDVC (Wang et al., 2021) uses a pretrained RGB frame encoder followed by a transformer, along with N learnable queries to generate N events. After predicting the number of events in the video, it selects the most probable proposals as final events. This work utilizes a deformable transformer (Zhu et al., 2020) for faster convergence. GVL (Wang et al., 2023) also employs learnable queries after extracting features from RGB frames. This paper extracts features from ground truth labels and trains the model using two tasks: event-to-text generation and text-to-event generation and introduce semantic cost in addition to localization cost to enhance robustness against annotation noise. Vid2Seq (Yang et al., 2023) leverages a vast amount of YouTube videos available in the HowTo100M (Miech et al., 2019) and YT-Temporal-1B (Zellers et al., 2022) datasets to pretrain a transformer model with two objectives: generation and denoising. A key contribution of this work is the use of time tokens to generate events in a single stage, which proves effective. In our work, we utilize the common two-stage model as training a model for directly predicting event times requires a substantial amount of data.

2.2 Compressed Video Processing

Compressed videos have primarily been used in the action recognition task. Wu et al. (2017) first demonstrated that processing videos in the compressed domain improves both model speed and accuracy in the context of action recognition. Previous work on compressed domain action recognition can be categorized into three main approaches: using I-frames + residuals (e.g. Battash et al., 2020 and Abdari et al., 2019), using I-frames + motion vectors (e.g. Wang and Torresani, 2022 and He et al., 2022), and using I-frames + motion vectors + residuals (e.g. Wu et al., 2017 and Mou et al., 2024). There are also a few rare works that utilize macro-blocks (e.g. Chadha et al., 2017) or DCT coefficients (e.g. Ming et al., 2023). However, the common methods primarily rely on the three main categories mentioned above. Our best model uses I-frames and motion vectors only, as our experiments show that, at least for the SoccerNet dataset, including residuals has a negative effect.

3 Method

As mentioned above, the goal of our proposed method is to leverage compressed videos to en-

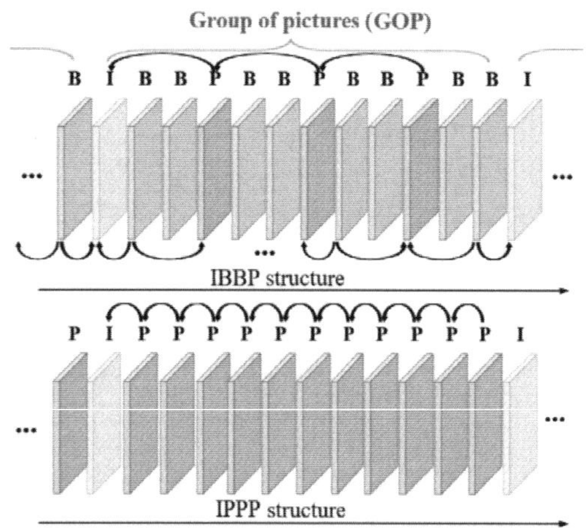

Figure 2: Two different possible structures of compressed videos. P-frames only refer to their previous frame, while B-frames can refer to any frame before or after them within their GOP. (Ming et al., 2024)

hance processing speed and reduce GPU memory usage. To achieve this, we first explain the structure of compressed videos in section 3.1. Then, we introduce the proposed model in section 3.2.

3.1 Compressed Video Structure

Modern video codecs like H.264 utilize temporal redundancy between successive video frames to compress video data. These codecs break down the video into multiple groups of pictures (GOPs) based on the differences between frames. Each GOP can be reconstructed independently without relying on other GOPs. Higher rates of change result in smaller GOPs, while lower rates of change produce larger GOPs. The first frame of each GOP is always an I-frame, which is a complete RGB image that can be reconstructed independently. The remaining frames can be either P-frames (predictive coded frames) or B-frames (bi-predictive coded frames). Both types of frames consist of a motion vector and a residual. The motion vector represents the movement of each macro-block in the current frame relative to the reference frame, and the residual captures the difference in color between frames after applying the motion vector to the reference frame. The reconstruction process can be formulated as follows:

$$F_{rec} = ApplyMV(F_{ref}, mv) + res \quad (1)$$

where F_{rec} is the reconstructed frame, $ApplyMV$ applies the motion vector to the reference frame, F_{ref} is the reference frame, mv is the motion vector and res is the residual. Each macro-block typically consists of a group of 4×4 pixels, so the number of elements in the motion vector is $16\times$ lower than in the original RGB frame. The difference between P-frames and B-frames is that a B-frame can refer to any frame before or after it within its GOP, whereas a P-frame only refers to the previous frame. Using B-frames provides higher compression rates but makes it more challenging for the model to learn patterns. Therefore, we configure the FFMPEG package (Tomar, 2006) to use only P-frames.

3.2 Model Architecture

Figure 3 presents an overview of the proposed architecture. After preprocessing, extracting I-frames, motion vectors, and residuals, and dividing the input video into chunks, each chunk is processed through the following stages: 1. Encoding I-frames, motion vectors, and residuals separately. 2. Encoding the past, present, and future periods separately using a common transformer encoder (Vaswani et al., 2017). 3. Encoding the entire chunk and predicting each event individually. 4. If an event has occurred, generating a caption using the encoded frames of the entire chunk and transcript features from the present period.

Each of these steps is explained in more detail in the following sections.

3.2.1 Preprocess Videos

First, we preprocess the original videos using the FFMPEG package. After this processing, the videos are H.264 encoded, include only I-frames and P-frames, and have a resolution of 224×224 with a frame rate of 2. Typically, the H.264 codec creates GOPs of varying lengths based on the rate of change between frames. We investigated the impact of this behavior by comparing it to a setup where we enforced a GOP size equal to our short memory length. The experiments indicate that using a dynamic GOP size benefits the model. For more details, refer to section 4.6.3.

3.2.2 Extract I/P-frames

We extract I-frames, motion vectors, and residuals using the tool described in (Shen, 2023). I-frames and residuals are saved in .jpg format, while motion vectors are saved in .png format. This is because

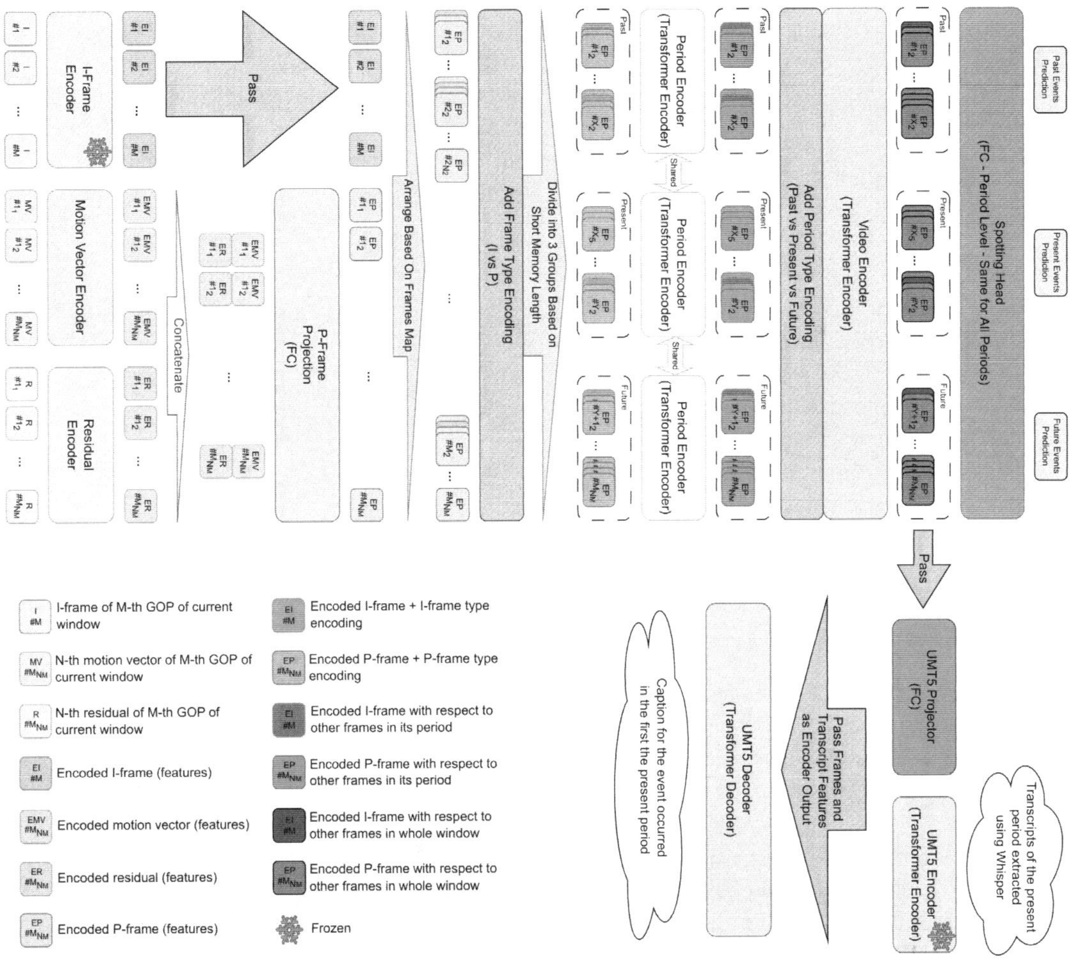

Figure 3: Architecture overview. The process involves multiple stages: Encoding I-frames, motion vectors, and residuals separately; Encoding the past, present, and future periods using a common transformer encoder; Encoding the entire chunk and predicting events individually; and, if any event occurs, generating captions using the encoded frames of the entire chunk and transcript features from the present period.

motion vectors are more sensitive to noise, which can be damaged through .jpg compression.

3.2.3 Extract I-frames Features

We use the pooler output of the CLIP-vit-base-patch32 model (Radford et al., 2021), available on HuggingFace (Wolf et al., 2020). Given that soccer game frames share many common elements, such as the ball, players, and pitch, we selected the CLIP model over ResNet (He et al., 2015). CLIP is more likely to provide well-distinguishable features for different frames of a soccer game due to its training on image-caption pairs, which consider the relative positions of entities within an image—important for generating captions. In contrast, ResNet is trained solely to predict the presence of a class in an image. To expedite the training process, we save the extracted features to disk.

3.2.4 Extract Transcripts Features

Since the videos are multilingual, we extract their transcripts using the Whisper-large-v3 model (Radford et al., 2022), which can detect the language of the input audio and perform automatic speech recognition (ASR). We utilize the 'return_timestamps' argument of this model to obtain the timestamps for transcript chunks. These timestamps are then used to align the transcript chunks with the corresponding video frames. To extract features from the transcripts, we first divide them into chunks and then use the UMT5 encoder (Chung et al., 2023) , a multilingual version of T5. As with the video features, we save the extracted transcript features to expedite the training process.

3.2.5 Video Encoder

The video encoder has three stages:

1. Encode frames individually: I-frame features are pre-extracted. Motion vectors and residuals are encoded using two separate ResNet-18 models as they can be processed using lightweight neural networks. Each frame in the current chunk is encoded using its respective encoder. The motion vectors and residuals of a P-frame are concatenated and projected to match the I-frame feature size using a fully connected layer. Finally, frames are arranged according to their positions in the original video.

2. Encode periods: Frame type encodings, which are learnable and help the model differentiate between I-frames and P-frames, are added to the frames. The frames are then divided into three periods (past, present, future) of equal size (short memory length). A common period encoder, a transformer encoder, is used to encode the frames within each period concerning each other.

3. Encode the whole chunk: Period type encodings, which are learnable and help the model distinguish different periods, are added. A final transformer encoder encodes the frames of the entire chunk with respect to each other.

Note that all transformer encoders are standard, utilizing sinusoidal positional encoding.

3.2.6 Event Spotting

A fully connected layer with a sigmoid activation function is applied to the mean of the encoded frames of each period to predict whether an event has occurred in the current period. The present period is the primary focus, while the past and future periods aid in feature extraction. A softmax is not used because events can occur simultaneously (e.g., a penalty and a yellow card).

3.2.7 Decoder

The decoder uses the UMT5 architecture and pretrained weights to generate captions. The input consists of encoded video frames concatenated with transcript features from the present period in time dimension. The output is the caption corresponding to the present period. Multiple captions for different events within the same period are separated by the '@' symbol. The decoder is trained solely on positive samples.

4 Experiments

All experiments were conducted using a single NVIDIA A100-SXM4-80GB GPU.

4.1 Two-stage Training

We use a standard two-stage training process: first, training the encoder and the spotting head, then freezing them and fine-tuning the decoder. End-to-end training yielded worse results. In the first stage, a weighted random sampling strategy is used, and in the second stage, all positive samples are utilized.

4.2 Sampling Strategy

As mentioned earlier, the video is divided into chunks of length equal to the short memory length (a hyperparameter). The model is also provided with the previous and next chunks to utilize past and future information. The SoccerNet dataset is highly imbalanced, with far fewer chunks containing events than those without. To mitigate this, we assign higher weights to positive samples during sampling. The weights are calculated as follows:

$$ew_c = (E - E_c)/E \tag{2}$$

$$w_i = \sum_{c=0}^{C} y_{i_c} \times ew_c \tag{3}$$

where E is the total number of events in chunks, E_c is the number of events in class c, ew_c is the weight of event class c, y_{i_c} is the c-th class of the i-th sample's label, and w_i is i-th sample's weight.

And negative sample weights are calculated as follows:

$$nw = \sum_{i=0}^{N} w_i/NS \tag{4}$$

$$w_i = nw/NS \tag{5}$$

where nw is the total weight of the negative samples, which equals the total weight of positive samples, and NS is the number of negative samples. As a result, each epoch contains an equal number of positive and negative samples.

4.3 Loss Function

Despite this sampling strategy, the model still encounters more zeros than ones, as the number of ones in a label is significantly smaller. Therefore, we use the focal loss function to further address the dataset imbalance, experimenting with different values of alpha while keeping gamma fixed at 2.

4.4 Implementation Details

Our model is implemented using PyTorch. As mentioned, videos are resized to 224×224 resulting in motion vectors of size 56×56 and residuals of size 224×224. The residuals are resized to 56×56 to match the size of the motion vectors. For ablation studies, the model is trained on the SoccerNet training set and evaluated on the validation set. Each training epoch in this phase contains 18,000 samples. For comparison with state-of-the-art models, the model is trained on the combined training, validation, and test sets and evaluated on the challenge set using the Eval.ai platform (EvalAI). Each training epoch in this part has 29000 samples for the first training stage. Each training epoch in this phase contains 29,000 samples. The batch size is fixed at 16 for all experiments. Both the period encoder and the video encoder are 2-layer transformer encoders with a hidden size of 1536 and 32 attention heads. We use the AdamW (Loshchilov and Hutter, 2017) optimizer with $\beta_1 = 0.9$ and $\beta_1 = 0.999$. The cosine learning rate scheduler starts from $1e - 4$ and ends at 0.35 of the cosine cycle, yielding a final learning rate of $2e - 5$.

4.5 Evaluation Metrics

We use the SoccerNet challenge metrics: METEOR, BLEU@1, BLEU@2, BLEU@3, BLEU@4, ROUGE_L, CIDEr, recall, and precision. BLEU@N measures n-gram precision, METEOR assesses semantic accuracy, ROUGE evaluates word order, and CIDEr measures the degree to which the caption conveys key information.

4.6 Ablation Study

We conducted multiple ablation studies to evaluate the impact of various changes on model performance. The best model from each part was selected for further evaluation. In the tables, **bold = best**, underline = second best, TS = 1 stage training or 2 stage training, SML = short memory length, GOP = size of each group of pictures, Res = Use residuals, Trans = Use transcripts.

4.6.1 Residuals and Transcripts

The first experiment assessed the usefulness of residuals and transcripts. We tested all four possible combinations, and Table 1 shows the results.

As shown, using residuals degrades the model accuracy a lot, possibly because this reason: as residuals have visual structure as I-frames and the differences between successive frames in soccer videos are negligible, the residuals cannot add any information.

Using transcripts, however, can be beneficial, as indicated by the higher CIDEr score, which reflects better key point capture in generated captions. Other metrics can be ignored for comparison, as they are nearly identical and do not follow a consistent pattern.

4.6.2 Short Memory Length

We cannot use a short memory length greater than 60 (30s) as the challenge evaluation uses a 30s window around the ground truth. Table 2 shows the results for two different short memory lengths.

Most metrics improve with a short memory length of 60 as a larger chunk size provides the model with more information for caption generation.

4.6.3 GOP Size

As mentioned earlier, the H.264 codec typically uses a dynamic GOP (Group of Pictures) size, which adjusts according to the frequency of changes between successive frames. A higher frequency of changes results in a smaller GOP size, leading to more I-frames in areas with significant changes, and vice versa. To evaluate the impact of this, we conducted an experiment where we forced the FFMPEG package to set the GOP size to a short memory length. Table 3 presents the results.

The results demonstrate that forcing a short GOP size significantly degrades performance, particularly in the CIDEr metric, which measures the alignment of key concepts. Thus, allowing FFMPEG to use a dynamic GOP size is beneficial for the model's performance.

4.6.4 Two Stage Training

We also investigated whether a two-stage training approach is more effective than training the model all at once. As shown in Table 4, two-stage training yields better results. This is because negative samples can negatively impact the decoder component of the model when trained simultaneously.

TS	SML	GOP	Res	Trans	α	B@1	B@2	B@3	B@4	M	R@L	C	recall	precision
2	60	auto	✗	✗	0.9	33.29	**27.50**	**24.11**	**21.63**	19.21	**26.40**	18.38	82.95	**62.11**
2	60	auto	✗	✓	0.9	**33.30**	27.17	23.63	21.05	**19.87**	26.31	**19.23**	82.92	**62.11**
2	60	auto	✓	✗	0.9	30.24	25.13	22.28	20.09	18.00	22.48	13.61	**91.86**	60.30
2	60	auto	✓	✓	0.9	30.01	25.48	22.83	20.78	17.71	23.61	15.98	**91.86**	60.29

Table 1: Ablation study about impact of using residuals and transcripts.

TS	SML	GOP	Res	Trans	α	B@1	B@2	B@3	B@4	M	R@L	C	recall	precision
2	60	auto	✗	✓	0.9	**33.30**	27.17	23.63	21.05	**19.87**	**26.31**	**19.23**	82.92	**62.11**
2	40	auto	✗	✓	0.9	32.33	**27.22**	**24.17**	**21.85**	19.11	25.16	17.03	**91.61**	59.44

Table 2: Ablation study about impact of different length of short memory.

4.6.5 Focal Loss Alpha

We experimented with three different values of the alpha parameter in focal loss. The results indicate that a higher alpha increases recall at the cost of lower precision, and vice versa. According to Table 5 the optimal alpha value is 0.6. The experiments reveal a strong correlation between precision and generation metrics.

4.6.6 Generation Method

Initially, we observed that samples with multiple events often resulted in empty captions. We examined whether filtering these out would be beneficial. Additionally, we experimented with different generation strategies, including beam search and top-k+top-p sampling. Table 6 shows that the best configuration is to use greedy generation while ignoring blank captions.

4.7 Comparison with RGB

To assess the utility of using compressed videos, we compared our proposed model with an RGB variant where original RGB frames were used instead of I/P-frames. Results in Table 7 show that our proposed method achieves competitive results compared to its RGB variant.

Moreover, to understand the impact of using compressed videos on speed and GPU memory consumption, we conducted another comparison against the RGB variant. The results in Table 8 indicate approximately $5.4\times$ faster training speed and $5.1\times$ lower GPU memory usage, as well as $4.7\times$ faster inference speed and $7.8\times$ lower GPU memory usage compared to the RGB-based approach, which is significant. These results were obtained using the PyTorch profiler.

4.8 Comparison with SOTA methods

We evaluated our proposed model against state-of-the-art (SOTA) models on the challenge set of the SoccerNet dataset. The evaluation was conducted using the best configuration, which includes two-stage training, a short memory length of 60, auto GOP size, no residuals, inclusion of transcripts, a focal loss alpha of 0.6, and greedy generation while ignoring blank captions.

Table 9 presents the results, where our model ranks second in almost all metrics and exhibits performance comparable to SOTA models. Once again, a positive correlation between precision and generation metrics is evident. These results suggest that compressed video retains most of the necessary information with minimal redundancy.

4.9 Qualitative Results

As discussed in the appendix, Table 10 provides examples comparing the model's output to the ground truth, highlighting the model's bias towards corner events and events with no comments. Similar results are shown in Figure 4, which presents the confusion matrix. Further examples, along with frames from the time intervals used for predictions, are shown in Figures 5, 6, 7, and 8.

5 Conclusion

In this paper, we introduce a CNN-Transformer architecture for dense video captioning using compressed videos for the first time. The experiments demonstrate that our proposed model not only achieves competitive performance with SOTA models but also significantly reduces GPU memory usage and improves processing speed. This suggests that compressed videos could potentially become the standard for video processing, replacing traditional RGB frames processing.

TS	SML	GOP	Res	Trans	α	B@1	B@2	B@3	B@4	M	R@L	C	recall	precision
2	60	auto	✗	✓	0.9	**33.30**	**27.17**	23.63	21.05	**19.87**	**26.31**	**19.23**	82.92	**62.11**
2	60	60	✗	✓	0.9	29.66	26.22	**24.13**	**22.43**	18.21	24.33	11.91	**91.77**	56.86

Table 3: Ablation study about impact of different different GOP sizes.

TS	SML	GOP	Res	Trans	α	B@1	B@2	B@3	B@4	M	R@L	C	recall	precision
2	60	auto	✗	✓	0.9	**33.30**	**27.17**	**23.63**	**21.05**	19.87	**26.31**	**19.23**	82.92	**62.11**
1	60	auto	✗	✓	0.9	32.17	26.31	23.02	20.57	**20.24**	25.20	17.02	**93.60**	56.86

Table 4: Ablation study about impact of different training strategies.

TS	SML	GOP	Res	Trans	α	B@1	B@2	B@3	B@4	M	R@L	C	recall	precision
2	60	auto	✗	✓	0.9	33.30	27.17	23.63	21.05	19.87	26.31	19.23	**82.92**	62.11
2	60	auto	✗	✓	0.6	**36.70**	**30.12**	**26.24**	**23.32**	21.94	**32.48**	**28.77**	32.44	72.46
2	60	auto	✗	✓	0.4	34.66	28.33	24.60	21.80	**22.54**	32.25	28.54	23.99	**74.81**

Table 5: Ablation study about impact of different values of alpha in focal loss.

IB	NB	TOP_K	TOP_P	α	B@1	B@2	B@3	B@4	M	R@L	C	recall	precision
✗	1	0	0	0.9	33.30	27.17	23.63	21.05	19.87	26.31	19.23	82.92	**62.11**
✓	1	0	0	0.9	**33.89**	**27.65**	**24.06**	**21.43**	**21.53**	**28.49**	**21.33**	**82.92**	61.12
✓	5	0	0	0.9	28.40	22.38	19.32	17.12	20.18	25.99	15.64	82.92	61.10
✓	1	50	0.95	0.9	30.27	24.34	21.19	18.87	19.81	25.90	13.24	82.92	61.18

Table 6: Ablation study about impact of different generation strategies. (IB = Ignore blanks, NB = Number of beams)

RGB	TS	SML	GOP	Res	Trans	α	B@1	B@2	B@3	B@4	M	R@L	C	recall	precision
-	2	60	auto	✗	✓	0.9	33.30	27.17	23.63	21.05	19.87	26.31	19.23	82.92	**62.11**
✓	2	60	auto	-	-	0.9	**34.05**	**28.60**	**25.32**	**22.78**	**20.39**	**26.84**	**22.04**	**86.26**	60.79

Table 7: Accuracy comparison with RGB variant of the same architecture.

Video Encoder	Train Time (s)	Train GPU Mem. (TB)	Inference Time (s)	Inference GPU Mem. (TB)
Compressed Video	**15.13**	**1.5**	**8.67**	**0.29**
RGB	81.77	7.63	40.90	2.26

Table 8: Speed and GPU memory footprint comparison with RGB variant of the same architecture. The values shows the total time and total amount of GPU memory spent to encode the frames of all of the samples of a match (Encoder part only).

Team	B@1	B@2	B@3	B@4	M	R@L	C	recall	precision
OPPO	35.55	**31.03**	**28.13**	**25.65**	**26.66**	**32.33**	**69.73**	24.59	68.59
HZC	29.73	24.52	21.44	19.13	21.30	24.56	24.76	98.68	51.19
Baseline 2	30.01	24.80	21.74	19.44	21.25	24.65	25.68	98.68	51.21
justplay	29.83	24.68	21.66	19.38	21.20	24.34	25.89	98.68	50.99
aisoccer	29.53	24.42	21.42	19.15	21.02	24.31	23.72	98.63	50.83
Baseline 1	11.91	9.97	8.83	7.97	15.24	10.69	16.33	**98.97**	23.92
CVT5 (Ours)	**36.64**	29.60	25.55	22.59	22.17	32.02	26.84	42.16	**72.97**

Table 9: Comparison with state-of-the-art models (Leaderboard 2023) (Cioppa et al., 2023).

6 Limitations

The primary limitation of this work is that it was only evaluated on a single dataset. The results may vary significantly on other benchmarks, as events in a soccer game differ greatly from, for example, cooking events. It would be beneficial to evaluate the model on additional datasets.

Another limitation is that the quality of generated captions is heavily influenced by the low precision in event detection. This issue arises for several reasons: 1. Low precision means the model may predict an event where there is none, leading to incorrect captions. 2. Low precision also makes it difficult for the encoder to distinguish between events, complicating the task of generating distinct captions for different events. 3. The SoccerNet dataset has a highly imbalanced distribution of events, where the model's outputs are often biased toward the majority class. As shown in Table 9 on the 2023 leaderboard, achieving a certain accuracy level is easy, but improving beyond that is challenging due to the difficulty in accurately predicting minority class events. Future work could focus on strategies to better learn and predict minority classes.

References

Ali Abdari, Pouria Amirjan, and Azadeh Mansouri. 2019. Action recognition in compressed domain using residual information. In *2019 4th International Conference on Pattern Recognition and Image Analysis (IPRIA)*, pages 130–134.

Barak Battash, Haim Barad, Hanlin Tang, and Amit Bleiweiss. 2020. Mimic the raw domain: Accelerating action recognition in the compressed domain. In *2020 IEEE/CVF Conference on Computer Vision and Pattern Recognition Workshops (CVPRW)*, pages 2926–2934.

Aaron Chadha, Alhabib Abbas, and Yiannis Andreopoulos. 2017. Compressed-domain video classification with deep neural networks: "there's way too much information to decode the matrix". In *2017 IEEE International Conference on Image Processing (ICIP)*, pages 1832–1836.

Hyung Won Chung, Xavier Garcia, Adam Roberts, Yi Tay, Orhan Firat, Sharan Narang, and Noah Constant. 2023. Unimax: Fairer and more effective language sampling for large-scale multilingual pretraining. In *The Eleventh International Conference on Learning Representations*.

Anthony Cioppa, Silvio Giancola, Vladimir Somers, Floriane Magera, Xin Zhou, Hassan Mkhallati, Adrien Deliège, Jan Held, Carlos Hinojosa, Amir M. Mansourian, Pierre Miralles, Olivier Barnich, Christophe De Vleeschouwer, Alexandre Alahi, Bernard Ghanem, Marc Van Droogenbroeck, Abdullah Kamal, Adrien Maglo, Albert Clapés, Amr Abdelaziz, Artur Xarles, Astrid Orcesi, Atom Scott, Bin Liu, Byoungkwon Lim, Chen Chen, Fabian Deuser, Feng Yan, Fufu Yu, Gal Shitrit, Guanshuo Wang, Gyusik Choi, Hankyul Kim, Hao Guo, Hasby Fahrudin, Hidenari Koguchi, Håkan Ardö, Ibrahim Salah, Ido Yerushalmy, Iftikar Muhammad, Ikuma Uchida, Ishay Be'ery, Jaonary Rabarisoa, Jeongae Lee, Jiajun Fu, Jianqin Yin, Jinghang Xu, Jongho Nang, Julien Denize, Junjie Li, Junpei Zhang, Juntae Kim, Kamil Synowiec, Kenji Kobayashi, Kexin Zhang, Konrad Habel, Kota Nakajima, Licheng Jiao, Lin Ma, Lizhi Wang, Luping Wang, Menglong Li, Mengying Zhou, Mohamed Nasr, Mohamed Abdelwahed, Mykola Liashuha, Nikolay Falaleev, Norbert Oswald, Qiong Jia, Quoc-Cuong Pham, Ran Song, Romain Hérault, Rui Peng, Ruilong Chen, Ruixuan Liu, Ruslan Baikulov, Ryuto Fukushima, Sergio Escalera, Seungcheon Lee, Shimin Chen, Shouhong Ding, Taiga Someya, Thomas B. Moeslund, Tianjiao Li, Wei Shen, Wei Zhang, Wei Li, Wei Dai, Weixin Luo, Wending Zhao, Wenjie Zhang, Xinquan Yang, Yanbiao Ma, Yeeun Joo, Yingsen Zeng, Yiyang Gan, Yongqiang Zhu, Yujie Zhong, Zheng Ruan, Zhiheng Li, Zhijian Huang, and Ziyu Meng. 2023. Soccernet 2023 challenges results. *Preprint*, arXiv:2309.06006.

EvalAI. Evalai: Evaluating state of the art in ai.

Kaiming He, Xiangyu Zhang, Shaoqing Ren, and Jian Sun. 2015. Deep residual learning for image recognition. *CoRR*, abs/1512.03385.

Lijun He, Miao Zhang, Sijin Zhang, Liejun Wang, and Fan Li. 2022. Mtrfn: Multiscale temporal receptive field network for compressed video action recognition at edge servers. *IEEE Internet of Things Journal*, 9(15):13965–13977.

Gabriel Huang, Bo Pang, Zhenhai Zhu, Clara Rivera, and Radu Soricut. 2020. Multimodal pretraining for dense video captioning. *CoRR*, abs/2011.11760.

Ranjay Krishna, Kenji Hata, Frederic Ren, Li Fei-Fei, and Juan Carlos Niebles. 2017. Dense-captioning events in videos. *CoRR*, abs/1705.00754.

Ilya Loshchilov and Frank Hutter. 2017. Fixing weight decay regularization in adam. *CoRR*, abs/1711.05101.

Antoine Miech, Dimitri Zhukov, Jean-Baptiste Alayrac, Makarand Tapaswi, Ivan Laptev, and Josef Sivic. 2019. Howto100m: Learning a text-video embedding by watching hundred million narrated video clips. *CoRR*, abs/1906.03327.

Yue Ming, Lu Xiong, Xia Jia, Qingfang Zheng, Jiangwan Zhou, Fan Feng, and Nannan Hu. 2023. Frequency enhancement network for efficient compressed video action recognition. In *2023 IEEE In-*

ternational Conference on Image Processing (ICIP)*, pages 825–829.

Yue Ming, Jiangwan Zhou, Nannan Hu, Fan Feng, Panzi Zhao, Boyang Lyu, and Hui Yu. 2024. Action recognition in compressed domains: A survey. *Neurocomputing*, 577:127389.

Hassan Mkhallati, Anthony Cioppa, Silvio Giancola, Bernard Ghanem, and Marc Van Droogenbroeck. 2023. SoccerNet-caption: Dense video captioning for soccer broadcasts commentaries. abs/2304.04565.

Yuting Mou, Xinghao Jiang, Ke Xu, Tanfeng Sun, and Zepeng Wang. 2024. Compressed video action recognition with dual-stream and dual-modal transformer. *IEEE Transactions on Circuits and Systems for Video Technology*, 34(5):3299–3312.

Alec Radford, Jong Wook Kim, Chris Hallacy, Aditya Ramesh, Gabriel Goh, Sandhini Agarwal, Girish Sastry, Amanda Askell, Pamela Mishkin, Jack Clark, Gretchen Krueger, and Ilya Sutskever. 2021. Learning transferable visual models from natural language supervision. *CoRR*, abs/2103.00020.

Alec Radford, Jong Wook Kim, Tao Xu, Greg Brockman, Christine McLeavey, and Ilya Sutskever. 2022. Robust speech recognition via large-scale weak supervision. *arXiv preprint*.

Yaojie Shen. 2023. Github - acherstyx/compressed-video-reader: A video reader for extracting motion vectors and residuals from encoded h.264 videos.

Suramya Tomar. 2006. Converting video formats with ffmpeg. *Linux Journal*, 2006(146):10.

Ashish Vaswani, Noam Shazeer, Niki Parmar, Jakob Uszkoreit, Llion Jones, Aidan N. Gomez, Lukasz Kaiser, and Illia Polosukhin. 2017. Attention is all you need. *CoRR*, abs/1706.03762.

Jue Wang and Lorenzo Torresani. 2022. Deformable video transformer. In *2022 IEEE/CVF Conference on Computer Vision and Pattern Recognition (CVPR)*, pages 14033–14042.

Teng Wang, Jinrui Zhang, Feng Zheng, Wenhao Jiang, Ran Cheng, and Ping Luo. 2023. Learning grounded vision-language representation for versatile understanding in untrimmed videos. *CoRR*, abs/2303.06378.

Teng Wang, Ruimao Zhang, Zhichao Lu, Feng Zheng, Ran Cheng, and Ping Luo. 2021. End-to-end dense video captioning with parallel decoding. *CoRR*, abs/2108.07781.

Thomas Wolf, Lysandre Debut, Victor Sanh, Julien Chaumond, Clement Delangue, Anthony Moi, Perric Cistac, Clara Ma, Yacine Jernite, Julien Plu, Canwen Xu, Teven Le Scao, Sylvain Gugger, Mariama Drame, Quentin Lhoest, and Alexander M. Rush. 2020. Transformers: State-of-the-Art Natural Language Processing. pages 38–45. Association for Computational Linguistics.

Chao-Yuan Wu, Manzil Zaheer, Hexiang Hu, R. Manmatha, Alexander J. Smola, and Philipp Krähenbühl. 2017. Compressed video action recognition. *CoRR*, abs/1712.00636.

A. Yang, A. Nagrani, P. Seo, A. Miech, J. Pont-Tuset, I. Laptev, J. Sivic, and C. Schmid. 2023. Vid2seq: Large-scale pretraining of a visual language model for dense video captioning. In *2023 IEEE/CVF Conference on Computer Vision and Pattern Recognition (CVPR)*, pages 10714–10726, Los Alamitos, CA, USA. IEEE Computer Society.

Rowan Zellers, Jiasen Lu, Ximing Lu, Youngjae Yu, Yanpeng Zhao, Mohammadreza Salehi, Aditya Kusupati, Jack Hessel, Ali Farhadi, and Yejin Choi. 2022. MERLOT reserve: Neural script knowledge through vision and language and sound. *CoRR*, abs/2201.02639.

Xizhou Zhu, Weijie Su, Lewei Lu, Bin Li, Xiaogang Wang, and Jifeng Dai. 2020. Deformable DETR: deformable transformers for end-to-end object detection. *CoRR*, abs/2010.04159.

A Qualitative Results

Table 10 shows examples of the model's output compared to the ground truth. The model's bias towards corner events and events with no comments is evident in these examples. Similar results are shown in Figure 4 which presents the confusion matrix of the model's output and ground truth. Additionally, when the spotting head is uncertain about the occurrence of an event, the captioner module often generates incorrect captions. Occasional language modeling errors, such as repetitive tokens, are also observed.

Examples of the model's output, along with the frames from the time intervals used for predictions, are shown in Figures 5, 6, 7, and 8. The frame rate is 4 times lower than the model's input sampling rate, meaning one frame is shown every 2 seconds. The images start from the top left and end at the bottom right. As observed in these examples, even when the model makes a mistake, the images closely resemble the generated descriptions, meaning that these examples are challenging. However, it can also be seen that the model does not pay enough attention to small details within the frames.

Confidence	GT Event	G Event	GT Caption	G Caption
0.88	corner	corner	[PLAYER] ([TEAM]) attempts to find a teammate with the corner, but the effort is snuffed out by the goalkeeper.	[PLAYER] ([TEAM]) takes the corner, but it's intercepted by the defender.
0.52	-	corner	[PLAYER] ([TEAM]) smashes the ball towards goal from the edge of the penalty box, but it fails to bother the goalkeeper as it hits the defensive wall.	[PLAYER] ([TEAM]) takes the corner, but it's intercepted by the defender.
0.59	soccer-ball	soccer-ball	Goal! [PLAYER] feeds [PLAYER] ([TEAM]), who taps the ball into an empty net. He makes it 1:0.	[PLAYER] ([TEAM]) is unable to feed a low pass into the path of one of his teammates. The ball goes out of play and [TEAM] will have a goal kick.
0.81	corner	corner	[PLAYER] ([TEAM]) launches a powerful cross from the corner into the box, but the ball is intercepted by the defender. The linesman makes the right call and [TEAM] will have a corner.	[PLAYER] ([TEAM]) takes the corner, but it's intercepted by the defender.
0.89	substitution	substitution	The referee allows time for a substitution. [PLAYER] will be replaced by [PLAYER] ([TEAM]).	[COACH] has decided to introduce fresh legs, with [PLAYER] ([TEAM]) replacing [PLAYER].
0.66	-	-	[PLAYER] ([TEAM]) is having a lively performance. He is causing problems and wanting the ball at every opportunity.	[PLAYER] ([TEAM]) sends a cross into the box, [TEAM]]]] ([TEAM]]), [TEAM]] will have a chance to score from a free kick. [TEAM] will have a chance
0.54	-	-	[PLAYER] ([TEAM]) whips the ball in from the long-range free kick, but the first man gets it clear.	[PLAYER] ([TEAM]) sends a pass into the box, [PLAYER] ([TEAM]) is REFEREE]REFEREE] REFEREE]REFEREE] REFEREE]REFEREE] REFEREE]REFEREE]
0.68	-	-	[PLAYER] ([TEAM]) picks up a rebound inside the penalty area and drills a shot to the bottom right corner, but is denied by a reflex save from [PLAYER]. [TEAM] have been awarded a corner kick. The referee and one of his assistants both point at the corner flag.	[PLAYER] ([TEAM]) sends a cross into the box, but the opposition's defence clears the ball away to eliminate the danger. The referee blows his whistle, [TEAM] are awarded a corner kick
0.58	-	-	[PLAYER] ([TEAM]) receives a pass and decides to smash the ball from long range, but his poor effort sails high over the bar.	[PLAYER] ([TEAM]) sends a cross into the box, but [PLAYER] comes off his line to gather the ball.
0.86	substitution	substitution	The manager makes a subsitution with [PLAYER] ([TEAM]) coming on for [PLAYER].	[COACH] has decided to introduce fresh legs, with [PLAYER] ([TEAM]) replacing [PLAYER].
0.67	-	-	[PLAYER] ([TEAM]) was trying to get to the ball but clattered into the legs of the opponent as well. [REFEREE] blows his whistle for an infringement. [TEAM] are awarded a free kick. Let's see what they create from this.	[PLAYER] ([TEAM]) sends a cross into the box, but the opposition's defence clears the ball away to eliminate the danger.
0.82	corner	corner	[PLAYER] ([TEAM]) takes the resulting corner which is well defended.	[PLAYER] ([TEAM]) sends a cross into the box, but the opposition's defence clears the ball away to eliminate the danger. The referee and his assistant both point at the corner flag. [TEAM] will
0.69	-	corner	[PLAYER] ([TEAM]) whips the ball in, but it fails to reach any of his teammates as the opposition's defence averts the threat. The linesman points to the corner flag, [TEAM] are going to take it.	[PLAYER] ([TEAM]) sends a cross into the box, but the opposition's defence clears the ball away to eliminate the danger. The referee and his assistant both point at the corner flag. [TEAM] will
0.85	corner	corner	[PLAYER] ([TEAM]) swings in a cross from the corner, but [PLAYER] reads it well and gathers the ball.	[PLAYER] ([TEAM]) sends a cross into the box, but the opposition's defence clears the ball to safety. The ball goes out of play and [TEAM] have been awarded a corner kick.
0.53	-	-	He should have done better. [PLAYER] ([TEAM]) is afforded space to connect with a [PLAYER] cross, but his header from the centre of the box flies well wide of the left post.	[PLAYER] ([TEAM]) sends a cross into the box, but the opposition's defence clears the ball to safety.
0.68	corner	-	[PLAYER] ([TEAM]) goes over to take the corner kick and it looks like he will send the ball into the penalty box.	[PLAYER] ([TEAM]) sends a cross into the box, but the opposition's defence clears the ball away to eliminate the danger. The referee and his assistant both point at the corner flag. [TEAM] will
0.54	-	-	What a goal-scoring opportunity! [PLAYER] ([TEAM]) finds some space inside the box and gets in a strike, but the shot is brilliantly blocked by one of the defending players sliding in.	[PLAYER] ([TEAM]) sends a pass into the box, [PLAYER] ([TEAM]) is REFEREE]REFEREE] REFEREE]REFEREE] REFEREE]REFEREE] REFEREE]REFEREE]
0.50	-	-	[PLAYER] ([TEAM]) produces a lovely ball into the penalty area but the defender manages to intercept and comfortably averts the danger.	[PLAYER] ([TEAM]) sends a pass into the box, [PLAYER] ([TEAM]) is REFEREE]REFEREE] REFEREE]REFEREE] REFEREE]REFEREE] REFEREE]REFEREE]
0.50	-	-	[PLAYER] ([TEAM]) attempts to slip the ball through the defence, but is unable to find any of his teammates.	[PLAYER] ([TEAM]) sends a cross into the box, but [PLAYER] comes off his line to gather the ball.
0.58	corner	corner	[PLAYER] ([TEAM]) swings in the corner kick, but one of the defenders leaps highest to head the ball away.	[PLAYER] ([TEAM]) takes the corner kick and sends a lovely ball into the penalty area, but the opposition's defence is ready and knocks the ball to safety.
	penalty		Poor challenge! [PLAYER] ([TEAM]) is penalised for tripping and [REFEREE] blows his whistle. PENALTY to [TEAM]! Great chance to score.	
0.58	y-card	-	[PLAYER] ([TEAM]) commits a foul and is shown a yellow card without any hesitation from the referee.	[PLAYER] ([TEAM]) is penalised for holding. [REFEREE] signals a set piece.
	soccer-ball		[PLAYER] ([TEAM]) sends [PLAYER] the wrong way and fires the penalty into the middle of the goal!	

Table 10: Some examples of the model's output compared to the ground truth

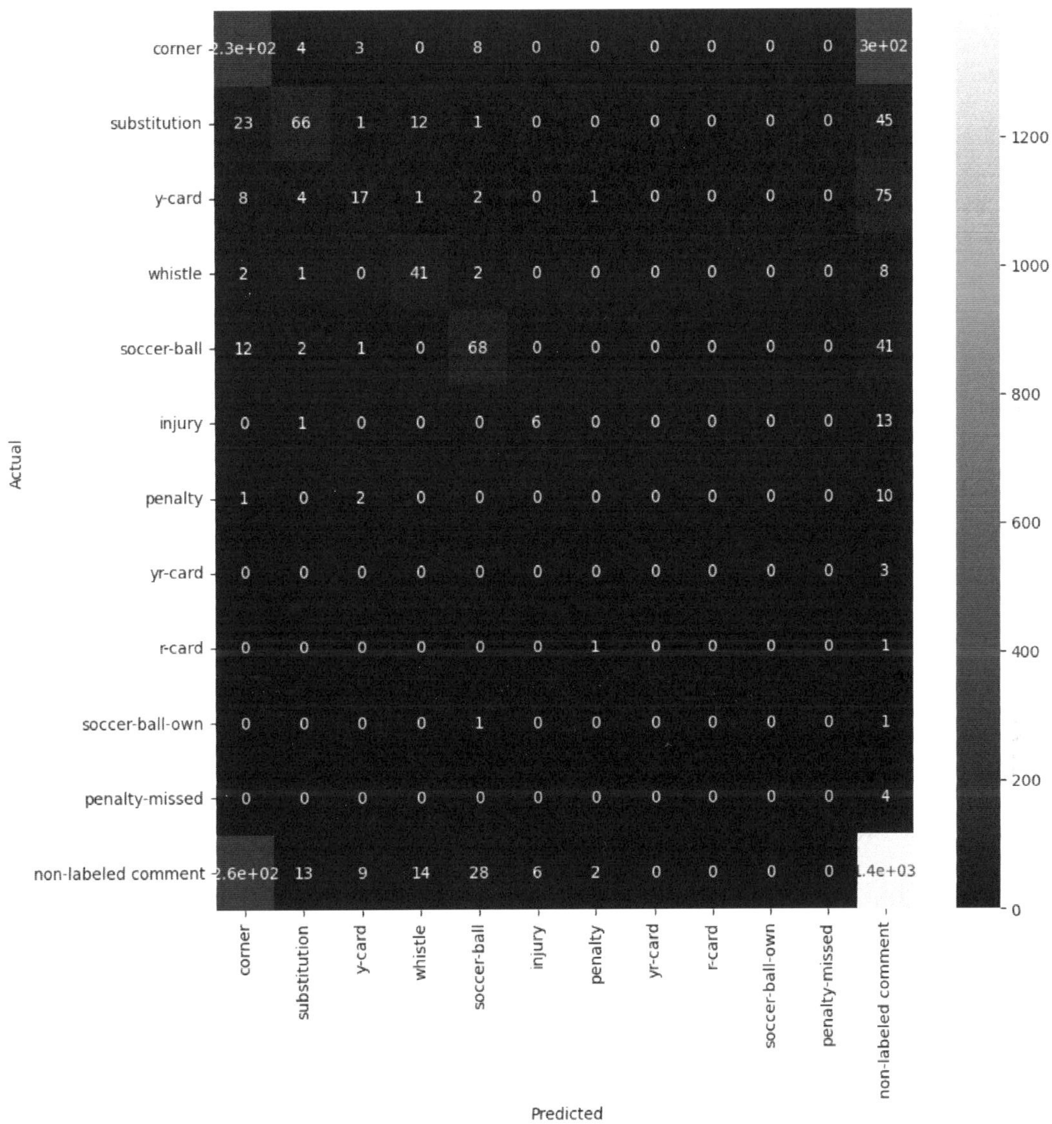

Figure 4: Confusion matrix on the SoccerNet validation set

Figure 5: Model output: [PLAYER] ([TEAM]) takes the corner, but it's intercepted by the defender. Ground truth: [PLAYER] ([TEAM]) attempts to find a teammate with the corner, but the effort is snuffed out by the goalkeeper.

Figure 6: Model output: [PLAYER] ([TEAM]) takes the corner, but it's intercepted by the defender. Ground truth: [PLAYER] ([TEAM]) smashes the ball towards goal from the edge of the penalty box, but it fails to bother the goalkeeper as it hits the defensive wall.

Figure 7: Model output: [PLAYER] ([TEAM]) is unable to feed a low pass into the path of one of his teammates. The ball goes out of play and [TEAM] will have a goal kick. Ground truth: Goal! [PLAYER] feeds [PLAYER] ([TEAM]), who taps the ball into an empty net. He makes it 1:0.

Figure 8: Model output: [COACH] has decided to introduce fresh legs, with [PLAYER] ([TEAM]) replacing [PLAYER]. Ground truth: The referee allows time for a substitution. [PLAYER] will be replaced by [PLAYER] ([TEAM]).

If I feel smart, I will do the right thing: Combining Complementary Multimodal Information in Visual Language Models

Yuyu Bai
Vrije Universiteit Amsterdam
stacybai1122@gmail.com

Sandro Pezzelle
Institute for Logic, Language and Computation
University of Amsterdam
s.pezzelle@uva.nl

Abstract

Generative visual language models (VLMs) have recently shown potential across various downstream language-and-vision tasks. At the same time, it is still an open question whether, and to what extent, these models can properly understand a multimodal context where language and vision provide *complementary* information—a mechanism routinely in place in human language communication. In this work, we test various VLMs on the task of generating action descriptions consistent with both an image's visual content and an intention or attitude (not visually grounded) conveyed by a textual prompt. Our results show that BLIP-2 is not far from human performance when the task is framed as a generative multiple-choice problem, while other models struggle. Furthermore, the actions generated by BLIP-2 in an open-ended generative setting are better than those by the competitors; indeed, human annotators judge most of them as plausible continuations for the multimodal context. Our study reveals substantial variability among VLMs in integrating complementary multimodal information, yet BLIP-2 demonstrates promising trends across most evaluations, paving the way for seamless human-computer interaction.

1 Introduction

In recent years, transformer-based generative visual language models (VLMs) have shown outstanding results in many downstream tasks. Similar to what has happened in NLP, where pre-trained generative models have supplanted previous architectures thanks to their flexibility and portability, VLMs have proven effective in solving language-and-vision tasks by turning them into generative problems. This is possible thanks to their massive multimodal pre-training, which typically builds on a pre-trained language model and image processing model. This has enabled systems that can, in zero-shot mode and without further fine-tuning, seamlessly describe the content of an image, answer

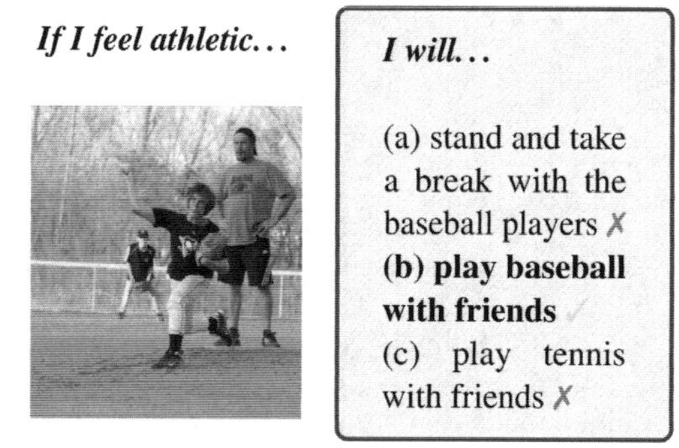

Figure 1: We test generative visual language models' (VLMs) abilities to combine *complementary* information brought into context by the two modalities. In this example from the BD2BB dataset (Pezzelle et al., 2020) (slightly edited for space reasons), only one of the actions on the right, (b), is consistent with both the textual prompt and the image on the left. As for (a) and (c), they are plausible based on the image or the textual prompt, respectively, but not on the combination of both.

questions about it, or engage in a dialogue (see Caffagni et al., 2024, for an overview). This might suggest that VLMs have skills similar to those needed for meaningful multimodal communication.

In real-life multimodal communication, human speakers continuously integrate complementary information from various modalities, including language and vision, to understand and convey messages and properly act in various situations (Partan and Marler, 1999; Benoît et al., 2000; Forceville, 2020). An example of such complementarity is shown in Figure 1: If someone observing the scene depicted in the image *feels athletic*, they would likely take an action that is consistent with both the visual content and their attitude or intention, i.e., *play baseball with friends*. In contrast, actions that are plausible given either the image or the textual intention, but not both, would not be considered. Note that making this type of inference is also key for any multimodal model that aims to be communicatively plausible and useful. Consider the

Proceedings of the First Workshop of Evaluation of Multi-Modal Generation, pages 24–39
January 20, 2025.

case of a virtual assistant that has access to the visual context and a spoken or written request from a user. If asked to recommend an appropriate activity to do—*Hey, I feel adventurous today. What do you recommend I do?*—the assistant should suggest something appropriate to the context surrounding the user and obviously in line with their attitude. Despite the relevance of the problem, only a few studies have investigated, to date, whether language-and-vision models master this ability. Before the generative 'revolution' that has recently affected VLMs, Pezzelle et al. (2020) proposed the *Be Different to Be Better* (BD2BB) benchmark (see an example in Figure 1) to test the ability of multimodal encoders such as LXMERT (Tan and Bansal, 2019) to integrate complementary information. In that study, these models were shown to lag far behind human intuitions, leaving ample room for improvement in future systems. To the best of our knowledge, no subsequent work addressed whether generative VLMs have filled this gap.

In this research, we use the BD2BB benchmark and test how several generative VLMs deal with it. We do so employing two main experiments. First, we challenge the models to solve the task in its original multiple-choice format, i.e., by picking, for a given image, one among 5 candidate actions (*I will...*) that we give to the model via prompting together with the intention (*If I...*). We evaluate model performance in terms of accuracy, that we measure both *extrinsically* (considering the label, corresponding to a given action, that is output by the model) and *intrinsically* (looking at the probability assigned by a model to each action following the same intention). Second, we test VLMs in the setup that best suits them, that is, by letting them generate an action based on the image and the intention. In this case, we assess model performance using both a *reference-based*, automatic metric (we compute BERTScore similarity between the generated action and the target one from BD2BB) and a *reference-free*, human-based evaluation (we ask annotators to judge whether a certain action is good for a given <image, intention> pair).

The results of our first experiment show that, while most tested models hover around the chance level, BLIP-2 achieves fairly high accuracy, much closer to human performance than LXMERT (reported in Pezzelle et al., 2020). Similarly, in our second experiment, the actions generated by BLIP-2 are deemed plausible by human participants in most cases, which is not the case for other models. Taken together, these results highlight substantial variability across VLMs in their ability to combine complementary multimodal information. At the same time, the promising trends exhibited by BLIP-2 reveal that this model is capable of understanding—to some extent—the visual scene, the intention, and their complex interaction.

2 Related Work

2.1 Generative Language-and-Vision Models

With the introduction of Transformers (Vaswani et al., 2017), NLP research has experienced unprecedented development. This, in turn, influenced the work on language and vision processing, which followed the same 'evolutionary' steps. First, based on Masked Language Models such as BERT (Devlin et al., 2019) and RoBERTa (Liu et al., 2019), the community proposed many multimodal encoders, either single-stream (i.e., jointly processing language and vision from the beginning), such as UNITER (Chen et al., 2020), VL-BERT (Su et al., 2019), and VisualBERT (Li et al., 2019), or dual-stream (i.e., processing language and vision separately, and later combining them through a series of multimodal layers), such as LXMERT (Tan and Bansal, 2019) and ViLBERT (Lu et al., 2019).

Later, in the wake of the success of autoregressive Large Language Models (LLMs) such as GPT (Radford et al., 2019), OPT (Zhang et al., 2022) or LLaMA (Touvron et al., 2023), the language-and-vision community has taken a generative direction. With such an approach, answering questions about an image (VQA) or describing its content (IC) can be done by simply feeding the model with the image and the appropriate prompt. Various generative language-and-vision models have been proposed in recent years, such as BLIP-2 (Li et al., 2023), Flamingo (Alayrac et al., 2022), FROMAGe (Koh et al., 2023), MAPL (Mañas et al., 2022), and IDEFICS (Laurençon et al., 2023). In general, a common feature of all these models is that they leverage a pre-trained text-only LLM and a visual encoder, on top of which a relatively lightweight trainable network is learned. Such a network—which can consist of a bunch of Transformer (BLIP-2, Flamingo, IDEFICS), fully connected (MAPL), or linear layers (FROMAGe)—is responsible for connecting the two modalities and making the model capable of solving multimodal tasks. Using this strategy, generative language and vision models have achieved results never approached before (e.g., when introduced, Flamingo was the best-performing model on 16 multimodal tasks). Furthermore, their architecture makes these models much more flexible and portable than their predecessors, as they can be applied, without any fine-tuning, to virtually any unseen task.

2.2 Complementary Language and Vision

The models described above have been quite extensively tested in various downstream tasks, such as Visual Question Answering (Antol et al., 2015) and Image Captioning (Bernardi et al., 2016), which typically require dealing with *aligned* information from language and vision. To illustrate, these tasks challenge the models to locate a phrase or sentence in the image, retrieve information from it, or verify that what is depicted complies with a description. Comparably less attention has been paid to assessing whether, and to what extent, they can genuinely combine *complementary* information from the two modalities—something necessary, e.g., to generate a plausible action for the example in Figure 1.

This ability is certainly necessary for tasks such as Visual Dialog (Das et al., 2017; Mostafazadeh et al., 2017) or Visual Storytelling (Huang et al., 2016; Hong et al., 2023). In the former, multimodal models are asked to maintain a meaningful conversation starting from the contents of an image, which requires more than simply describing visible aspects. As for the latter, the goal is to produce a story based on a sequence of images. Again, this task requires not only understanding the visual content (which is, however, crucial; see Surikuchi et al., 2023), but also making inferences over people's emotions and feelings, understanding social dynamics, and so on. These are challenging tasks for large multimodal models, which were recently shown to have little social awareness and struggle with recognizing subtle and culturally diverse emotions (Deng et al., 2023). Similarly, these models face difficulties in handling semantically underspecified language (where the language signal needs to be complemented by extra information, e.g., visual info; see Pezzelle, 2023); moreover, they have trouble understanding humor (Hessel et al., 2023), an aspect of multimodal language use that can only be mastered by going beyond the literal (i.e., image-aligned) meaning of a sentence.

To explore more complementary scenarios, various directions have been taken. These include approaches to Image Captioning that are sensitive to the context and communicative purpose of the captions (Kreiss et al., 2021, 2022); tasks that challenge the models to predict something *external* to the multimodal sample, such as the motivation or intent of a social media post (Kruk et al., 2019), or the cause or consequence of an event (Hessel et al., 2022); datasets to test complex inference abilities in multimodal setups, such as predicting the next utterance or frame in a comic strip (Iyyer et al., 2017). BD2BB (Pezzelle et al., 2020) also belongs to this latter category, as it challenges models to predict *what comes next* based on both grounded (the image contents) and non-grounded information (the textual intention). In this work, for the first time, we study how generative visual language models deal with complementary multimodal information.

3 Methods

3.1 Data

We use the BD2BB dataset and corresponding multiple-choice task (Pezzelle et al., 2020). The task is exemplified in Figure 1: given an image and a textual intention (*If I...*), a model must select the correct action (*I will...*), i.e., the one that complies with both the visual and textual information. Note that, in BD2BB (and differently from what is shown in the figure), each sample comes with 5 candidate options—two that are valid given the image only (so-called *visual decoys*), two that are valid given the intention only (*language decoys*), and the correct one. The images in BD2BB come from a subset of COCO images (Lin et al., 2014) depicting at least one person.[1] The dataset, collected via crowdsourcing and further post-processed, includes around 10K <image, intention, candidate actions> samples. In this work, we test models in a zero-shot setup (without training or fine-tuning them) on the test set, which includes 4081 samples.

3.2 Models

We experiment with four state-of-the-art, open-source generative VLMs, i.e., MAPL, FROMAGe, BLIP2, and IDEFICS. As mentioned in Section 2.1, these models are all based on a similar architecture that leverages two frozen pre-trained unimodal models (a language and a vision one) and learns a relatively lightweight mapping network on top of them. Below, we briefly describe these models

[1]This choice is meant to increase the likelihood of interacting with these images by performing some action.

	MAPL	FROMAGe	BLIP-2	IDEFICS
Underlying language model	GPT-J	OPT	OPT / FlanT5	LLaMA
Underlying vision model	Vit-L14	Vit-L14	Vit-L14 / Vit-G14	OpenClip[5]
Mapping network's architecture	Fully connected layers	Linear layers	Transformer	Transformer
# trainable parameters	3.4M	5.5M	188M	1.4B
Generated output	Text	Text / Image	Text	Text
COCO images in VLM training?	No	No	Yes	No
COCO images in vision model training?	No	No	No	No

Table 1: A comparison of the four VLMs used in this work concerning some of their main features.

from smallest to largest in terms of learnable parameters. For convenience, we provide an overview of their most important features in Table 1. We refer the reader to the original papers for further details on each model's architecture, training data, and optimization strategies.

MAPL (Mañas et al., 2022) builds on CLIP (Radford et al., 2021) and GPT-J (Wang and Komatsuzaki, 2021) as a visual and language frozen model, respectively. The trainable network to map visual features into token embeddings consists of a few fully connected layers with ReLU activations (Nair and Hinton, 2010) and dropout regularization (Srivastava et al., 2014). With only trainable 3.4M parameters, this network is the lightest of the four we use in this work.

FROMAGe (Koh et al., 2023) leverages CLIP Vit-L14 (Radford et al., 2021) and OPT (Zhang et al., 2022) as its frozen visual and language model, respectively. The projection of the image and text representations into a common latent space is done through several trainable linear layers. This makes this model lightweight, with only 5.5M trainable parameters. Among the four models we use, FROMAGe is the only one capable of producing outputs including both text and images.

BLIP2 (Li et al., 2023) bootstraps language-and-vision representations from the underlying frozen pre-trained unimodal models via a Transformer-based network. It allows using various underlying frozen models: CLIP Vit-L14 (Radford et al., 2021) or Vit-G14 from EVA-CLIP (Fang et al., 2023) on the vision side; OPT (Zhang et al., 2022) or FlanT5 (Chung et al., 2022) on the language side (here, we use the version with FlanT5 and Vit-G).

The multimodal mapping is carried out by a trainable Querying Transformer (Q-Former) network. The Q-Former includes two transformer submodules sharing self-attention layers: an image transformer interacting with the frozen image encoder for visual feature extraction, and a language transformer serving as both a text encoder and decoder. It is worth noting that, among the four models here considered, BLIP-2 is the only one also trained with images from COCO (Lin et al., 2014), i.e., the images used to build the BD2BB dataset. Though the model has not seen the BD2BB data, it could still have an advantage over other architectures.

IDEFICS (Laurençon et al., 2023) is an open-access re-implementation of the Flamingo model (Alayrac et al., 2022) which leverages LLaMA as the language model (Touvron et al., 2023) and OpenClip[5] (a model pre-trained with a contrastive text-image approach, similar to CLIP Radford et al., 2021) as the vision model. Similar to BLIP-2, IDEFICS uses a Transformer-based architecture to connect language and vision. In particular, it employs a Perceiver Resampler module to map varied-size vision features to a few tokens, which are then used to condition the frozen LM through cross-attention layers. We employ the 9B parameter instructed version with 1.4B trainable parameters, nearly 10 times more than BLIP-2. This makes IDEFICS the largest model we consider.

3.3 Experimental Settings

We test the four models in two experiments: a multiple-choice experiment (Section 4) and an open-ended generative experiment (Section 5). In both experiments, we test the pre-trained models in a zero-shot manner.[2] That is, we do not further train or fine-tune them.[3] We ran the models on an A1000 GPU using their default hyperparameters to ensure deterministic results. We also conducted

[2]The pre-trained models can be downloaded from: `https://github.com/octarinesec/MAPL` (MAPL) `https://github.com/kohjingyu/fromage` (FROMAGe) `https://huggingface.co/docs/transformers/en/model_doc/blip-2` (BLIP-2) `https://huggingface.co/docs/transformers/en/model_doc/idefics` (IDEFICS)

[3]Data and code available at: `https://github.com/baiyuyu/VL-complementary-infomation`

the multiple-choice experiment with other hyperparameter settings (see Appendix A).

4 Multiple-Choice Experiment

We test the four generative models in the original BD2BB multiple-choice classification task. Here, together with the intention and the image, we provide the model with the five candidate actions and task the model to select the correct one. We evaluate model performance in terms of accuracy, which we measure both *intrinsically* and *intrinsically*. Below, we describe the two evaluations in more detail.

Extrinsic evaluation Given an <image, intention, actions> sample, we ask the models to provide the correct action via prompting. Since we present the candidate actions as options preceded by an alphabet letter *(A-E)*, models are expected to output the letter corresponding to the action they consider correct. To elicit model responses, we used the following template, filled with the intention, the five actions, and a prompt describing the task: "[intention], [prompt]: A. [action_1] B. [action_2] C. [action_3] D. [action_4] E. [action_5]". Given this template, we experiment with 30 prompts (provided in Appendix B) and compute average accuracy and standard deviation over them. An example of a template filled with all information for one dataset's sample is the following (we give the prompt in italic): "If I feel adventurous, *what should I do? Choose the best option from the following:* A. I will ride an elephant. B. I will merely watch my friend fly an animal kite. C. I will go bird watching on an outdoor public patio. D. I will ride a horse like the man. E. I will stand and observe the zebras." Such experimental setup assumes that each of the four models can provide answers in the form of a single letter. However, in practice, the raw outputs often contained additional text that required some post-processing to extract the relevant letter. For instance, the IDEFICS model generated responses structured as "Question: ...Assistant: E". For those cases, we employed a cleaning step based on hard-coded rules to remove the surrounding text, ensuring only the answer ("E") was retained.

Intrinsic evaluation Given an <image, intention, actions> sample, we consider its 5 <intention, action> pairs and compute the cross-entropy loss between each of these sequences (we concatenate the intention and the action) and the image. To do so, we first obtain the logits from the model's final hidden layer for the current input sequence. Then, we calculate the cross-entropy loss between these logits and the target tokens. The total cross-entropy loss for a sequence is the sum of the losses at each word position. The sequence with the lowest cross-entropy loss is selected as the model answer. These predictions are used to compute model accuracy.

Model	Accuracy	
	intrinsic	*extrinsic*
LXMERT*	62.2	
CLIP	53.2	
MAPL	63.1	22.0±0.8
FROMAGe	47.9	20.0±0.5
BLIP-2	42.0	**75.7±0.8**
IDEFICS	**63.7**	35.5±7.2
Humans*	79.0	

Table 2: Multiple-choice experiment. Intrinsic and extrinsic model accuracy. Numbers in bold are the highest in the column. *Results from Pezzelle et al. (2020).

4.1 Results

In Table 2, we report the extrinsic and intrinsic accuracy of each tested model. We compare our results with those by humans and the pre-trained LXMERT (Tan and Bansal, 2019) (best-performing in Pezzelle et al., 2020), as they are given in the BD2BB paper. As an additional baseline, we report the results by CLIP (Radford et al., 2021), which we obtain by computing the CLIPScore (Hessel et al., 2021) (quantifying the plain degree of alignment between the visual and textual inputs) between the image and each of the <intention, action> pairs, fed to the model as a sequence. By looking at the numbers in the table, we identify a few key findings, that we summarize below.

BLIP-2 approaches human performance in the extrinsic evaluation The first key finding of our experiment concerns the performance of BLIP-2 in the extrinsic evaluation: the model achieves an average accuracy of 75.7%, i.e., only 3 accuracy points far from human performance. This means that, for more than 3 samples out of 4, the model identifies the correct action for a given <image, intention> pair. This result is even more remarkable considering that the other three models do not fare much better than chance in this evaluation setting. As mentioned in Section 3.2, BLIP-2 is the only model trained with COCO images (though, crucially, none of the tested models, in-

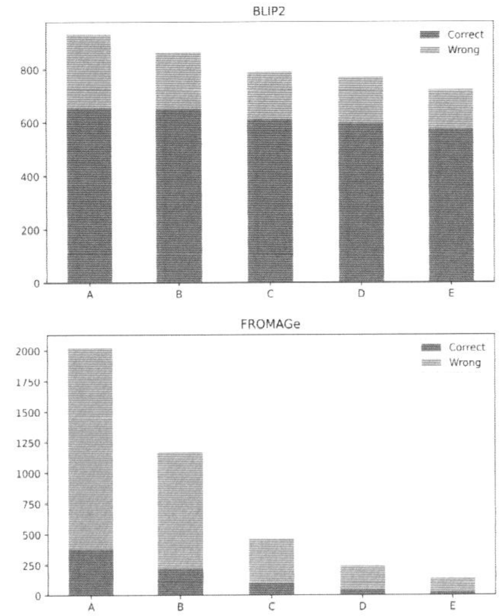

Figure 2: Multiple-choice experiment. Distribution of correct and wrong answers by BLIP-2 (top) and FROMAGe (bottom) against their position (A-E) in the template. While BLIP-2 has only a minor bias toward first-position answers, FROMAGe is heavily biased.

cluding BLIP-2, have ever seen the BD2BB data). Moreover, BLIP-2 is the only one leveraging a language model, FlanT5, which was instruction-finetuned on a mixture of tasks. Therefore, it is reasonable to hypothesize both these aspects could give an advantage to BLIP-2 over the other models. We leave to future work an extensive exploration of this issue, which is outside the scope of this work.

Some VLMs are biased towards early-presented options Upon manual inspection of the model-generated outputs in the extrinsic evaluation, we noticed a bias of MAPL, FROMAGe, and IDEFICS toward predicting the actions presented earlier in the template; that is, these models appeared to prefer A over E. To quantify this effect, we calculated, for each model, the percentage of predicted responses based on their position. In Figure 2, we visualize the results for FROMAGe (MAPL and IDEFICS exhibit a very similar pattern), which we plot against the behavior of BLIP-2. As can be seen, FROMAGe is heavily biased toward the first positions/letters in the template, while BLIP-2 is not, or to a much lesser extent. This striking difference highlights that, while BLIP-2 can treat each action in the template (almost) equally, this is not the case for the other models. This is likely one of the reasons for the success of this model.

	BLIP-2	Humans*
multimodal	75.7±0.8	79.0
language-only	59.1±0.4	50.0
vision-only	57.0±2.5	72.3

Table 3: BLIP-2 and human accuracy in three settings: multimodal, language-only, and vision-only, evaluated extrinsically. *From Pezzelle et al. (2020).

VLMs do not overtly outperform LXMERT in the intrinsic evaluation When evaluated intrinsically on the task, generative VLMs do not exhibit a generalized advantage over the previous-generation models. While MAPL and IDEFICS do perform slightly better than LXMERT (see Table 2), this is not the case for FROMAGe and BLIP-2 (note, though, that in an additional experiment, we found that BLIP-2 with underlying OPT achieves better accuracy: 62.4%). This suggests that generative VLMs may not, by default, be necessarily better encoders than previous models, in line with what was discussed by BehnamGhader et al. (2024) for text-only LMs. At the same time, all VLMs except FROMAGe outperform CLIP, which reveals that the cross-modal scores we obtain from them encode more than simple image-text alignment, which is all that CLIP captures. This provides indirect proof that VLMs can, to some extent, combine complementary information from the two modalities.

4.2 Is BLIP-2 Using the Multimodal Context?

As discussed above, BLIP-2 achieves near-human accuracy in the multiple-choice experiment when evaluated extrinsically. In this analysis, we explore whether this performance is due to genuine integration of language and vision or biases and shortcuts exploited in one of the two modalities. To do so, we run the same experiment in two additional settings: (1) a language-only one, where we provide the model with the intention and the actions, but not the image; (2) a vision-only one, where we provide the model with the image and the actions, but not the intention (see the prompts in Appendix C). If the model genuinely leverages the two modalities, it should perform worse in both these settings than the multimodal one, where both the image and the intention are given as input. The results of this analysis are presented in Table 3.

As can be seen, the model fed with the multimodal input neatly outperforms both unimodal settings. This reveals that jointly leveraging information conveyed by the image and the intention is beneficial to solving the task, a pattern that is also observed in human behavior. Compared to humans, however, BLIP-2 exhibits a slight advantage in the language-only setting and a large disadvantage in the vision-only setting. This pattern suggests, on the one hand, that the underlying FlanT5 language model might be driven by some biases and default choices when performing the inference task; on the other hand, its image processor is less capable than humans to understand the subtleties of a scene and which actions it pragmatically licenses.

In Appendix D, we present the results of an additional analysis that further investigates whether, and when, the model leverages complementary information or simply counts on a single modality.

5 Open-Ended Generative Experiment

In the multiple-choice experiment, only BLIP-2, but none of the other models, is extrinsically good. At the same time, most VLMs can assign a higher probability to the correct action in many cases. This discrepancy is likely due more to how the different models have been trained and designed than to what the models do or do not know. Moreover, we acknowledge that a multiple-choice scenario is not the most naturalistic way to interrogate these models. To overcome these issues, in the second experiment, we feed the VLMs with the image and the intention and let them generate an open-ended continuation. This is a more straightforward way to assess the models, but it poses challenges on the evaluation side. Below, we describe the two methods we use to evaluate model performance.

Reference-based evaluation In this evaluation, we take the continuation generated by a model and compare it to each of the five candidate actions in the sample. We make the simplistic assumption that, if the generated action is good, it should be more similar to the correct action than the decoy actions. This assumption allows us to compute model accuracy: we consider the model correct every time the similarity between the generated and correct actions is the highest in the batch.

Intuitively, the choice of the prompt to use to elicit a continuation from a model plays a big role. Indeed, we noticed that some prompts may be effective for some models, but not for others. After a careful, manual exploration of prompts, we focused on four that appeared to be good-performing across models. We provide further details about this exploration and the actual prompts in Appendix C.

Model	Accuracy
MAPL	32.9±8.7
FROMAGe	32.7±4.8
BLIP-2	**49.5±2.6**
IDEFICS	31.5±10.9

Table 4: Open-ended generative experiment. Reference-based accuracy is computed using BERTScore similarity. Average and std. over results for 4 different prompts.

To compute similarities, we used various common NLG metrics, including BLEU4 (Papineni et al., 2002), ROUGE (Lin, 2004), CIDER (Vedantam et al., 2015), Meteor (Banerjee and Lavie, 2005), and the more recent BERTScore (Zhang et al., 2019). While the scores by various metrics can be different, we observed that various metrics led to similar patterns. Therefore, from now on, we only focus on BERTScore and refer the reader to Appendix E for further details on other metrics.

Reference-free evaluation Evaluating model outputs using automatic, reference-based metrics is simplistic as it assumes that only an action that is similar to the target one is a good one. To evaluate the plausibility of the actions in a reference-free manner, we therefore carried out a human evaluation. We sampled 50 <image, intention, generated action> datapoints per model and presented them, one at a time, to six participants.[4] We asked them to judge whether the second part of the sentence (displayed in bold), i.e., the generated action, was a plausible continuation of the first part, i.e., the ground-truth intention, based on the contents of the image. As the question was binary, they could choose between the options *Yes* or *No*. To ensure the quality of human annotations, we added 20 clear-cut cases to the data (10 correct, 10 wrong), that we used as a control group. All participants achieved high accuracy ($\geq 75\%$) on these control samples. In total, each participant assessed 220 samples (200 model-generated + 20 control ones).

5.1 Results

Table 4 and Figure 3 report, respectively, the results of the reference-based and reference-free evaluation. Below, we summarize the main findings.

[4]Participants were recruited among colleagues at our institution and carried out the annotation voluntarily. They were informed about the use of the annotations they provided and agreed to their use through informed consent.

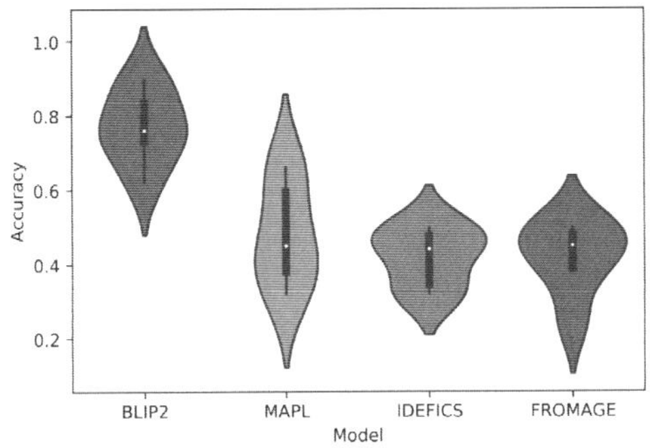

Figure 3: Open-ended generative experiment. Reference-free accuracy is based on human judgments, 300 per model (i.e., one per assessed sample).

BLIP2 is the best-performing model according to both evaluations Based on the results of both evaluations, BLIP-2 appears to be the best-performing model in this experiment. Indeed, this model achieves the highest average reference-based accuracy (49.5%) across the board, outperforming the other models by nearly 20 accuracy points. As for the reference-free evaluation, human participants judge BLIP-2's generated actions as plausible in 77% cases. This is a remarkably higher accuracy than the one obtained by the other models, whose accuracy ranges between 40 and 45%. These results confirm the superiority of BLIP-2 in generating actions consistent with both a visual context and a non-grounded textual intention.

BLIP-2's abilities can also be appreciated by looking at cases where it generates actions that are judged implausible by human annotators, as the one in Figure 4. Here, given the intention *If I want to socialize*, the model generates a good action, which is also consistent with the scene content—a pool in the foreground and several people standing around it. However, in this case, this action is *pragmatically* implausible, as the people in the image are busy playing video games. From this single example, it appears that the strengths of BLIP-2 lie in its ability to understand the scene, the intention, and their complex interaction. On the other hand, there is room for improvement in understanding the dynamics of events and relationships between people conveyed by an image. Improving this aspect can be a good direction to develop semantically valid and pragmatically plausible models.

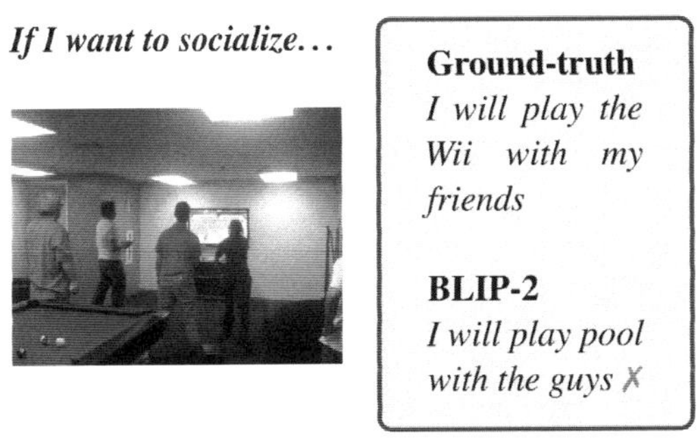

Figure 4: An example of an action generated by BLIP-2. In this case, the human annotators considered this action implausible given the intention and the image.

Other models perform similarly (poorly) As for MAPL, IDEFICS, and FROMAGe, it can be noted that their performance is similar according to both evaluations. This is interesting as the models build on different language and vision models, have varying sizes, and are trained with different data. Once again, this observation seems to reiterate the peculiarity of BLIP-2 compared to other architectures, from which it differs by the instruction-tuned LM and the presence of COCO in the training data.

6 Conclusion

In this work, we focused on the problem of combining complementary information brought to a context by language and vision. We used a benchmark proposed for previous-generation multimodal models, i.e., language-and-vision encoders based on the Masked Language Modeling objective, and tested, for the first time, how state-of-the-art generative visual language models deal with it. We presented a set of innovative analytical methods designed to assess the ability of multimodal generative models to integrate complementary information effectively. Through both multiple-choice evaluations and open-ended generative experiments, our approach offers a novel perspective on the challenges and capabilities of these models in achieving true multimodal integration. In our experiments, we found that the BLIP-2 performs consistently and significantly better than competing models. While most generative VLMs struggle, this model achieves both near-human accuracy in the multiple-choice experiment and high human judgments in the open-ended generative experiment. This reveals the superiority of this model on the task, likely due to instruction finetuning and having seen COCO images in training. These two ingredients appear to be key for the model, which exhibits a deep understanding of the image, the textual intention, and the complex interaction between them. Based on these findings, we conjecture that this recipe—and, particularly, instruction finetuning—may help models develop better generalized semantic and pragmatic abilities. These skills are crucial to language-mediated communication; future work might extend our investigation to other scenarios, including more naturalistic ones. Similarly, future work should focus on a comprehensive evaluation of the impact of seeing the same images encountered during training. While the BD2BB task here explored is a different one than plain image captioning, this aspect surely deserves further attention.

We argue that future work should focus on building more datasets and resources that encompass complex interactions between image content and its accompanying text. This implies taking a more communicative perspective on the study of language in multimodal contexts, which is what is needed to develop linguistic technologies ready to communicate seamlessly with human users.

Limitations

Our investigation is limited to one (English) dataset and a handful of models. This narrows the scope of the findings we presented. While our approach can be easily applied to other resources, languages, and models, we acknowledge that the claims made in this paper may not necessarily generalize. Another limitation is the choice of prompts used to elicit the responses from the models. There is growing evidence of the significant role of prompt wording on model generation, that we fully recognize. Although we believe we conducted a fairly comprehensive prompt search, our results can only speak for the prompts we used. Furthermore, the human evaluation we conducted is arguably small-scale as it involves few participants and a relatively small number of samples. We cannot fully exclude that the reported patterns may not replicate when increasing the number of participants and stimuli.

References

Jean-Baptiste Alayrac, Jeff Donahue, Pauline Luc, Antoine Miech, Iain Barr, Yana Hasson, Karel Lenc, Arthur Mensch, Katherine Millican, Malcolm Reynolds, et al. 2022. Flamingo: a visual language model for few-shot learning. *Advances in Neural Information Processing Systems*, 35:23716–23736.

Stanislaw Antol, Aishwarya Agrawal, Jiasen Lu, Margaret Mitchell, Dhruv Batra, C Lawrence Zitnick, and Devi Parikh. 2015. Vqa: Visual question answering. In *Proceedings of the IEEE international conference on computer vision*, pages 2425–2433.

Satanjeev Banerjee and Alon Lavie. 2005. Meteor: An automatic metric for mt evaluation with improved correlation with human judgments. In *Proceedings of the acl workshop on intrinsic and extrinsic evaluation measures for machine translation and/or summarization*, pages 65–72.

Parishad BehnamGhader, Vaibhav Adlakha, Marius Mosbach, Dzmitry Bahdanau, Nicolas Chapados, and Siva Reddy. 2024. Llm2vec: Large language models are secretly powerful text encoders. *arXiv preprint arXiv:2404.05961*.

C. Benoît, J. C. Martin, C. Pelachaud, L. Schomaker, and B. Suhm. 2000. Audio-visual and multimodal speech-based systems. pages 102–203.

Raffaella Bernardi, Ruket Cakici, Desmond Elliott, Aykut Erdem, Erkut Erdem, Nazli Ikizler-Cinbis, Frank Keller, Adrian Muscat, and Barbara Plank. 2016. Automatic description generation from images: A survey of models, datasets, and evaluation measures. *Journal of Artificial Intelligence Research*, 55:409–442.

Davide Caffagni, Federico Cocchi, Luca Barsellotti, Nicholas Moratelli, Sara Sarto, Lorenzo Baraldi, Marcella Cornia, and Rita Cucchiara. 2024. The (r)evolution of multimodal large language models: A survey. *arXiv preprint arXiv:2402.12451*.

Yen-Chun Chen, Linjie Li, Licheng Yu, Ahmed El Kholy, Faisal Ahmed, Zhe Gan, Yu Cheng, and Jingjing Liu. 2020. UNITER: Universal image-text representation learning. In *European conference on computer vision*, pages 104–120. Springer.

Hyung Won Chung, Le Hou, Shayne Longpre, Barret Zoph, Yi Tay, William Fedus, Eric Li, Xuezhi Wang, Mostafa Dehghani, Siddhartha Brahma, et al. 2022. Scaling instruction-finetuned language models. *arXiv preprint arXiv:2210.11416*.

Abhishek Das, Satwik Kottur, Khushi Gupta, Avi Singh, Deshraj Yadav, José MF Moura, Devi Parikh, and Dhruv Batra. 2017. Visual dialog. In *Proceedings of the IEEE conference on computer vision and pattern recognition*, pages 326–335.

Katherine Deng, Arijit Ray, Reuben Tan, Saadia Gabriel, Bryan A. Plummer, and Kate Saenko. 2023. Socratis: Are large multimodal models emotionally aware?

Jacob Devlin, Ming-Wei Chang, Kenton Lee, and Kristina Toutanova. 2019. BERT: Pre-training of deep bidirectional transformers for language understanding. In *Proceedings of the 2019 Conference of the North American Chapter of the Association for Computational Linguistics: Human Language Technologies, Volume 1 (Long and Short Papers)*, pages 4171–4186, Minneapolis, Minnesota. Association for Computational Linguistics.

Yuxin Fang, Wen Wang, Binhui Xie, Quan Sun, Ledell Wu, Xinggang Wang, Tiejun Huang, Xinlong Wang, and Yue Cao. 2023. Eva: Exploring the limits of masked visual representation learning at scale. In *Proceedings of the IEEE/CVF Conference on Computer Vision and Pattern Recognition*, pages 19358–19369.

C. Forceville. 2020. Introduction. *Visual and Multimodal Communication*.

Jack Hessel, Ari Holtzman, Maxwell Forbes, Ronan Le Bras, and Yejin Choi. 2021. Clipscore: A reference-free evaluation metric for image captioning. *arXiv preprint arXiv:2104.08718*.

Jack Hessel, Jena D Hwang, Jae Sung Park, Rowan Zellers, Chandra Bhagavatula, Anna Rohrbach, Kate Saenko, and Yejin Choi. 2022. The abduction of sherlock holmes: A dataset for visual abductive reasoning. In *European Conference on Computer Vision*, pages 558–575. Springer.

Jack Hessel, Ana Marasovic, Jena D. Hwang, Lillian Lee, Jeff Da, Rowan Zellers, Robert Mankoff, and Yejin Choi. 2023. Do androids laugh at electric sheep? humor "understanding" benchmarks from the new yorker caption contest. In *Proceedings of the 61st Annual Meeting of the Association for Computational Linguistics (Volume 1: Long Papers)*, pages 688–714, Toronto, Canada. Association for Computational Linguistics.

Xudong Hong, Asad Sayeed, Khushboo Mehra, Vera Demberg, and Bernt Schiele. 2023. Visual writing prompts: Character-grounded story generation with curated image sequences. *Transactions of the Association for Computational Linguistics*, 11:565–581.

Ting-Hao Kenneth Huang, Francis Ferraro, Nasrin Mostafazadeh, Ishan Misra, Aishwarya Agrawal, Jacob Devlin, Ross Girshick, Xiaodong He, Pushmeet Kohli, Dhruv Batra, C. Lawrence Zitnick, Devi Parikh, Lucy Vanderwende, Michel Galley, and Margaret Mitchell. 2016. Visual storytelling. In *Proceedings of the 2016 Conference of the North American Chapter of the Association for Computational Linguistics: Human Language Technologies*, pages 1233–1239, San Diego, California. Association for Computational Linguistics.

Mohit Iyyer, Varun Manjunatha, Anupam Guha, Yogarshi Vyas, Jordan Boyd-Graber, Hal Daume, and Larry S Davis. 2017. The amazing mysteries of the gutter: Drawing inferences between panels in comic book narratives. In *Proceedings of the IEEE Conference on Computer Vision and Pattern recognition*, pages 7186–7195.

Jing Yu Koh, Ruslan Salakhutdinov, and Daniel Fried. 2023. Grounding language models to images for multimodal generation. *arXiv preprint arXiv:2301.13823*.

Elisa Kreiss, Cynthia Bennett, Shayan Hooshmand, Eric Zelikman, Meredith Ringel Morris, and Christopher Potts. 2022. Context matters for image descriptions for accessibility: Challenges for referenceless evaluation metrics. *arXiv preprint arXiv:2205.10646*.

Elisa Kreiss, Fei Fang, Noah D Goodman, and Christopher Potts. 2021. Concadia: Towards image-based text generation with a purpose. *arXiv preprint arXiv:2104.08376*.

Julia Kruk, Jonah Lubin, Karan Sikka, Xiao Lin, Dan Jurafsky, and Ajay Divakaran. 2019. Integrating text and image: Determining multimodal document intent in instagram posts. In *Proceedings of the 2019 Conference on Empirical Methods in Natural Language Processing and the 9th International Joint Conference on Natural Language Processing (EMNLP-IJCNLP)*, pages 4622–4632.

Hugo Laurençon, Lucile Saulnier, Léo Tronchon, Stas Bekman, Amanpreet Singh, Anton Lozhkov, Thomas Wang, Siddharth Karamcheti, Alexander M. Rush, Douwe Kiela, Matthieu Cord, and Victor Sanh. 2023. Obelics: An open web-scale filtered dataset of interleaved image-text documents.

Junnan Li, Dongxu Li, Silvio Savarese, and Steven Hoi. 2023. Blip-2: Bootstrapping language-image pre-training with frozen image encoders and large language models. *arXiv preprint arXiv:2301.12597*.

Liunian Harold Li, Mark Yatskar, Da Yin, Cho-Jui Hsieh, and Kai-Wei Chang. 2019. VisualBERT: A simple and performant baseline for vision and language. *arXiv e-prints*, pages arXiv–1908.

Chin-Yew Lin. 2004. Rouge: A package for automatic evaluation of summaries. In *Text summarization branches out*, pages 74–81.

Tsung-Yi Lin, Michael Maire, Serge Belongie, James Hays, Pietro Perona, Deva Ramanan, Piotr Dollár, and C Lawrence Zitnick. 2014. Microsoft coco: Common objects in context. In *Computer Vision–ECCV 2014: 13th European Conference, Zurich, Switzerland, September 6-12, 2014, Proceedings, Part V 13*, pages 740–755. Springer.

Yinhan Liu, Myle Ott, Naman Goyal, Jingfei Du, Mandar Joshi, Danqi Chen, Omer Levy, Mike Lewis, Luke Zettlemoyer, and Veselin Stoyanov. 2019. RoBERTa: A robustly optimized BERT pretraining approach.

Jiasen Lu, Dhruv Batra, Devi Parikh, and Stefan Lee. 2019. Vilbert: Pretraining task-agnostic visiolinguistic representations for vision-and-language tasks. *Advances in neural information processing systems*, 32.

Oscar Mañas, Pau Rodriguez, Saba Ahmadi, Aida Nematzadeh, Yash Goyal, and Aishwarya Agrawal. 2022. Mapl: Parameter-efficient adaptation of unimodal pre-trained models for vision-language few-shot prompting. *arXiv preprint arXiv:2210.07179*.

Nasrin Mostafazadeh, Chris Brockett, William B Dolan, Michel Galley, Jianfeng Gao, Georgios Spithourakis, and Lucy Vanderwende. 2017. Image-grounded conversations: Multimodal context for natural question and response generation. In *Proceedings of the Eighth International Joint Conference on Natural Language Processing (Volume 1: Long Papers)*, pages 462–472.

Vinod Nair and Geoffrey E Hinton. 2010. Rectified linear units improve restricted boltzmann machines. In *Proceedings of the 27th international conference on machine learning (ICML-10)*, pages 807–814.

Kishore Papineni, Salim Roukos, Todd Ward, and Wei-Jing Zhu. 2002. Bleu: a method for automatic evaluation of machine translation. In *Proceedings of the 40th annual meeting of the Association for Computational Linguistics*, pages 311–318.

Sarah Partan and Peter Marler. 1999. Communication goes multimodal. *Science*, 283(5406):1272–1273.

Sandro Pezzelle. 2023. Dealing with semantic underspecification in multimodal NLP. In *Proceedings of the 61st Annual Meeting of the Association for Computational Linguistics (Volume 1: Long Papers)*, pages 12098–12112, Toronto, Canada. Association for Computational Linguistics.

Sandro Pezzelle, Claudio Greco, Greta Gandolfi, Eleonora Gualdoni, and Raffaella Bernardi. 2020. Be different to be better! a benchmark to leverage the complementarity of language and vision. In *Findings of the association for computational linguistics: EMNLP 2020*, pages 2751–2767.

Alec Radford, Jong Wook Kim, Chris Hallacy, Aditya Ramesh, Gabriel Goh, Sandhini Agarwal, Girish Sastry, Amanda Askell, Pamela Mishkin, Jack Clark, et al. 2021. Learning transferable visual models from natural language supervision. In *International conference on machine learning*, pages 8748–8763. PMLR.

Alec Radford, Jeffrey Wu, Rewon Child, David Luan, Dario Amodei, Ilya Sutskever, et al. 2019. Language models are unsupervised multitask learners. *OpenAI blog*, 1(8):9.

Nitish Srivastava, Geoffrey Hinton, Alex Krizhevsky, Ilya Sutskever, and Ruslan Salakhutdinov. 2014. Dropout: a simple way to prevent neural networks from overfitting. *The journal of machine learning research*, 15(1):1929–1958.

Weijie Su, Xizhou Zhu, Yue Cao, Bin Li, Lewei Lu, Furu Wei, and Jifeng Dai. 2019. Vl-bert: Pre-training of generic visual-linguistic representations. *arXiv preprint arXiv:1908.08530*.

Aditya Surikuchi, Sandro Pezzelle, and Raquel Fernández. 2023. GROOViST: A metric for grounding objects in visual storytelling. In *Proceedings of the 2023 Conference on Empirical Methods in Natural Language Processing*, pages 3331–3339, Singapore. Association for Computational Linguistics.

Hao Tan and Mohit Bansal. 2019. Lxmert: Learning cross-modality encoder representations from transformers. *arXiv preprint arXiv:1908.07490*.

Hugo Touvron, Thibaut Lavril, Gautier Izacard, Xavier Martinet, Marie-Anne Lachaux, Timothée Lacroix, Baptiste Rozière, Naman Goyal, Eric Hambro, Faisal Azhar, et al. 2023. LLaMA: Open and efficient foundation language models. *arXiv preprint arXiv:2302.13971*.

Ashish Vaswani, Noam Shazeer, Niki Parmar, Jakob Uszkoreit, Llion Jones, Aidan N Gomez, Łukasz Kaiser, and Illia Polosukhin. 2017. Attention is all you need. *Advances in neural information processing systems*, 30.

Ramakrishna Vedantam, C Lawrence Zitnick, and Devi Parikh. 2015. Cider: Consensus-based image description evaluation. In *Proceedings of the IEEE conference on computer vision and pattern recognition*, pages 4566–4575.

Ben Wang and Aran Komatsuzaki. 2021. Gpt-j-6b: A 6 billion parameter autoregressive language model.

Susan Zhang, Stephen Roller, Naman Goyal, Mikel Artetxe, Moya Chen, Shuohui Chen, Christopher Dewan, Mona Diab, Xian Li, Xi Victoria Lin, et al. 2022. OPT: Open pre-trained transformer language models. *arXiv e-prints*, pages arXiv–2205.

Tianyi Zhang, Varsha Kishore, Felix Wu, Kilian Q Weinberger, and Yoav Artzi. 2019. Bertscore: Evaluating text generation with bert. *arXiv preprint arXiv:1904.09675*.

A Different Parameter Combinations for Multiple-Choice Experiment

We tested each model's most promising prompt with 4 different parameter combinations. The results are shown in table 5.

-	FROMAGe	BLIP2	IDEFICS
Default parameter	20.5	77.1	42.1
Temp = 0.8,topp = 0.8	19.7	75.9	33.1
Temp = 0.8,topp = 0.9	17.8	74.3	30.0
Temp = 0.8,topp = 0.8	17.7	75.2	30.5
Temp = 0.8,topp = 0.8	17.7	73.5	28.3

Table 5: The results for 3 generative models in discriminative setting across different parameter combinations

B 30 Prompts for Multipul-Choice Experiment

1. What am I supposed to do <intention>? <candidate actions>
2. What am I supposed to do <intention>? Pick the best option from the following ones: <candidate actions>
3. Question: What am I supposed to do <intention>? Pick the best option from the following ones: <candidate actions> Answer:
4. Given this visual context, what am I supposed to do <intention>? Pick the best option from the following ones: <candidate actions>
5. What am I supposed to do given this visual context, <intention>? Pick the best option from the following ones: <candidate actions>
6. Suppose I am faced with this situation. What am I supposed to do <intention>? Pick the best option from the following ones: <candidate actions>
7. What action will I perform <intention>? Pick the best option from the following ones: <candidate actions>
8. Suppose I am faced with this situation. What actions should I perform <intention>? Pick the best option from the following ones: <candidate actions>
9. Imagine I am in this visual scenario. What action should I perform <intention>? Pick the best option from the following ones: <candidate actions>
10. What actions should I perform <intention>? Considering both my feeling and the image, pick the best option from the following ones: <candidate actions>
11. Considering both my feeling and the image, what will I do <intention>? Pick the best option from the following ones: <candidate actions>
12. What will I do <intention>? Pick the best option from the following ones: <candidate actions>
13. <intention>, what's the best step to take? Select the optimal choice from the options provided.<candidate actions>
14. <intention>, what's the most suitable action to choose? Select the best option from the following list.<candidate actions>
15. <intention>, what's the recommended action to perform? Choose the best option from the following ones.<candidate actions>
16. Which action is most advisable <intention>? Choose from the following options. <candidate actions>
17. What's the best step to follow <intention>? Pick from the following options. <candidate actions>
18. <intention>, what's the most appropriate decision to make? Select the right choice from the options provided. <candidate actions>
19. What's the recommended response <intention>? Choose from the following options. <candidate actions>
20. What should I do <intention>? Choose from the following options considering both my feeling and the image.<candidate actions>
21. Taking into account both my feeling and the image, what's the recommended step to take <intention>? Pick from the following options. <candidate actions>
22. Considering equally the image and my feeling, what should be my action <intention>? Choose the right action from the following list.<candidate actions>

23. With both the image and my feeling in mind, how should I react <intention>? Select the best choice from the following options. <candidate actions>

24. With both the image and my feeling in mind, what action is most advisable <intention>? Choose from the following options. <candidate actions>

25. When taking both the image and my feeling into consideration, what's the best step to follow <intention>? Pick from the following options.

26. <intention>. <candidate actions>

27. <intention>, what happens next? <candidate actions>

28. <intention>, what will I do? <candidate actions>

29. What will I do <intention>? <candidate actions>

30. How should I behave <intention>? <candidate actions>

C 4 Prompts For Open-Ended Generative Experiment

1. What am I supposed to do <intention>? I will...
2. <intention>, what will I do? I will...
3. What should I do <intention>? I will...
4. What action will I perform <intention>? I will...

For this open-ended generative experiment, it is important to note that the optimal prompt may vary for each model. For instance, the prompt "What am I supposed to do + [intention]+? " can yield results for BLIP2 but did not work well for the MAPL and FROMAGe models. For the MAPL model, "Question:... Answer:", and for the FROMAGe model, "Q:... \nA: " are the template prompts provided by the model developer. Additionally, adding "I will" at the end of the prompt is proved to be effective for both models. After a careful manual inspection of several prompts and their outputs, we focused on the 4 most promising ones as in this appendix.

Actions generated using these prompts also need to be further processed to ensure they conform to the same format as the target action and other optional actions. For example, IDEFICS consistently generates sentences prefixed with "Assistant:". To calculate the similarity score of these answers with other actions, it is necessary to remove the "Assistant:" prefix and retain only the main action, which typically begins with a verb.

D Error Analysis

We performed an error analysis aiming to compare the outputs of the three versions of BLIP2: multimodal, language-only, and vision-only. By doing so, we aimed to gain insights into how, and when, BLIP2 effectively leveraged information from language and vision to achieve better performance in the task. We observed that, in 1,350 cases (33%), all three model versions provided a true prediction. In such cases, the model could make a correct assessment by relying only on one single modality, which suggests that, in these cases, the information conveyed by the multimodal input may be redundant.

In 221 cases (around 5%), only the multimodal BLIP2 could correctly predict the right answer, while no unimodal model versions could. In these cases, BLIP2 genuinely leveraged complementary information from the two modalities, which was necessary but not sufficient on their own to perform the task.

The entire test dataset, comprising 4,081 samples, was categorized into eight different groups based on the consensus of model predictions under three conditions. The categories are as follows:

- TTT: The model correctly produces the answer in LV, L, and V.
- TTF: The model correctly produces the answer in LV, L, but not in V.
- ...and so on for the remaining categories.

For each category, a manual inspection of 100 cases was conducted to identify the sources of errors in the models. The results of this analysis are summarized in Table 6.

This error analysis table reveals a wealth of information. The second and third rows of the table indicate that when there is correct information in one modality, the multimodal model knows how to utilize it effectively. Furthermore, the examples in the fourth row demonstrate that these cases can only be predicted correctly using complementary information.

Is the prediction correct?	Number of Cases	Percentage	Comments
BLIP_LV: T BLIP_V: T BLIP_L: T	1350	0.3308	No errors were found in these cases, indicating that they may be too easy for the multimodality model to handle.
BLIP_LV: T BLIP_V: T BLIP_L: F	581	0.1424	The model in the L setting gave incorrect predictions due to the absence of image information.
BLIP_LV: T BLIP_V: F BLIP_L: T	808	0.1980	The model in the V setting gave incorrect predictions due to the absence of intention information.
BLIP_LV: T BLIP_V: F BLIP_L: F	222	0.0544	Only multimodality setting can give true predictions.
BLIP_LV: F BLIP_V: T BLIP_L: T	11	0.0027	The model's incorrect predictions can be attributed to the following reasons: 1. Problematic/borderline cases; 2. Wrong object detection; 3. Failure to understand the intention; 4.Only considering one modality;
BLIP_LV: F BLIP_V: T BLIP_L: F	221	0.0542	
BLIP_LV: F BLIP_V: F BLIP_L: T	117	0.0287	
BLIP_LV: F BLIP_V: F BLIP_L: F	771	0.1889	

Table 6: Error Analysis Table: Each row provides information on some specific cases, indicating whether the BLIP2 model can produce a correct prediction under three different conditions and the potential reasons for such results.

E Exploring Different Metrics for Similarity Measurement

We tested different metrics to conduct the Reference-based evaluation for the open-ended generative experiment. We tested in three settings: multimodal, language-only, and vision-only. The result are reported in Table 7.

F Degree of Visual Grounding

In our previous analysis, we evaluated the BLIP2 model's performance in the BD2BB task by examining the accuracy of the generated actions. However, accuracy alone does not fully capture the model's ability to utilize the information from two modalities. Therefore, we can also evaluate the model from a different perspective by considering its ability to incorporate information only from the image. We assumed that if the model successfully utilizes the image information, it will explicitly mention objects from the image in the generated actions. This indicates that the action is grounded in the visual content.

Thanks to the labeling of golden nouns in the image data, we can easily determine whether the generated action mentions any objects from the image. Based on how many actions are grounded in the visual content, we can calculate the grounding rate by following the formula:

$$\text{grounding\_rate} = \frac{N_{\text{grounded}}}{N_{\text{total}}} \qquad (1)$$

We calculated the grounding rate for generated actions using 15 manually selected prompts. These prompts were carefully crafted to vary in their focus: some directed the model's attention toward language aspects, others toward visual elements, and some involved variations in linguistic forms. The prompts we use are shown in Table 8. The grounding rate varied across different prompts. Interestingly, we found that by changing the prompt, we could easily influence the grounding rate while accuracy remain stable. Although we cannot suppress a modality by altering the prompt (prompt 6), we can effectively focus selectively on one modality by being explicit (prompts 7, 8, 9, and 14). Figure 5 is the bar plot about both accuracy and grounding rate. The pink bar represents the accu-

Setting	BERTScore	BLEU-4	CIDER	METEOR	ROUGE
LV	0.53	0.54	0.52	0.48	0.51
L	0.39	0.49	0.38	0.29	0.36
V	0.42	0.37	0.41	0.38	0.4

Table 7: Results for BLIP2 in three different settings using different metrics.

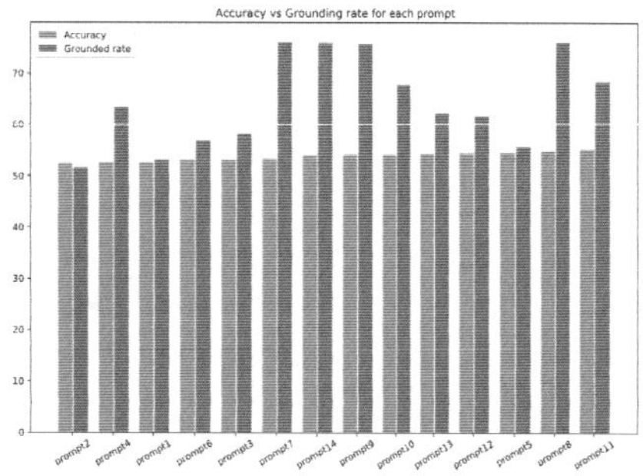

Figure 5: A bar plot illustrates the accuracy and grounding rate across different prompts. Accuracy increases from left to right. The bar with the highest grounding rate corresponds to Prompt 8: "Suppose I am in this specific visual context. What actions should I take [intention]? Please mention at least one object from the image." The bar with the lowest grounding rate corresponds to Prompt 2: "Q: What am I supposed to do [intention]? A:" This variation highlights the impact of prompt design on model performance.

racy of different prompts in an ascending order. It is shown that the grounding rate does not always align with the accuracy.

By introducing the grounding rate as an evaluation metric, we provide an additional perspective to assess the performance of multimodal models. It highlights the model's ability to ground its generated actions in visual information, offering insights beyond accuracy alone (Surikuchi et al., 2023).

	Prompt	Accuracy	Grounding rate
prompt1	Question: What am I supposed to do + [intention]? Answer:	52.66	53.10
prompt2	Q: What am I supposed to do + [intention]? \nA:	52.34	51.58
prompt3	What am I supposed to do + [intention]?	53.20	58.25
prompt4	What am I supposed to do + [intention]+? I will	52.63	63.44
prompt5	What am I supposed to do + [intention]+? Answer in the format "I will"	54.57	55.67
prompt6	What am I supposed to do + [intention]+? Please provide an answer based solely on the intention, without considering the image.	53.08	56.82
prompt7	What action should I take +[intention]+? Please base your response solely on the image. Additionally, kindly mention at least one object visible in the image.	53.32	75.97
prompt8	Suppose I am in this specific visual context. What actions should I take+ [intention]+? Please mention at least one object from the image.	54.76	76.06
prompt9	Imagine I am in the given visual scenario. What actions should I take regarding +[intention]+'? Please mention at least one object from the image.	54.06	75.74
prompt10	Imagine yourself in this specific visual context. Considering both the intention and the image, what actions should be taken +[intention]+?	54.06	67.78
prompt11	Considering both the intention and the image, what will you do +[intention]+?	55.16	68.41
prompt12	What will I do +[intention]+?	54.47	61.67
prompt13	What will you do +[intention]+? I will	54.37	62.23
prompt14	What will you do +[intention]+? Please give a plausible reason by mentioning at least one object from the image.	53.96	75.89

Table 8: The accuracy and grounding rate across different variations of the prompts.

LLaVA-RE: Binary Image-Text Relevancy Evaluation with Multimodal Large Language Model

Tao Sun*
Stony Brook University
tao@cs.stonybrook.edu

Oliver Liu, JinJin Li, Lan Ma
Amazon
{olivlius,jinjinli,mamlm}@amazon.com

Abstract

Multimodal generative AI usually involves generating image or text responses given inputs in another modality. The evaluation of image-text relevancy is essential for measuring response quality or ranking candidate responses. In particular, binary relevancy evaluation, *i.e.*, "Relevant" *vs.* "Not Relevant", is a fundamental problem. However, this is a challenging task considering that texts have diverse formats and the definition of relevancy varies in different scenarios. We find that Multimodal Large Language Models (MLLMs) are an ideal choice to build such evaluators, as they can flexibly handle complex text formats and take in additional task information. In this paper, we present LLaVA-RE, a first attempt for binary image-text relevancy evaluation with MLLM. It follows the LLaVA architecture and adopts detailed task instructions and multimodal in-context samples. In addition, we propose a novel binary relevancy data set that covers various tasks. Experimental results validate the effectiveness of our framework.

1 Introduction

Multimodal generative AI such as GPT-4V (Achiam et al., 2023), Gemini (Team et al., 2023), and Stable Diffusion (Rombach et al., 2022) has shown remarkable ability to generate image or text responses. A typical scenario is an AI assistant where *agent* responses to *user* instructions during a conversation. For example, *user* inputs a textual query, and *agent* returns an image that is generated or retrieved from some database. To measure response quality or rank candidate responses, an essential component is evaluating the relevancy between text and image. However, this is not an easy task. The texts can have diverse formats such as a long description, a multi-turn conversation, or a structured document digest. Such complex texts usually contain rich information, and the definition of relevancy varies in different scenarios. It requires to specify attributes that lead to a 'relevant' image. For example, a multi-turn conversation and an image may talk about the same product but have some controversial details, such as color or size; when describing fine-grained bird species, one image can match common attributes of the bird genus but not specie-wise details. In both cases, the image can be labeled either as 'relevant' or 'not relevant', depending on the particular goal. Traditional retrieval models (Frome et al., 2013; Lee et al., 2018; Qu et al., 2021) rely on image and text embeddings. They are not suitable for this complex evaluation task with long texts. Methods like CLIP (Radford et al., 2021) and BLIP (Li et al., 2022) fall apart for long and ambiguous texts.

These challenges motivate us to build an effective relevancy evaluation model for complex image-text pairs. We focus on binary image-text relevancy, *i.e.*, "Relevant" *vs.* "Not Relevant". Although it is possible to add intermediate relevancy labels such as "Somewhat Relevant", binary relevance labels are more common in practical usage and it enforces evaluators to make less ambiguous labeling.

Multimodal Large Langauge Models (MLLMs) such as LLaVA (Liu et al., 2024c) are an ideal choice for the above-mentioned purposes. Compared with traditional models that rely on similarity scores between image and text embeddings (Wang et al., 2018), MLLMs exhibit much more flexibility. As MLLMs are pre-trained on huge image-text corpus, they can easily handle diverse text formats. Besides, additional task information such as the relevancy definition or demonstration examples can be readily integrated into model inputs. However, even with contextual information, a direct extension of state-of-the-art MLLMs does not perform effectively on relevancy tasks.

In this paper, we present **L**arge **L**anguage **a**nd

*Work done during internship at Amazon.

Proceedings of the First Workshop of Evaluation of Multi-Modal Generation, pages 40–51
January 20, 2025. ©2025 Association for Computational Linguistics

Vision **A**ssistant for binary image-text **R**elevancy **E**valuation (LLaVA-RE), a first attempt for relevancy evaluation with MLLM. Our model builds upon the LLaVA 1.5 architecture (Liu et al., 2024a), which shows excellent performances among open-sourced MLLMs and can be easily extended owing to its light-weight design. To handle ambiguity in relevancy, we adopt detailed task instructions. Furthermore, we leverage multimodal in-context-learning (Doveh et al., 2024) to include few-shot demonstration examples. These designs empower LLaVA-RE to generalize to unseen relevancy tasks and achieve more accurate predictions. Since there are no publicly available datasets focusing on complex image-text relevancy, we propose a novel binary relevancy dataset covering diverse tasks. For each task, a strategy to sample positive and negative image-text pairs is delicately designed. We train our model on the curated datasets and evaluate on unseen and fine-grained relevancy tasks.

We summarize the contributions as follows:

- To the best of our knowledge, LLaVA-RE is the first work to build MLLM for binary image-text relevancy evaluation.
- We create a novel binary relevancy dataset covering diverse tasks, where positive and negative image-text pairs are delicately sampled.
- Experimental results validate the effectiveness of our framework over the vanilla LLaVA 1.5 by incorporating novel designs of task instructions and multimodal in-context learning.

2 Related Work

Image-Text Retrieval is a common task that retrieves the most related image or text giving the counterpart (Cao et al., 2022). Traditional methods (Frome et al., 2013; Lee et al., 2018; Qu et al., 2021) built visual semantic embeddings and model dense cross-modal interactions to get similarity scores. CLIP (Radford et al., 2021) is a pioneering work that aligns image and text modalities via contrastive learning on abundant imaga-text pairs. This is later improved with bootstrapping (Li et al., 2022) and Query Transformer (Li et al., 2023b). InternVL (Chen et al., 2024) scaled up the vision foundation model and progressively aligns it with LLM. Although these works aim to match image and text, their texts are often short image captions. In contrast, we tackle relevancy evaluation tasks that involve significantly longer texts, greater ambiguity, and more complex formats.

MLLM and Binary VQA. Recently, numerous MLLM models have been introduced (Achiam et al., 2023; Laurençon et al., 2024), with the LLaVA family (Liu et al., 2024c) being the most closely related to our work. LLaVA model connected a pretrained vision encoder and an LLM with a linear layer, and trains on visual instruction-following data generated by GPT-4. LLaVA 1.5 enhances performance with an MLP projector and academic-task VQA datasets (Liu et al., 2024a), while Liu et al. (2024b) introduce dynamic image resolution and stronger LLM backbones. MLLM models achieve impressive performances on diverse Visual Question Answering (VQA) tasks, and binary VQA that has a "yes/no" answer is an important subset. However, these existing binary VQA questions hae simple forms and it is unclear how MLLMs generalize to the challenging text-image relevancy tasks studied in this paper.

Multimodal In-Context-Learning utilizes multimodal context to improve model inference. Li et al. (2023a) construct an interleaved multi-modal ICL dataset and train a Flamingo-based model to demonstrate ICL capability. Zhao et al. (2023) introduce a novel context scheme that incorporates an additional image declaration section and includes image proxy tokens to enhance model's ICL ability. Doveh et al. (2024) extend LLaVA with ICL capability by tuning on few-shot instruction data. Despite these innovations, the effectiveness to incorporate ICL in binary relevancy tasks is under-explored. Our work finds current multimodal ICL solutions struggling to adapt effectively to this specific relevancy evaluation task.

3 Approach

3.1 Binary Relevancy Evaluation Formulation

Given a pair of image I and text T, we want to evaluate whether they are relevant or not. Formally, a relevancy evaluator $\mathcal{M}$ maps (I, T) into a binary label $r \in \{\text{"Relevant"}, \text{"Not Relevant"}\}$. Usually, this is not a well-defined task as the meaning of relevancy depends on specific scenarios. We assume that there exists an additional task instruction S, which is a paragraph of natural language describing the data and clarifying the relevancy definition. Meanwhile, there could be a few demonstration examples $\{(I_i, T_i, r_i)\}$ from the same task. Binary relevancy evaluation can be formulated as follows:

$$r = \mathcal{M}(I, T; S, \{(I_i, T_i, r_i)\}) \quad (1)$$

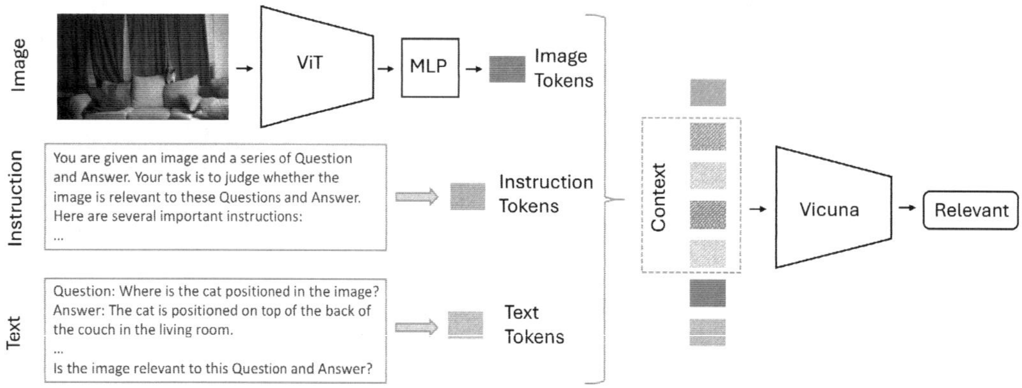

Figure 1: Framework of LLaVA-RE model. We use ViT and Vicuna as the image and text encoder, respectively. Context samples are selected from the same relevancy evaluation task.

Task	Train	Test	Text format
llava	$10k$	$6k$	Conversations
wiki	$20k$	300	Plain paragraph
recipe	$12k$	$1k$	Ingredients description
textvqa	$33k$	$1k$	Question, answer, reasoning
tdiuc	$7k$	300	Question, answer, reasoning
chartqa	–	$1k$	Question, answer, reasoning
infographics	–	$1k$	Question, answer, reasoning
fine-grained	–	$6k$	Category description

Table 1: List of created binary relevancy datasets.

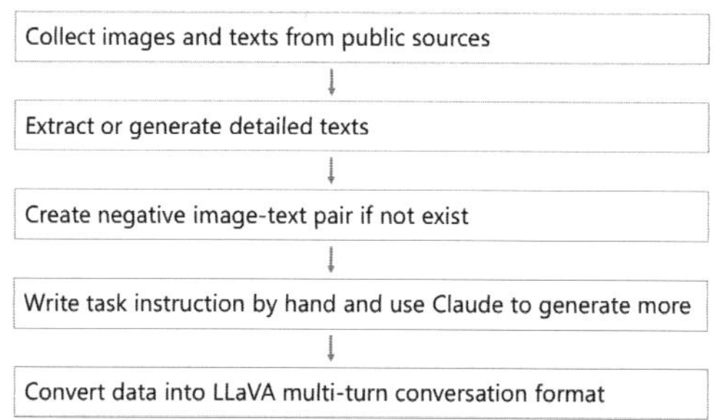

Figure 2: Data creation pipeline.

3.2 LLaVA-RE

In this paper, we present **L**arge **L**anguage **a**nd **V**ision **A**ssistant for binary image-text **R**elevancy **E**valuation (LLaVA-RE). It is built upon the LLaVA 1.5 architecture (Liu et al., 2024a), which uses a conversation data format and can readily integrate task instructions and demonstration text-image examples. One data sample is as follows:

$$\begin{aligned}
&\texttt{Human}: S \\
&\texttt{Human}: I_1, T_1 \quad \texttt{Assistant}: r_1 \\
&\ldots \\
&\texttt{Human}: I_C, T_C \quad \texttt{Assistant}: r_C \\
&\texttt{Human}: I, T \quad \texttt{Assistant}: r
\end{aligned} \tag{2}$$

where C is the number of demonstration examples.

The model training includes two stages: first, we train the image projector using the same methodology as LLaVA 1.5 (Liu et al., 2024a); second, we train the language backbone with multimodal ICL instruction tuning (Doveh et al., 2024) using binary relevancy data. To increase diversity during training, random task instructions are generated with Claude 3 Sonnet based on hand-crafted templates. The demonstration examples are sampled from training data of the same relevancy task. The task instruction together with demonstration examples form the prompt input for MLLMs. It can vary across different samples.

3.3 Binary Relevancy Data Creation

As there are no available complex binary relevancy datasets for training and evaluation, we create data from diverse public datasets listed in Tab. 1. These are for preliminary experiments and we plan to expand them in a future work. The datasets will be released upon approval.

The data creation pipeline consists of 5 stages, as shown in Fig. 2. We first collect public data with image and text correspondences. As we focus on texts with complex formats and rich details, we select VQA datasets whose questions require some reasoning, and structured data like Wikipedia pages. Having more diverse data sources would certainly be helpful. The images are ready to use, while texts need additional processing. We extract related texts from the raw data, and format them with predefined templates. For short texts, we use

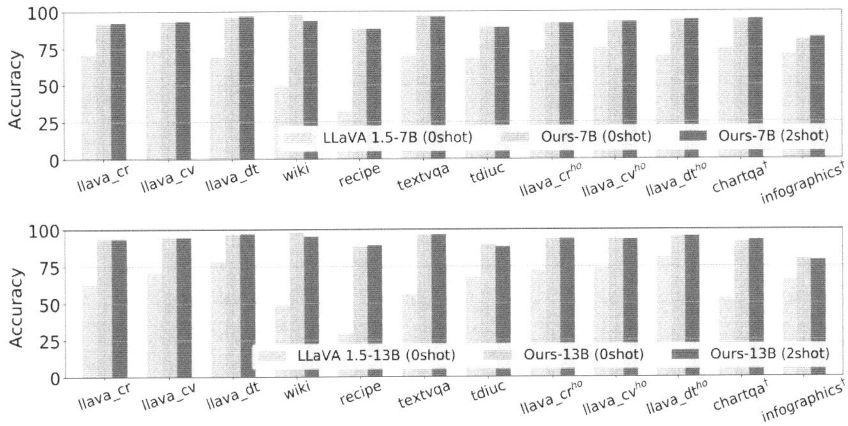

Figure 3: Evaluation results on training and unseen tasks. (^{ho}hold-out test data, †unseen test tasks)

Claude 3 Sonnet to generate detailed reasoning words or descriptions. After that, a key step is to define positive and negative image-text pairs. Positive pairs are easy to obtain as they can be derived from the raw data correspondences, while negative pairs may not exist. We create negative pairs by sampling images (or texts) from the same category. The specific strategies depend on the datasets. It is worth mentioning that defining proper negative pairs is a challenging task, as there are no human annotations. If using more strict rules (*e.g.*, higher similarity score thresholds), some relevant image-text pairs may be mislabeled as 'hard' negative samples. Finally, we use Claude 3 Sonnet to generate task instructions for each dataset and convert data into LLaVA multi-turn conversation format. Due to page length limit, more details can be found in Sec. A.1.

3.4 Framework

The framework of LLaVA-RE model is plotted in Fig. 1. Given a pair of image and text, and a task instruction, we use ViT model (Dosovitskiy, 2021) to extract image tokens. The text and instruction are transformed using a default tokenizor. An MLP module maps original image tokens into text space. In addition, there are several context samples tokenized in the same way. The Vicuna model (Chiang et al., 2023) takes the entire token sequence and predicts a binary relevancy label.

4 Experiments

4.1 Setup

Model Settings. Following LLaVA 1.5, we use CLIP-Large of 336×336 image resolution as vision encoder and Vicuna as LLM backbone. We experiment with both 7B and 13B Vicuna models.

Training Details. We use the same pretraining setting as LLaVA 1.5 to learn the image projector. During instruction tuning phase, we conduct 4-shot ICL tuning. The 4 context samples are randomly selected from the same task. For each ICL training sample, losses are applied to both context samples and training sample. Thus, the effective training shot ranges from 0 to 4. We also include LLaVA-Instruct-665k into training to preserve general VQA capability, but only train with 0-shot. While the goal is to do relevancy evaluation, we find that ICL training with only relevancy data is prone to overfitting. To alleviate this, we add $24k$ ICL samples of general VQA tasks created from TDIUC. The training is conducted with LoRA using 8× A100s. Input token length limit is set to 4096. As one image takes 576 tokens, it allows for 4 context samples in most cases. The learning rate of instruction tuning phase is 1.5e-4. Other hyper-parameters are kept the same as LLaVA 1.5.

Evaluation Details. We evaluate binary prediction accuracies on the test split of training tasks, hold-out and unseen tasks. During inference, each dataset uses a hand-crafted task instruction that is unseen during training. The in-context samples are sampled from training data in a balanced manner, *i.e.*, relevant and not relevant samples alternatively. In some rare cases where 4-shot inference exceeds 4096 tokens, we adjust token limit to 5120 to achieve a valid prediction.

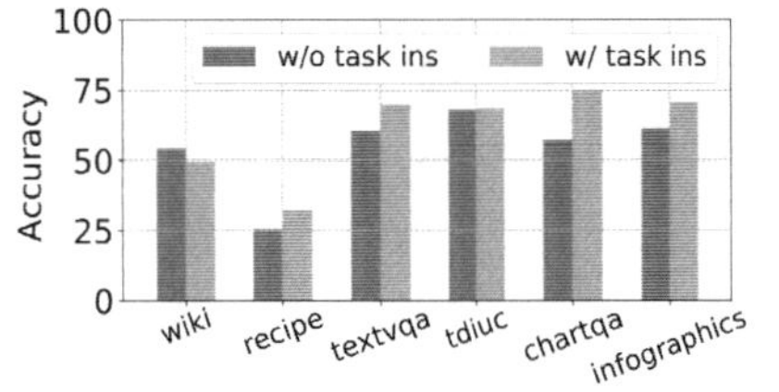

Figure 4: Effect of task instructions on LLaVA 1.5-7B.

4.2 Results

Effect of Task Instructions. We first study the effect of task instructions during inference on LLaVA 1.5 model. From Fig. 4, it can be seen that using task instructions achieves better accuracies on 5 out of 6 tasks. Since LLaVA 1.5 is not trained specifically for our binary image-text relevancy task, relevancy instructions provide useful information.

Evaluation on Training and Unseen Tasks. Figure 3 plots the evaluation results of LLaVA 1.5 and our LLaVA-RE model. On the test split of 5 training tasks, LLaVA-RE achieves much higher accuracies than LLaVA 1.5 with both 7B and 13B Vicuna backbones. LLaVA 1.5's accuracies are below 50% on some challenging tasks such as `wiki` and `recipe`, showing that binary image-text relevancy evaluation can sometimes be hard for off-the-shelf state-of-the-art models. The improvement of our models is consistent on 3 hold-out training tasks and 2 unseen tasks, which validates the generalization capability of LLaVA-RE. In the evaluations, 2-shot inference does not show much difference compared to 0-shot. One reason is that the ICL instruction tuning also optimizes 0-shot loss on the training tasks. Another reason is that 2-shot context samples are randomly selected and not semantically related to the test example.

Evaluation on Fine-grained Tasks. To further study the influence of ICL context examples, we evaluate LLaVA-RE on 6 fine-grained tasks. It is worth mentioning that these tasks are very different from the training and unseen test tasks in the previous subsection. The fine-grained classes have subtle definition and merely overlap with our training data. The left part of Fig. 5 plots the averaged accuracies under different numbers of shots. The ICL contexts are either random or semantic-related. In the former situation, context examples are randomly sampled from the whole dataset; in the latter situation, context examples share the same texts as the test example. The accuracy for 0-shot inference

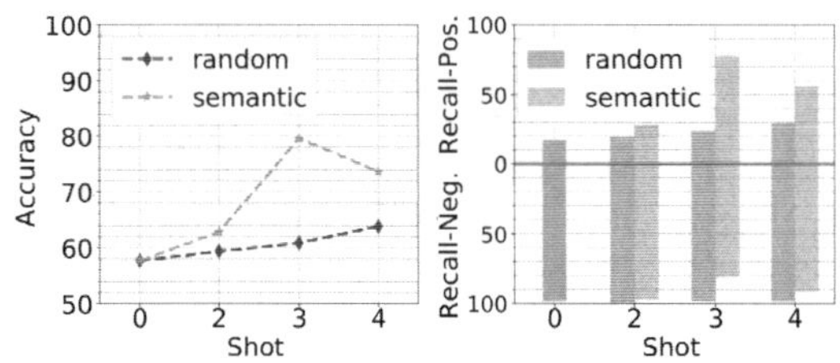

Figure 5: Evaluation results averaged over 6 fine-grained tasks on Ours-7B, using random or sematic-related ICL context examples, (left): accuracies, (right): recalls for negative and positive samples. 0-shot results are shown in a red bar for a comparison.

is unsatisfactory. From the recall plots on the right part of Fig. 5, we see that the predictions are biased towards a negative answer (*i.e.*, "Not Relevant"). This could be attributed to the distribution shift between training and fine-grained tasks. When doing evaluation with ICL contexts (Shot>0), the predictions become more balanced and the overall accuracies improve over 0-shot results. Using semantic-related contexts clearly outperforms random contexts. These observations validate the effectiveness of ICL in our image-text relevancy evaluation.

5 Conclusion

In this paper, we study the important task of binary image-text relevancy evaluation. We present LLaVA-RE, a first attempt based on MLLM. It leverages task instructions and multimodal in-context samples to handle complex relevancy tasks. Furthermore, we create a novel binary relevancy dataset for training and evaluation. Experimental results validate the effectiveness of our framework. In future work, we plan to compare our model with more MLLMs and traditional semantic embedding models.

Limitations

Relevancy task instructions. This paper studies the evaluation of relevancy between image and complex text. In some scenarios, the definition of relevancy can be ambiguous if we focus on different aspects. For example, an image of a husky and a text of corgi can be regarded as relevant in terms of the general dog category, but irrelevant if focusing on the dog breeds. We use a few sentences of task instructions as the model input. However, how well an MLLM can follow those fine-grained instructions relies on the foundational capability of the LLM backbone. In NLP, an LLM foundation model usually requires a sufficient model size (*i.e.* 13B) to have a good understanding of complex texts. Our training process does not own control of this instruction following capability. It will be necessary to understand how different LLM model sizes affect the understanding of easy and challenging relevancy tasks. Besides, the task instructions we use are written by human. It is helpful to explore the best form of task instructions for MLLM in our relevancy evaluation situation.

Context samples size. Due to the 4096 input tokens limitation of LLM backbones, we can only use up to four context samples (image-text pairs). However, four samples may not be enough for some ambiguous relevancy tasks. One image takes 576 tokens, which has a large redundancy. There are some works showing that the number of image tokens can be even reduced from 576 to 9 without affecting the performance much (Cai et al., 2024). In future work, it is meaningful to study how to combine these techniques into LLaVA-RE to incorporate more context samples.

Label noises. We constructed multiple binary relevancy tasks from existing public datasets. The most challenging part is how to define negative pairs. In this paper, we use some heuristic ideas, such as sampling another image from the same category based on image similarities. However, the image similarity scores may not necessarily reflect the true fine-grained correlations, and this procedure inevitably introduces some noisy labels. Existing public multi-modal datasets mostly are not built to evaluate relevancy. How to construct high-quality relevancy labels, *e.g.*, by expert annotations, is a challenging yet important problem for our future explorations.

References

Josh Achiam, Steven Adler, Sandhini Agarwal, Lama Ahmad, Ilge Akkaya, Florencia Leoni Aleman, Diogo Almeida, Janko Altenschmidt, Sam Altman, Shyamal Anadkat, et al. 2023. Gpt-4 technical report. *arXiv preprint arXiv:2303.08774*.

Lukas Bossard, Matthieu Guillaumin, and Luc Van Gool. 2014. Food-101–mining discriminative components with random forests. In *European Conference on Computer vision*, pages 446–461. Springer.

Mu Cai, Jianwei Yang, Jianfeng Gao, and Yong Jae Lee. 2024. Matryoshka multimodal models. *arXiv preprint arXiv:2405.17430*.

Min Cao, Shiping Li, Juntao Li, Liqiang Nie, and Min Zhang. 2022. Image-text retrieval: A survey on recent research and development.

Zhe Chen, Jiannan Wu, Wenhai Wang, Weijie Su, Guo Chen, Sen Xing, Muyan Zhong, Qinglong Zhang, Xizhou Zhu, Lewei Lu, et al. 2024. Internvl: Scaling up vision foundation models and aligning for generic visual-linguistic tasks. In *Proceedings of the IEEE/CVF Conference on Computer Vision and Pattern Recognition*, pages 24185–24198.

Wei-Lin Chiang, Zhuohan Li, Zi Lin, Ying Sheng, Zhanghao Wu, Hao Zhang, Lianmin Zheng, Siyuan Zhuang, Yonghao Zhuang, Joseph E. Gonzalez, Ion Stoica, and Eric P. Xing. 2023. Vicuna: An open-source chatbot impressing gpt-4 with 90%* chatgpt quality.

Alexey Dosovitskiy. 2021. An image is worth 16x16 words: Transformers for image recognition at scale. In *International Conference on Learning Representations*.

Sivan Doveh, Shaked Perek, M Jehanzeb Mirza, Amit Alfassy, Assaf Arbelle, Shimon Ullman, and Leonid Karlinsky. 2024. Towards multimodal in-context learning for vision & language models. *arXiv preprint arXiv:2403.12736*.

Andrea Frome, Greg S Corrado, Jon Shlens, Samy Bengio, Jeff Dean, Marc'Aurelio Ranzato, and Tomas Mikolov. 2013. Devise: A deep visual-semantic embedding model. *Advances in Neural Information Processing Systems*, 26.

Kushal Kafle and Christopher Kanan. 2017. An analysis of visual question answering algorithms. In *Proceedings of the IEEE International Conference on Computer Vision*, pages 1965–1973.

Aditya Khosla, Nityananda Jayadevaprakash, Bangpeng Yao, and Li Fei-Fei. 2011. Novel datasets for fine-grained image categorization. In *First Workshop on Fine Grained Visual Categorization*, volume 5, page 2. Citeseer.

Jonathan Krause, Michael Stark, Jia Deng, and Li Fei-Fei. 2013. 3d object representations for fine-grained categorization. In *Proceedings of the IEEE International Conference on Computer Vision Workshops*, pages 554–561.

Hugo Laurençon, Léo Tronchon, Matthieu Cord, and Victor Sanh. 2024. What matters when building vision-language models? *arXiv preprint arXiv:2405.02246*.

Kuang-Huei Lee, Xi Chen, Gang Hua, Houdong Hu, and Xiaodong He. 2018. Stacked cross attention for image-text matching. In *Proceedings of the European Conference on Computer Vision*, pages 201–216.

Bo Li, Yuanhan Zhang, Liangyu Chen, Jinghao Wang, Fanyi Pu, Jingkang Yang, Chunyuan Li, and Ziwei Liu. 2023a. Mimic-it: Multi-modal in-context instruction tuning. *arXiv preprint arXiv:2306.05425*.

Junnan Li, Dongxu Li, Silvio Savarese, and Steven Hoi. 2023b. Blip-2: Bootstrapping language-image pretraining with frozen image encoders and large language models. In *International Conference on Machine Learning*, pages 19730–19742. PMLR.

Junnan Li, Dongxu Li, Caiming Xiong, and Steven Hoi. 2022. Blip: Bootstrapping language-image pretraining for unified vision-language understanding and generation. In *International Conference on Machine Learning*, pages 12888–12900. PMLR.

Tsung-Yi Lin, Michael Maire, Serge Belongie, James Hays, Pietro Perona, Deva Ramanan, Piotr Dollár, and C Lawrence Zitnick. 2014. Microsoft coco: Common objects in context. In *Proceedings of the European Conference on Computer Vision*, pages 740–755. Springer.

Haotian Liu, Chunyuan Li, Yuheng Li, and Yong Jae Lee. 2024a. Improved baselines with visual instruction tuning. In *Proceedings of the IEEE/CVF Conference on Computer Vision and Pattern Recognition*, pages 26296–26306.

Haotian Liu, Chunyuan Li, Yuheng Li, Bo Li, Yuanhan Zhang, Sheng Shen, and Yong Jae Lee. 2024b. Llava-next: Improved reasoning, ocr, and world knowledge.

Haotian Liu, Chunyuan Li, Qingyang Wu, and Yong Jae Lee. 2024c. Visual instruction tuning. *Advances in Neural Information Processing Systems*, 36.

Ahmed Masry, Do Xuan Long, Jia Qing Tan, Shafiq Joty, and Enamul Hoque. 2022. Chartqa: A benchmark for question answering about charts with visual and logical reasoning. In *Findings of the Association for Computational Linguistics*.

Minesh Mathew, Viraj Bagal, Rubèn Tito, Dimosthenis Karatzas, Ernest Valveny, and CV Jawahar. 2022. Infographicvqa. In *Proceedings of the IEEE/CVF Winter Conference on Applications of Computer Vision*, pages 1697–1706.

Maria-Elena Nilsback and Andrew Zisserman. 2008. Automated flower classification over a large number of classes. In *Indian Conference on Computer Vision, Graphics & Image Processing*, pages 722–729. IEEE.

Omkar M Parkhi, Andrea Vedaldi, Andrew Zisserman, and CV Jawahar. 2012. Cats and dogs. In *Proceedings of the IEEE Conference on Computer Vision and Pattern Recognition*, pages 3498–3505. IEEE.

Leigang Qu, Meng Liu, Jianlong Wu, Zan Gao, and Liqiang Nie. 2021. Dynamic modality interaction modeling for image-text retrieval. In *Proceedings of the 44th International ACM SIGIR Conference on Research and Development in Information Retrieval*, pages 1104–1113.

Alec Radford, Jong Wook Kim, Chris Hallacy, Aditya Ramesh, Gabriel Goh, Sandhini Agarwal, Girish Sastry, Amanda Askell, Pamela Mishkin, Jack Clark, et al. 2021. Learning transferable visual models from natural language supervision. In *International Conference on Machine Learning*, pages 8748–8763. PMLR.

Robin Rombach, Andreas Blattmann, Dominik Lorenz, Patrick Esser, and Björn Ommer. 2022. High-resolution image synthesis with latent diffusion models. In *Proceedings of the IEEE/CVF Conference on Computer Vision and Pattern Recognition*, pages 10684–10695.

Amanpreet Singh, Vivek Natarajan, Meet Shah, Yu Jiang, Xinlei Chen, Dhruv Batra, Devi Parikh, and Marcus Rohrbach. 2019. Towards vqa models that can read. In *Proceedings of the IEEE/CVF Conference on Computer Vision and Pattern Recognition*, pages 8317–8326.

Krishna Srinivasan, Karthik Raman, Jiecao Chen, Michael Bendersky, and Marc Najork. 2021. Wit: Wikipedia-based image text dataset for multimodal multilingual machine learning. In *Proceedings of the 44th international ACM SIGIR Conference on Research and Development in Information Retrieval*, pages 2443–2449.

Gemini Team, Rohan Anil, Sebastian Borgeaud, Yonghui Wu, Jean-Baptiste Alayrac, Jiahui Yu, Radu Soricut, Johan Schalkwyk, Andrew M Dai, Anja Hauth, et al. 2023. Gemini: a family of highly capable multimodal models. *arXiv preprint arXiv:2312.11805*.

Catherine Wah, Steve Branson, Peter Welinder, Pietro Perona, and Serge Belongie. 2011. The caltech-ucsd birds-200-2011 dataset.

Liwei Wang, Yin Li, Jing Huang, and Svetlana Lazebnik. 2018. Learning two-branch neural networks for image-text matching tasks. *IEEE Transactions on Pattern Analysis and Machine Intelligence*, 41(2):394–407.

Semih Yagcioglu, Aykut Erdem, Erkut Erdem, and Nazli Ikizler-Cinbis. 2018. Recipeqa: A challenge dataset for multimodal comprehension of cooking recipes. In *Proceedings of the Conference on Empirical Methods in Natural Language Processing*.

Haozhe Zhao, Zefan Cai, Shuzheng Si, Xiaojian Ma, Kaikai An, Liang Chen, Zixuan Liu, Sheng Wang, Wenjuan Han, and Baobao Chang. 2023. Mmicl: Empowering vision-language model with multi-modal in-context learning. *arXiv preprint arXiv:2309.07915*.

A Appendix

A.1 Data Creation Details

We created several binary relevancy datasets for training and evaluation, based on public data sources. Below we present creation details for each task.

LLaVA. LLaVA-Visual-Instruct 150K (Liu et al., 2024a) is constructed for visual instruction tuning by prompting GPT-4 API. It contains three subtasks: detailed description, conversation and complex reasoning. The images are from COCO dataset (Lin et al., 2014). Each raw sample contains one image I and a series of questions and answers $\{(Q_i, A_i)\}$ related to the image. We convert the QA series into a long text T by applying a simple template of "Question: $\{Q\}$ Answer: $\{A\}$" on each QA. (I, T) thus defines a positive image-text pair. To create non-relevant data, we randomly sample another image $\tilde{I}$ that belongs to the same category as I and define $\{\tilde{I}, T\}$ as the negative pair. For evaluation purpose, we create hold-out test tasks using COCO `person` category, which is disjoint with the training categories.

Wiki. Wikipedia-based Image Text (WIT) Dataset (Srinivasan et al., 2021) is a large multimodal multilingual dataset extracted from Wikipedia pages. The original data is composed of 37.6 million entity rich image-text examples across 108 Wikipedia languages, while we only use a very small portion of English sources (20k). One WIT data entry includes several fields such as `page title`, `page description`, `section text`, `section image`, *etc.* Since `section text` and `section image` co-exist in the page, it is reasonable to define them as the positive image-text pair. On the other hand, `page description` describes the same topic as `section text` yet has different details, we define `page description` and `section image` as the negative image-text pair.

Recipe. RecipeQA (Yagcioglu et al., 2018) is a challenging dataset for multimodal comprehension of cooking recipes. Each recipe consists of textual descriptions of several steps to cook a particular food, and among them the first step usually talks about ingredients. Along with the recipe is a choice list of one positive image about this food and three negative images about other food. We filter out recipes whose first step has a title of "ingredients". Then we define positive image-text pair as positive food image and textual description of the first step, and similarly negative image-text pair with negative food images.

TextVQA. TextVQA (Singh et al., 2019) is a VQA dataset that requires models to read and reason about text in images to answer questions about them. For example, one question is "what kind of mushrooms are being advertised?", and the answer is "breaded". All questions and answers are short. To create a long text for our relevancy evaluation purpose, we send the image, question and answer to Claude 3 Sonnet and ask Claude to generate a few sentences to justify the answer, *e.g.*, *"The advertisement clearly states 'Try Our Enchanting Breaded Mushrooms' at the bottom, directly referring to breaded mushrooms as the featured item being promoted. The image reinforces this by depicting large, breaded mushroom-like structures alongside a character from Alice in Wonderland's whimsical setting, playing on the 'wonderland' theme mentioned. Therefore, based on the explicit text and visual context provided, the type of mushrooms being advertised are indeed breaded mushrooms."*. Given the question Q, answer A and reasoning R, we apply a template of "Question: $\{Q\}$ Answer: $\{A\}$. $\{R\}$" to create a long text. A positive pair is an image and the corresponding question and answer. To get a negative pair, we randomly sampled another image from the same category based on image similarity scores.

TDIUC. Task Driven Image Understanding Challenge (TDIUC) (Kafle and Kanan, 2017) is a VQA dataset organized into 12 different categories. Each category focuses on a particular task such as `object presence`, `sport recognition`, *etc.* It also introduces a category of `absurd` questions that are meaningless for a given image. To make binary relevancy tasks, we only use data from three categories: `activity recognition`, `sentiment understanding` and `utility/affordance` which require more reasoning capability. We use Claude 3 Sonnet to generate a few sentences of justification based on the image, question and answer. A positive pair is an image and the corresponding question and answer, using a similar template as `textvqa`. To get a negative pair, we randomly sample another question/answer from the same category based on text similarity scores.

ChartQA. ChartQA (Masry et al., 2022) is a benchmark for question answering about chart images. These images are different from training tasks, and used to evaluate models' generalization ability. We use Claude 3 Sonnet to generate a few sentences to justify the answer, and create positive/negative pairs in a similar manner as `textvqa`.

Infographics. InfographicVQA (Mathew et al., 2022) comprises a diverse collection of infographics with question-answer annotations. The questions require elementary reasoning and basic arithmetic skills over the document layout, textual content, graphical elements and data visualization. We use Claude 3 Sonnet to generate a few sentences to justify the answer, and create positive/negative pairs in a similar manner as `tdiuc`.

Fine-grained. We create 6 tasks from commonly used fine-grained classification datasets including cars (Krause et al., 2013), CUB (Wah et al., 2011), dogs (Khosla et al., 2011), pets (Parkhi et al., 2012), flowers (Nilsback and Zisserman, 2008) and food (Bossard et al., 2014). For each dataset, we ask Claude 3 Sonnet to generate useful visual features to distinguish one class. With this, each class label is converted into a long textual description focusing on fine-grained visual features. For example, give a car model "Dodge Caliber Wagon 2007", Claude responses with *"The Dodge Caliber Wagon 2007 has a distinctive boxy and upright shape with a tall stance and pronounced wheel arches. Its front end features a characteristic crosshair grille with the Dodge logo in the center, and angular headlights that sweep back towards the fenders. The side profile shows a long greenhouse with an upswept beltline and a rear quarter window, giving it a distinctive wagon silhouette. The wheels are typically five-spoke alloy rims, and the body color options range from bold shades like Infrared and Sunburst Orange to more subdued hues like Silver and Black. Distinctive badging on the rear liftgate and lower body panels proudly displays the 'Caliber' name and Dodge branding."* The positive pair is an image and the corresponding class description. To get a negative pair, we randomly sample another image from the same fine-grained class.

A.2 Detailed Accuracies

Table A.1 lists the detailed accuracies of comparison models on training and unseen tasks.

A.3 Sampled Task Instructions

Below we show some task instructions from sampled datasets.

LLaVA. *You are given an image and a series of Question and Answer. Your task is to judge whether the image is relevant to these Questions and Answer. Here are several important instructions:*
- Do not simply confirm the the object exists in image.
- Think about whether there is visual evidence supports or unrelated or contradicts the question and answer.
- In the textual question and answer, look for attributes such as color, size, shape, location, etc. And evaluate if the image matches these attributes.
- In the textual question and answer, look for context or settings of how the object is shown (background, neighboring objects, usage scenarios, etc.), and evaluate if the image shows the context.
- Use only the clear visual information that can be directly seen from image to determine the relevancy to question and answers.
- IMPORTANT: do not reason with your own knowledge or additional hallucination or guessing to determine relevancy.
- IMPORTANT: do not say 'yes' if certain aspects cannot be determined visually, Look very careful at the image!
- IMPORTANT: do not say 'yes' if answering requires knowledge beyond the image.
- Only say 'yes' if the image shows direct and obvious matching visual clues that supports the textual question and answer.
- If there are multiple question and answer, only say 'yes' if the image is relevant to all question and answer.
- If image is only related to the object and does not match the attributes, you should say 'no'.

Textvqa. *You are given an image and a pair of question and answer. Your task is to judge whether the image is relevant to the question and answer. Here are several important instructions:*
- The question focuses on text understanding. The image may be coherent or incoherent to this question.
- The answer includes an explanation to justify itself. It contains important details about a true relevant image.
- In the text, look for descriptions about objects, characters, colors, spatial relationships. Check

Table A.1: Detailed evaluation accuracies on training and unseen tasks. ('lv' short for 'llava', 'info.' short for infographics, ^{ho}hold-out test data, †unseen test tasks)

model	shot	lv_cr	lv_cv	lv_dt	wiki	recipe	textvqa	tdiuc	lv_cr^{ho}	lv_cv^{ho}	lv_dt^{ho}	chartqa†	info.†
LLaVA 1.5-7B	0	70.8	74.3	69.7	49.3	32.2	70.0	68.7	73.9	75.4	70.0	75.1	70.9
Ours-7B	0	91.9	93.5	96.0	97.7	88.3	97.1	89.3	92.2	93.1	94.1	94.6	80.8
Ours-7B	2	92.4	93.4	96.7	93.7	88.2	96.5	89.3	92.0	92.8	94.5	94.8	82.3
LLaVA 1.5-13B	0	63.0	70.6	78.4	49.0	29.6	55.9	68.0	72.5	74.0	80.9	53.1	65.4
Ours-13B	0	93.7	94.7	97.0	98.3	88.6	96.3	89.7	93.6	93.6	95.0	91.8	79.7
Ours-13B	2	93.6	94.6	97.0	95.3	89.3	96.4	88.3	93.7	93.3	95.2	93.0	79.1

whether these descriptions match the image.
- In the image, recognize existing characters such as digits, english letters, before making a judgement.
- Use only the clear visual information that can be directly seen from image to determine the relevancy to text.
- IMPORTANT: do not reason with additional hallucination or guessing to determine relevancy.
- IMPORTANT: do not say 'yes' if certain aspects cannot be determined visually, Look very careful at the image!
- Only say 'yes' if the image shows direct and obvious matching visual clues that supports the text.
- If image contradicts with answer regarding the question, you should say 'no'.
- The answer must be a single word of 'Yes' or 'No'.

Cars (fine-grained). *You are given a car image and a short description about a specific car model. Your task is to judge whether the image is relevant to the text. Here are several important instructions:*
- Carefully look at details in the image, such as car shape, decoration, color, number of doors, wheel sizes.
- The image may look similar to the described car model, but not exactly match it.
- Use your own knowledge to distinguish any visual differences between the image and the car description.
- Only say 'yes' if the image shows exactly the same fine-grained attributes as the description. Otherwise, say 'no'.
- The answer must be a single word of 'yes' or 'no'.

A.4 Sampled Image-Text pairs

We show some sampled image-text pairs from training and test tasks in Tables A.2,A.3.

Table A.2: Sampled image-text pairs from different tasks.

Task: llava; Label: 'relevant' 	Question: What role might a ferry play in a location like this? Answer: In this oceanic scene with a view of the mountains, a ferry might play a significant role in providing transportation services between various coastal points, including towns, cities, and islands. As the landscape is surrounded by a large body of water, the ferry connects these locations and enables people to travel across the water efficiently and conveniently. It can be a preferred mode of transport for commuters, tourists, or locals who need to access services or visit attractions in different areas. Additionally, ferries might also accommodate vehicles and cargo, providing further convenience to travelers and playing a crucial role in the region's economy by facilitating trade and the movement of goods. Is the image relevant to this Question and Answer?
Task: llava; Label: 'not relevant' 	Question: Explain the visual content of the image in great detail. Answer: The image captures a city street scene at either dusk or dawn with a flock of birds flying high above. There are at least 15 birds scattered across the sky in various positions, creating a sense of motion and activity. Along the street, cars are parked on the side, and some are in motion, with one of the moving cars having its headlights on. The street itself is lined with trees and buildings, adding to the urban atmosphere. Traffic lights are also visible in the scene, with three on the left side and two on the right side of the street. The overall mood of the image is serene as the sun goes down, creating an end-of-the-day feeling in the city. Is the image relevant to this Question and Answer?
Task: wiki; Label: 'relevant' 	Text: A pantile is a type of fired roof tile, normally made from clay. It is S-shaped in profile and is single lap, meaning that the end of the tile laps only the course immediately below. Flat tiles normally lap two courses. A pantile-covered roof is considerably lighter than a flat-tiled equivalent and can be laid to a lower pitch. Pantiles are used in eastern coastal parts of England and Scotland including Norfolk, East Yorkshire, County Durham, Perthshire, Angus, Lothian and Fife, where they were first imported from the Netherlands in the early 17th century. They are rarely used in western England or western Scotland, except in Bristol and the Somerset town of Bridgwater. Roofing pantiles are not to be confused with a type used for paving, after which the Georgian colonnade in Tunbridge Wells is named. Whilst called pantiles, the paving tiles which were installed there in 1699 were one-inch-thick square tiles made from heavy wealden clay, so-named as shaped in a wooden pan before firing. The pantile paving in Tunbridge Wells was replaced with stone flag tiles in 1792. Is the image relevant to this Text?
Task: recipe; Label: 'relevant' 	Ingredients: First of all collect the following ingredients (this is what I used for mine but if you want bigger or smaller meat loaf use your own quantity): 700g Minced meat 2 Packages of bacon 4 eggs (1 raw, 3 boiled) Ham Salt Pepper Parmigiano Cheese Are the Ingredients necessary to make food in the image?
Task: textvqa; Label: 'not relevant' 	Question: what type of plane is this? Answer: lape. The image depicts an old propeller-driven aircraft sitting on a grassy field. The registration or name painted on the side of the aircraft fuselage clearly reads "EC-AGC LAPE", indicating that the type of plane shown is a Lape model. The black and white photograph captures this vintage aircraft in an outdoor setting, providing visual evidence that confirms the stated answer that this is indeed a Lape type of plane. Is the image relevant to this Question and Answer?

Table A.3: Sampled image-text pairs from different tasks.

Task: tdiuc; Label: 'relevant' 	Question: What are elephants thought to be afraid of? Answer: mice. While the image shows a group of elephants calmly walking together, it does not directly relate to what elephants may be afraid of. However, the provided answer that elephants are thought to be afraid of mice is an interesting folk belief or myth. This notion likely stems from observations or anecdotes of elephants appearing startled or reacting to the sudden movements or sounds of small rodents, which could seem disproportionate to their massive size. However, scientific evidence suggests that elephants' fear of mice is likely exaggerated, and they may simply be reacting to unexpected stimuli rather than being genuinely afraid of the mice themselves. While the origins of this belief are unclear, it persists as an enduring myth or legend about these majestic creatures. The image alone cannot confirm or deny this claim, as it simply depicts elephants in their natural habitat without any mice present. Is the Answer relevant to this Image and Question?
Task: infographics; Label: 'not relevant' 	Question: What is the majority percentage of females in the wholesale & retail industry of Canada? Answer: 21.0% Question: What percent of the women entrepreneurs in Canada work for 31-39 hours a week? Answer: 19.8% Question: What percent of the women employees in Canada work for 41-49 hours a week? Answer: 2.7% Question: How many hours per week is spend on work by 17.4% of the women entrepreneurs in Canada? Answer: 40 HOURS Is the image relevant to these Question and Answer?
Task: chartqa; Label: 'not relevant' 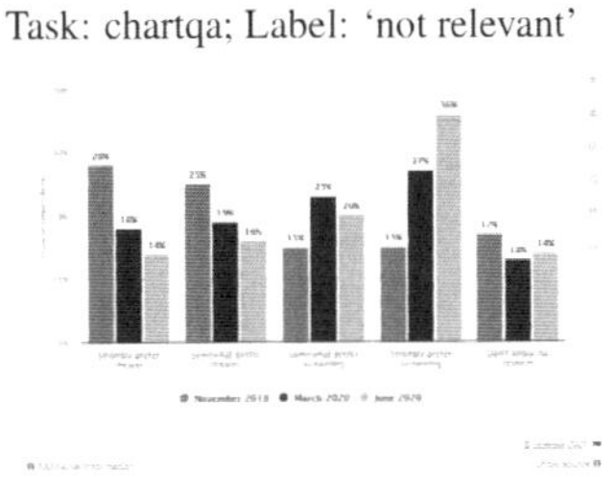	Question: What is the sum of making progress, losing ground and same in the year 2011? Answer: 99. The image shows a line graph depicting the perceptions of Mexicans regarding the government's progress against drug trafficking over the years 2011 to 2015. In 2011, the values for "Making progress," "Losing ground," and "Same" add up to 45, 30, and 19 respectively, which totals 94. However, the provided answer of 99 does not correspond to the sum of these three values in 2011 based on the information given in the graph. To justify the answer, I would need additional context or clarification on the data being referenced. Is the image relevant to this Question and Answer?
Task: flowers; Label: 'relevant' 	The prince of wales feathers is a perennial flowering plant with tall spikes of red, velvety flowers. The vibrant red petals are tightly clustered together in a cylindrical shape, forming a distinctive feather-like appearance. The flowers emerge from a terminal spike, with overlapping bracts that provide a protective covering. The lance-shaped leaves are mid-green in color and arranged oppositely along the stem. The plant can grow up to 1.5 meters tall, with multiple flowering spikes emerging from a single stem. Is the image relevant to this flower description?
Task: cars; Label: 'not relevant' 	The Ford Fiesta Sedan 2012 has a compact, three-box sedan body style with a distinct front grille featuring the iconic Ford blue oval logo in the center. Its headlights are swept back and have a distinctive shape, while the taillights have a distinctive LED light signature. The side profile features pronounced wheel arches and a character line running along the length of the car. The alloy wheels have a multi-spoke design and are typically 15 or 16 inches in diameter. Depending on the trim level, the exterior may feature body-colored door handles, side mirrors, and other accents, while higher trims may have chrome accents. Is the image relevant to this car description?

Persian in a Court: Benchmarking VLMs In Persian Multi-Modal Tasks

Farhan Farsi
Amirkabir University of Technology
farhan1379@aut.ac.ir

Shahriar Shariati Motlagh
University of Mazandaran
s.shariati21@umail.umz.ac.ir

Shayan Bali
King's College London
shayan.bali@kcl.ac.uk

Sadra Sabouri
University of Southern California
sabourih@usc.edu

Saeedeh Momtazi
Amirkabir University of Technology
momtazi@aut.ac.ir

Abstract

This study introduces a novel framework for evaluating Large Language Models (LLMs) and Vision-Language Models (VLMs) in Persian, a low-resource language. We develop comprehensive datasets to assess reasoning, linguistic understanding, and multimodal capabilities. Our datasets include Persian-OCR-QA for optical character recognition, Persian-VQA for visual question answering, Persian world-image puzzle for multimodal integration, Visual-Abstraction-Reasoning for abstract reasoning, and Iran-places for visual knowledge of Iranian figures and locations. We evaluate models like GPT-4o, Claude 3.5 Sonnet, and Llama 3.2 90B Vision, revealing their strengths and weaknesses in processing Persian. This research contributes to inclusive language processing by addressing the unique challenges of low-resource language evaluation. Additionally, we release samples of our dataset to support further research in Persian multi-modal tasks[1].

1 Introduction

Large Language Models (LLMs) have undergone rapid advancements in recent years, particularly in multimodal frameworks (Zhang et al., 2024; Wu et al., 2023) that integrate and process diverse data types such as text, audio, and images. These breakthroughs have expanded the applications of LLMs across various domains, from conversational AI to content generation (He et al., 2024) and knowledge retrieval (Long et al., 2024). Multimodal LLMs demonstrate remarkable capabilities in aligning and interpreting visual-textual information (Ataallah et al., 2024), making them powerful tools for tasks that span different modalities (Nguyen et al., 2023). However, as the capabilities of LLMs grow, so does the need for rigorous evaluation methods to measure their effectiveness and ensure their outputs align with the intended goals (Huang and Zhang, 2024). Evaluating LLMs became a crucial area of research, especially when considering other languages rather than high-resource ones, where resources are abundant (Chang et al., 2023).

Although Persian is the native or second language for around 130 million people, high-quality datasets and benchmarks for the language remain limited (Agic et al., 2016). While researchers have introduced foundational datasets for pretraining LLMs (Sabouri et al., 2022; Salmasi and Kabir, 2023; Farsi et al., 2024), these resources are often single-modality. Evaluating LLM capabilities, such as reasoning, verbal intelligence, and multimodal reasoning, remains underexplored. Multimodal frameworks compound this challenge by requiring datasets that effectively pair text with complementary modalities, such as images, videos, while maintaining linguistic nuances (Hedderich et al., 2020).

In this study, we address these challenges by creating a comprehensive dataset designed explicitly for the Persian language. These datasets are constructed from scratch and designed to evaluate LLMs on multiple dimensions, including reasoning and verbal intelligence similar to prior works (Fu et al., 2024). Furthermore, we assess a set of large language models' performance with our framework, which measures the relative difficulty of different datasets and ensures a uniform evaluation across tasks (Li et al., 2023b). By investigating the reasoning capabilities of LLMs and their ability to interact with Persian linguistic constructs and multimodal data, we aim to uncover the extent of their knowledge base and adaptability to low-resource

[1] https://huggingface.co/AUT-NLP

Proceedings of the First Workshop of Evaluation of Multi-Modal Generation, pages 52–56
January 20, 2025.

languages. To tackle these challenges, this study proposes a multimodal evaluation framework focusing on creating datasets tailored to the Persian language and evaluating the capabilities of LLMs and Vision-Language Models (VLMs) in processing Persian. The framework assesses models across key dimensions, including reasoning abilities and visual-textual comprehension, while considering the difficulty of the datasets (Zhu et al., 2023). This work aims to evaluate the performance of current LLMs in multimodal contexts, providing a comprehensive assessment of their capabilities in Persian. This research fills critical gaps in low-resource language evaluation while contributing to developing inclusive, adaptable, and effective language processing models for diverse applications.

2 Related Work

The work related to our study can be divided into three main areas, discussed in the following sections. Together, these areas offer a foundational understanding of the challenges and opportunities in developing and evaluating models in multimodal and low-resource language settings.

Benchmarking LLMs and Dataset Development for Low-Resource Languages. Multimodal evaluation frameworks are critical for assessing models integrating and processing diverse data modalities. MME introduces a comprehensive benchmark for multimodal language models (MLLMs), evaluating perception and cognition abilities across 14 subtasks, enabling comparisons among advanced MLLMs (Fu et al., 2024). Similarly, SEED-Bench-2 categorizes MLLM capabilities hierarchically, incorporating tasks like image generation and providing detailed insights into model strengths and weaknesses (Li et al., 2023a).

However, developing benchmarks and datasets for low-resource languages like Persian is challenging due to limited resources and linguistic diversity (Sabouri et al., 2022). Multilingual benchmarks, such as IGLUE (Bugliarello et al., 2022), support zero-shot and few-shot learning across 20 languages, highlighting the potential of multilingual datasets but often lacking specific resources for Persian. While comprehensive benchmarks like GAOKAO (Zhang et al., 2023a) showcase LLMs' strengths in objective tasks, they also expose limitations in domain-specific challenges. For Persian, benchmarking efforts remained scarce, underlining the need for evaluation frameworks that reflect its unique linguistic and cultural features.

Benchmarks and Visual Reasoning for Vision-Language Models. Vision-Language Models (VLMs) are evaluated using benchmarks designed to test their ability to handle both visual and textual inputs (Xu et al., 2024). Benchmarks like VisIT-Bench focus on tasks such as accessibility assessments and image-caption generation (Bitton et al., 2023), while GEM evaluates multilingual vision-language tasks, including image and video interactions (Su et al., 2021). Visual reasoning benchmarks like GRASP test language grounding and intuitive physics understanding in video-based tasks (Jassim et al., 2023), while Multimodal-CoT uses chain-of-thought prompting to improve structured reasoning (Zhang et al., 2023b). Together, these benchmarks comprehensively evaluate VLM capabilities across diverse tasks. For dataset creation, we studied these works to establish best practices.

3 Datasets

We focused on investigating the evaluation of the multimodality attribute in Large Language Models (LLMs). Multimodal datasets contain data from multiple modalities, such as text, images, audio, video, or other structured/unstructured data types. For this study, we prioritized text-image data, enabling in-depth exploration of the model's ability to process and reason across these two modalities.

To create a comprehensive benchmark for VLMs in the Persian language, particularly focusing on multimodal varieties, we emphasized several key aspects like their reasoning skills, creativity, familiarity with linguistics in images, and knowledge about places in Iran. Our dataset has five distinct sets that we describe in the following paragraphs.

Persian-VQA: To create a VQA (Visual Question Answering) dataset in Persian, we used the Zhang et al. (2016) dataset, which is one of the most popular VQA datasets in English. This dataset contains 7,764 yes/no questions derived from 1,023 images. We translated the entire dataset into Persian using the GPT-4o model. To ensure the quality of the translated questions, we conducted a manual review of the generated dataset. An example of a record of this dataset is shown in Figure 1.

Persian-OCR-QA: Nowadays, OCR (Optical Character Recognition) has become one of the most important tasks due to its numerous applications (Peng et al., 2013; Singh et al., 2012). To

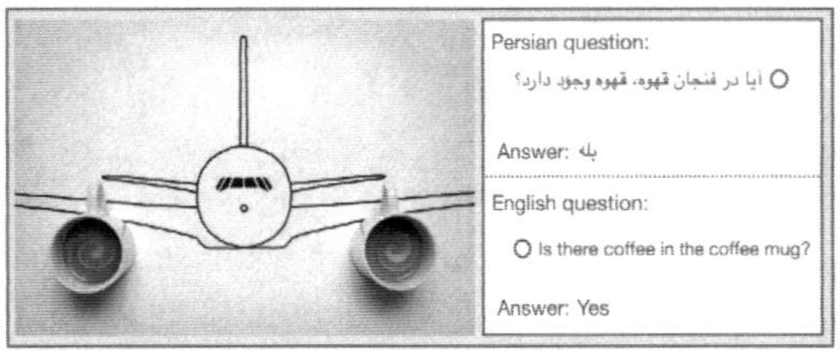

Figure 1: An example of Persian-VQA. Persian question-answer pair and its original English version.

evaluate the performance of current models on this task, we introduced new datasets to measure the performance of LLMs on OCR tasks in the Persian language. We used the Persian-OCR dataset, which contains 7,000 pages. Using GPT-4o-mini to make a question from the text and answer, we extracted ten question-answer pairs from each page, resulting in a comprehensive dataset of 70,000 entries.

Persian-VAR: To evaluate Vision Language Models (VLMs) in the domain of abstract reasoning, we introduce a novel dataset, Persian-VAR (Persian Visual-Abstraction-Reasoning), comprising 120 samples, inspired by Raven's Progressive Matrices (Carpenter et al., 1990). This non-verbal test is typically used to assess general human intelligence and abstract reasoning, and it serves as a non-verbal estimate of fluid intelligence. It is one of the most commonly administered tests to groups and individuals, from young children to the elderly. To create this dataset, we collected entrance exams for gifted middle and high schools in Iran, as illustrated in figure 2, providing a rich source of complex visual-abstraction-reasoning challenges that align with the cognitive capabilities assessed by Raven's matrices.

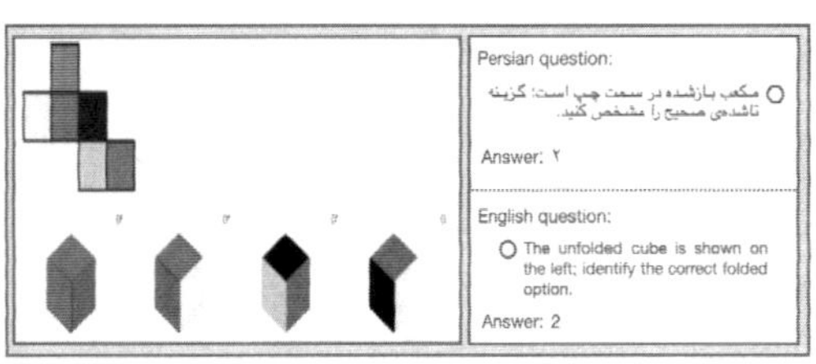

Figure 2: An Example of Persian-VAR. Persian question-answer pair and its original English version.

Persian-WIP: The Persian Word-Image Puzzle dataset assessed multimodal models' ability to integrate and process visual and textual information. By challenging models to combine visual cues with linguistic interpretation, this dataset evaluates their capability to manage complex inputs. Such tasks demand creative thinking and language skills, making it a robust framework for testing image recognition and language comprehension skills. This serves as both an educational tool and a benchmark for evaluating the effectiveness of multimodal systems. The dataset was compiled using crowdsourcing, crawling social apps like Telegram and Instagram, and generating images with AI models like Midjourney. Figure 3 displays a sample instance from the dataset.

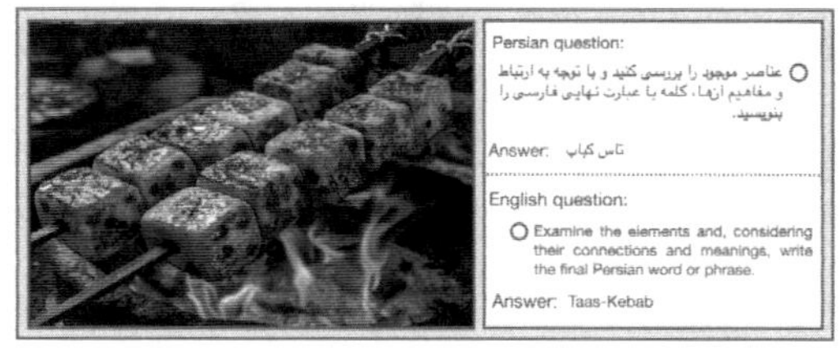

Figure 3: An Example of Persian-WIP. Taas-Kebab, a traditional Persian dish. The name combines "Taas" (dice) and "kebab" (grilled dish), referring to a dish made with diced kebab. When an image shows diced kebab, it represents Taas-Kebab in Persian.

Iran-Places: This dataset is designed to evaluate models on their knowledge of notable places in Iran, akin to the Persian version of (Weyand et al., 2020). It consists of over 500 images, with each province in Iran represented by at least seven images. This comprehensive coverage ensures a diverse representation of the country's geographical and cultural landmarks. An example of this is illustrated in Figure 4.

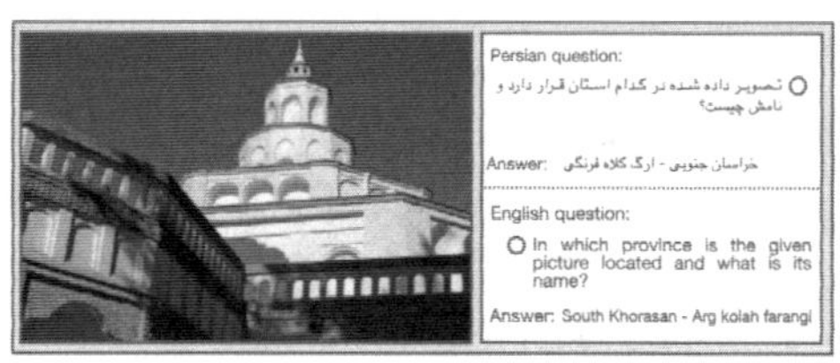

Figure 4: An Example of Iran-Places: Persian question-answer pair and its original English version.

4 Experiments

We tested current LLMs, such as ChatGPT-4o, Claude 3.5, and Llama 3.2, performance on the proposed benchmark. GPT-4o demonstrated superior performance in tasks requiring advanced reasoning and visual comprehension in Persian, indicating higher overall scores in cognitive tasks (Table 1). Claude 3.5 Sonnet excelled in text-based tasks like

Task	Metric	GPT-4o[a]	Claude 3.5 Sonnet[b]	Llama 3.2 90B Vision
P-VAR	Accuracy (%)	**16.22**	11.71	13.51
Persian-OCR-QA	BLEU-1 (%)	52.61	**57.53**	23.09
	ROUGE-L[c](%)	63.41	**77.47**	44.96
Persian-VQA	Accuracy (%)	**89.17**	85.86	82.89
	F1 Score (%)	**91.54**	87.82	86.78
Iran-Places	Relaxed Exact match[d](%)	16.44	**17.07**	16.43

[a] The GPT-4o-2024-09-03 version is used in this benchmark.

[b] The Claude-3.5-Sonnet-2024-10-22 version is used in this benchmark.

[c] We used the F1 score for ROUGE-L.

[d] We awarded 0.5 points if the name of the province or place was predicted correctly, 1 point if both were correct, and 0 points otherwise.

Table 1: Top 3 VLMs Performance on Different Multimodal Persian Tasks

OCR and text generation, suggesting strong textual processing capabilities. Llama 3.2 90B Vision showed balanced performance but with lower overall scores than the others.

All models struggled significantly with multimodal integration tasks, failing to achieve exact matches in the Persian Word-Image Puzzle, negatively impacting their overall multimodal scores. Similarly, low performance on tasks involving specific Iranian locations revealed limitations in culturally specific visual knowledge, affecting overall effectiveness in these areas.

These varied results, as detailed in Table 1, highlight the complexities of evaluating language models in Persian, showing strengths in specific areas but deficiencies in multimodal and culturally specific tasks. This underscores the need for further research and improved datasets to enhance model performance across diverse tasks.

5 Future Work

Our findings highlight the need for more specialized datasets for low-resource languages to improve model evaluation and performance. Future research should focus on developing new evaluation metrics, expanding multimodal datasets to include additional modalities like video and audio, and advancing model capabilities in handling complex multimodal tasks for the Persian language.

6 Conclusion

In this study, we introduced a framework for evaluating Large Language Models (LLMs) and Vision-Language Models (VLMs) in Persian, focusing on five specialized datasets: Persian-OCR-QA, Persian-VQA, Persian Word-Image Puzzle (P-WIP), Persian Visual-Abstraction-Reasoning (P-VAR), and Iran-Places. Our evaluations of GPT-4o, Claude 3.5 Sonnet, and Llama 3.2 90B Vision provided significant insights. GPT-4o excelled in abstract reasoning and visual question answering, highlighting its strong visual-linguistic integration capability. Claude 3.5 Sonnet showed superior performance in Persian-specific OCR tasks. Although all models performed similarly in geographical knowledge, they struggled with the Persian Word-Image Puzzle, revealing challenges in tasks needing creative multimodal synthesis.

References

Zeljko Agic, Anders Johannsen, Barbara Plank, Héctor Martínez Alonso, Natalie Schluter, and Anders Søgaard. 2016. Multilingual projection for parsing truly low-resource languages. *Transactions of the Association for Computational Linguistics*, 4:301–312.

Kirolos Ataallah, Xiaoqian Shen, Eslam Abdelrahman, Essam Sleiman, Deyao Zhu, Jian Ding, and Mohamed Elhoseiny. 2024. Minigpt4-video: Advancing multimodal llms for video understanding with interleaved visual-textual tokens. *arXiv preprint arXiv:2404.03413*.

Yonatan Bitton et al. 2023. Visit-bench: A benchmark for vision-language instruction following inspired by real-world use. *ArXiv*.

Emanuele Bugliarello et al. 2022. Iglue: A benchmark for transfer learning across modalities, tasks, and languages. *ArXiv*.

Patricia A Carpenter, Marcel A Just, and Peter Shell. 1990. What one intelligence test measures: a theoretical account of the processing in the raven progressive matrices test. *Psychological review*, 97(3):404.

Yu-Chu Chang, Xu Wang, Jindong Wang, Yuanyi Wu, Kaijie Zhu, Hao Chen, Linyi Yang, Xiaoyuan Yi,

Cunxiang Wang, Yidong Wang, Weirong Ye, Yue Zhang, Yi Chang, Philip S. Yu, Qian Yang, and Xingxu Xie. 2023. A survey on evaluation of large language models. *ArXiv*, abs/2307.03109.

Farhan Farsi, Sadra Sabouri, Kian Kashfipour, Soroush Gooran, Hossein Sameti, and Ehsaneddin Asgari. 2024. Syntran-fa: Generating comprehensive answers for farsi qa pairs via syntactic transformation.

Chaoyou Fu, Peixian Chen, Yunhang Shen, Yulei Qin, Mengdan Zhang, Xu Lin, Jinrui Yang, Xiawu Zheng, Ke Li, Xing Sun, Yunsheng Wu, and Rongrong Ji. 2024. Mme: A comprehensive evaluation benchmark for multimodal large language models. *Preprint*, arXiv:2306.13394.

Yingqing He, Zhaoyang Liu, Jingye Chen, Zeyue Tian, Hongyu Liu, Xiaowei Chi, Runtao Liu, Ruibin Yuan, Yazhou Xing, Wenhai Wang, et al. 2024. Llms meet multimodal generation and editing: A survey. *arXiv preprint arXiv:2405.19334*.

Michael A. Hedderich, Lukas Lange, Heike Adel, Jannik Strotgen, and D. Klakow. 2020. A survey on recent approaches for natural language processing in low-resource scenarios. pages 2545–2568.

Jiaxing Huang and Jingyi Zhang. 2024. A survey on evaluation of multimodal large language models. *arXiv preprint arXiv:2408.15769*.

Serwan Jassim et al. 2023. Grasp: A novel benchmark for evaluating language grounding and situated physics understanding in multimodal language models. *ArXiv*.

Bohao Li et al. 2023a. Seed-bench-2: Benchmarking multimodal large language models. *ArXiv*.

Zejun Li, Ye Wang, Mengfei Du, Qingwen Liu, Binhao Wu, Jiwen Zhang, Chengxing Zhou, Zhihao Fan, Jie Fu, Jingjing Chen, Xuanjing Huang, and Zhongyu Wei. 2023b. Reform-eval: Evaluating large vision language models via unified re-formulation of task-oriented benchmarks. *ArXiv*, abs/2310.02569.

Xinwei Long, Jiali Zeng, Fandong Meng, Zhiyuan Ma, Kaiyan Zhang, Bowen Zhou, and Jie Zhou. 2024. Generative multi-modal knowledge retrieval with large language models. In *Proceedings of the AAAI Conference on Artificial Intelligence*, volume 38, pages 18733–18741.

Xuan-Phi Nguyen, Sharifah Mahani Aljunied, Shafiq R. Joty, and Lidong Bing. 2023. Democratizing llms for low-resource languages by leveraging their english dominant abilities with linguistically-diverse prompts. *ArXiv*, abs/2306.11372.

Xujun Peng, Huaigu Cao, Srirangaraj Setlur, Venu Govindaraju, and Prem Natarajan. 2013. Multilingual ocr research and applications: an overview. In *Proceedings of the 4th International Workshop on Multilingual OCR*, pages 1–8.

Sadra Sabouri, Elnaz Rahmati, Soroush Gooran, and Hossein Sameti. 2022. naab: A ready-to-use plug-and-play corpus for farsi. *arXiv preprint arXiv:2208.13486*.

Ali Salmasi and Ehsanollah Kabir. 2023. Farsi text in scene: A new dataset. In *2023 13th International Conference on Computer and Knowledge Engineering (ICCKE)*, pages 510–514. IEEE.

Amarjot Singh, Ketan Bacchuwar, and Akshay Bhasin. 2012. A survey of ocr applications. *International Journal of Machine Learning and Computing*, 2(3):314.

Lin Su et al. 2021. Gem: A general evaluation benchmark for multimodal tasks. *ArXiv*.

Tobias Weyand, Andre Araujo, Bingyi Cao, and Jack Sim. 2020. Google landmarks dataset v2-a large-scale benchmark for instance-level recognition and retrieval. In *Proceedings of the IEEE/CVF conference on computer vision and pattern recognition*, pages 2575–2584.

Shengqiong Wu, Hao Fei, Leigang Qu, Wei Ji, and Tat-Seng Chua. 2023. Next-gpt: Any-to-any multimodal llm. *arXiv preprint arXiv:2309.05519*.

Peng Xu, Wenqi Shao, Kaipeng Zhang, Peng Gao, Shuo Liu, Meng Lei, Fanqing Meng, Siyuan Huang, Yu Qiao, and Ping Luo. 2024. Lvlm-ehub: A comprehensive evaluation benchmark for large vision-language models. *IEEE Transactions on Pattern Analysis and Machine Intelligence*.

Duzhen Zhang, Yahan Yu, Jiahua Dong, Chenxing Li, Dan Su, Chenhui Chu, and Dong Yu. 2024. Mm-llms: Recent advances in multimodal large language models. *arXiv preprint arXiv:2401.13601*.

Peng Zhang, Yash Goyal, Douglas Summers-Stay, Dhruv Batra, and Devi Parikh. 2016. Yin and yang: Balancing and answering binary visual questions. In *Proceedings of the IEEE conference on computer vision and pattern recognition*, pages 5014–5022.

Xiaotian Zhang, Chun-yan Li, Yi Zong, Zhengyu Ying, Liang He, and Xipeng Qiu. 2023a. Evaluating the performance of large language models on gaokao benchmark. *ArXiv*.

Zhuosheng Zhang et al. 2023b. Multimodal chain-of-thought reasoning in language models. *ArXiv*.

Mingwei Zhu, Leigang Sha, Yu Shu, Kangjia Zhao, Tiancheng Zhao, and Jianwei Yin. 2023. Benchmarking sequential visual input reasoning and prediction in multimodal large language models. *ArXiv*, abs/2310.13473.

TaiwanVQA:
A Benchmark for Visual Question Answering for Taiwanese Daily Life

Hsin-Yi Hsieh[†][1] **Shang-Wei Liu**[†][1] **Chih-Chang Meng**[‡][2] **Chien-Hua Chen**[‡][2]
Shuo-Yueh Lin[§][3] **Hung-Ju Lin**[⋆][4] **Hen-Hsen Huang**[¶][5] **I Chen Wu**[‡][2]

[†]National Center for High-performance Computing, Taiwan [§]National Central University, Taiwan
[‡]National Yang Ming Chiao Tung University, Taiwan [⋆]National Taiwan University, Taiwan
[¶]Institute of Information Science, Academia Sinica, Taiwan

[1]{2403055,2403056}@narlabs.org.tw [2]{mcc.cs11,chchen.cs12,icwu}@nycu.edu.tw
[3]johnnylin@g.ncu.edu.tw [4]r11922147@csie.ntu.edu.tw [5]hhhuang@iis.sinica.edu.tw

Abstract

We introduce **TaiwanVQA**, a novel visual question answering benchmark designed to evaluate vision language models' (VLMs) ability to recognize and reason about Taiwan-specific multimodal content. TaiwanVQA comprises 2,000 image-question pairs covering diverse topics relevant to Taiwanese culture and daily life. We categorize the questions into recognition and reasoning tasks, further subclassifying reasoning questions based on the level of external knowledge required. We conduct extensive experiments on state-of-the-art VLMs, including GPT-4o, Llama-3.2, LLaVA, Qwen2-VL, and InternVL2 models. Our findings reveal significant limitations in current VLMs when handling culturally specific content. The performance gap widens between recognition tasks (top score 73.60%) and reasoning tasks (top score 49.80%), indicating challenges in cultural inference and contextual understanding. These results highlight the need for more culturally diverse training data and improved model architectures that can better integrate visual and textual information within specific cultural contexts. By providing TaiwanVQA, we aim to contribute to the development of more inclusive and culturally aware AI models, facilitating their deployment in diverse real-world settings. TaiwanVQA can be accessed on our GitHub page.

1 Introduction

Multimodal vision-language models (VLMs) have achieved remarkable success in integrating visual and textual information, enabling applications ranging from image captioning to visual question answering (Li et al., 2023; Dai et al., 2023). Despite these advances, most existing benchmarks focus on general-domain knowledge and widely spoken languages, often overlooking the challenges posed by culturally specific content and underrepresented languages (Yue et al., 2024a,b; Fu et al., 2024).

Understanding and reasoning about culturally nuanced content is crucial for deploying AI systems in diverse real-world settings (Nayak et al., 2024). For instance, accurately interpreting traditional symbols, local customs, or region-specific artifacts requires models to possess not only visual recognition capabilities but also contextual and cultural knowledge (Hershcovich et al., 2022).

To address this gap, we introduce **TaiwanVQA**, a visual question answering benchmark specifically designed to evaluate VLMs' abilities to recognize and reason about Taiwan-specific content. TaiwanVQA comprises 1,000 images paired with 2,000 questions covering a diverse range of topics relevant to Taiwanese daily life and culture, such as traditional cuisine, local festivals, historical landmarks, and public signage. Our contributions are threefold:

- We introduce TaiwanVQA, the first VQA benchmark specifically designed for Taiwanese cultural content, with data categorized based on aspects of daily life
- We propose a taxonomy of culture-specific visual questions into recognition and reasoning types, with reasoning questions sub-classified based on required external knowledge levels
- We provide comprehensive experiments on state-of-the-art VLMs including GPT-4 (OpenAI, 2023), revealing their limitations in handling culture-specific content.

Our findings indicate that while models perform reasonably well on recognition tasks, their performance significantly drops on reasoning tasks that require deeper cultural understanding. This underscores the need for more culturally diverse training data and enhanced model architectures capable of integrating visual and textual information within specific cultural contexts.

Proceedings of the First Workshop of Evaluation of Multi-Modal Generation, pages 57–75
January 20, 2025.

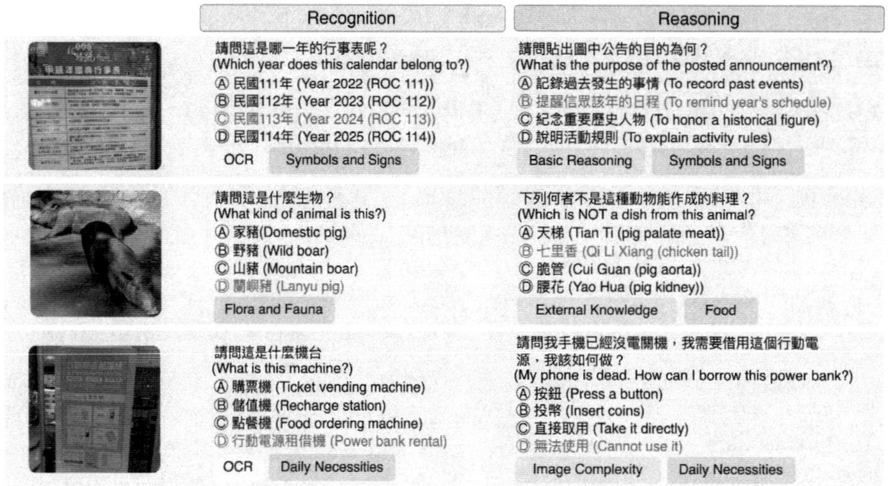

Figure 1: An Illustration of the TaiwanVQA Benchmark. Each row shows an image paired with two questions: a recognition question (left) and a reasoning question (right), both in multiple-choice format with the correct answers highlighted in red. Below each question, topic categories are labeled in purple (e.g., "Symbols and Signs", "Daily Necessities"), with additional labels in yellow for OCR requirements in recognition questions and in green for knowledge types in reasoning questions.

By providing TaiwanVQA, we aim to contribute to the development of more inclusive and culturally aware AI models, facilitating their deployment in diverse real-world scenarios and promoting research in underrepresented languages and cultures.

2 Related Work

The evaluation of VLMs has progressed from general visual recognition to understanding culturally specific content. Early datasets like DOLLAR STREET (Rojas et al., 2022) and GLDV2 (Weyand et al., 2020) provided extensive collections of images from diverse regions but focused primarily on recognition tasks without delving into cultural nuances.

Recent benchmarks have aimed to directly assess cultural understanding in VLMs. Burda-Lassen et al. (2024) introduced MOSAIC-1.5K, a culture-specific captioning dataset that includes images from various regions to test models' cultural awareness in captioning tasks. Similarly, Bhatia et al. (2024) proposed GLOBALRG, evaluating retrieval and grounding capabilities across 15 countries, emphasizing local concepts within a global context.

Nayak et al. (2024) introduced the CULTUREVQA dataset, a benchmark designed to evaluate VLMs on cultural understanding across multiple countries and cultures. CULTUREVQA comprises 2,378 image-question pairs from 11 countries spanning 5 continents, with questions focusing on traditions, rituals, and cultural artifacts. While this dataset advances the evaluation of cultural understanding in VLMs, it allocates a smaller proportion of its dataset to traditions and rituals compared to our benchmark and uses a multiple-choice evaluation format, which may not fully capture the depth of models' cultural reasoning capabilities.

Other efforts target more specific cultural domains. Li et al. (2024b) introduced FOODIEQA, which examines fine-grained understanding of Chinese food culture through multiple-choice tasks. Although it addresses a culturally rich dimension (food), current VLMs still lag behind human-level performance, especially on image-based tasks. Meanwhile, Liu et al. (2021) proposed MARVL, focusing on visually grounded reasoning across multiple languages and cultures, but it does not explicitly assess rich cultural common sense related to traditions and also utilizes a true/false format.

Our work differs by focusing specifically on the Taiwanese cultural context, providing an in-depth evaluation of VLMs' abilities to understand and reason about Taiwan-specific content. TaiwanVQA includes 2,000 image-question pairs with a significant emphasis on traditions, rituals, and daily life. We adopt a multiple-choice format, and ensure diverse and carefully designed distractors to challenge the models' cultural understanding. By categorizing questions into recognition and reasoning tasks, and further sub-classifying reasoning

	w/ OCR	w/o OCR	All
Recognition	339	661	1,000

	Basic	External Knowledge	Image Complexity	All
Reasoning	246	674	80	1,000

Table 1: Statistics of Recognition and Reasoning Questions by Types

questions based on the level of external knowledge required, our benchmark offers a comprehensive assessment of VLMs' cultural understanding within a specific regional context. This structured approach enables a more detailed analysis of models' capabilities and limitations in handling culturally rich content.

3 TaiwanVQA

3.1 Tasks

In constructing TaiwanVQA, we were inspired by two recent VLM evaluation benchmarks: MME(Fu et al., 2024) and TRANSPORTATIONGAMES(Zhang et al., 2024). MME's division of questions into perception and cognition guided our approach, as understanding Taiwan-related visual content requires both basic recognition and deeper reasoning. Thus, we structured TaiwanVQA by assigning two questions to each image to fully assess models' understanding of Taiwanese culture and knowledge:

- **Recognition Questions** – These questions evaluate models' ability to accurately identify Taiwan-specific visual elements, including local cuisine, transportation facilities, native ecology, and folk activities.
- **Reasoning Questions** – These questions test models' advanced analytical abilities, requiring them to not only identify visual elements but also understand relationships between them (such as spatial relations, usage contexts, and cultural implications), integrating local Taiwanese knowledge to reach accurate conclusions.

Within *recognition questions*, we specifically marked those requiring Optical Character Recognition (OCR) capabilities. These questions assess models' ability to recognize Traditional Chinese text in images, crucial for understanding Taiwan's visual elements such as public signs and notices.

Additionally, to better evaluate models' reasoning capabilities, we further categorize *reasoning questions* into three types:

- **Basic Reasoning Required** - Questions that can be answered through straightforward inference from the image content, requiring no external knowledge.
- **External Knowledge Required** - Questions that cannot be answered through image content alone, requiring specific knowledge about Taiwanese culture, customs, or context for accurate responses.
- **Image Complexity Required** - Images contain multiple visual elements or complex spatial relationships, requiring deep visual analysis for accurate judgment.

A detailed annotation process for both task types can be found in Appendix A, and Table 1 shows the statistical distribution across different types.

3.2 Data Collection

To construct the TaiwanVQA dataset, we selected 1,000 representative images of Taiwan, each paired with one identification and reasoning question, generating 2,000 questions in total. Due to licensing concerns, all images and questions were manually designed. We recruited 9 annotators from diverse backgrounds (varying in residence location, ethnic identity, gender, and academic fields), who underwent a week-long training before formal annotation. Detailed annotation guidelines can be found in Appendix A.

Beyond the task type classification in subsection 3.1, to ensure comprehensive coverage of Taiwan's daily life and cultural aspects, we established a question classification framework comprising 13 topics and 27 subtopics. We employed GPT-4o to perform the classification tasks to ensure consistency throughout the dataset. As shown in Figure 2, our questions primarily focus on signs and food culture, as these elements are most closely related to Taiwanese daily life. The remaining questions are evenly distributed across other categories, demonstrating the diversity of our data. Detailed classification criteria and prompts used can be found in Appendix B.

3.3 Data Quality

To validate the quality of TaiwanVQA benchmark, evaluation was performed by annotators on 10% randomly sampled data across three aspects:

- **Question Type Correctness** - compliance

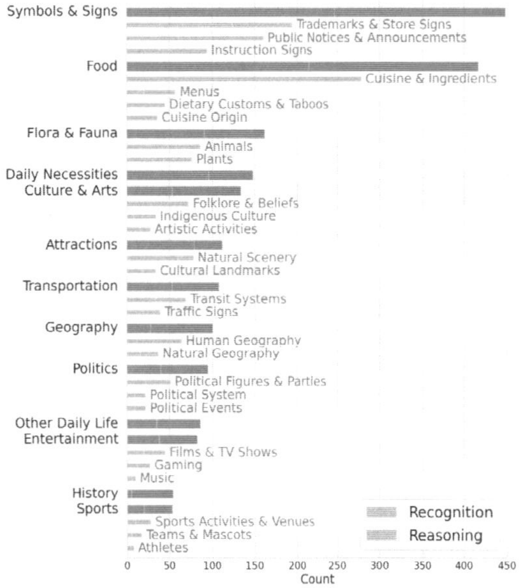

Figure 2: Distribution of Question Categories. The blue and red bars stand for the recognition and reasoning questions respectively. The darker bars represent the total number of questions in the topic, and the lighter bars represent the number of questions in the sub topics under the topic. If there are no shallower bars, it means that the topic has no sub topics, such as Daily Necessities.

	Q1: Recog. Compl.	Q2: Reas. Compl.	Q3: Topic Approp.	Q4: Subtopic Approp.	Q5: Question Clarity	Q6: Img Clarity	Q7: Img Need
A1	91	98	89.7	86.1	100	98	99.5
A2	88	99	88.1	85.1	99.5	100	100
A3	94	93	94.8	92.3	99	98.5	98
A4	93	91	96.4	90.2	98.5	94	98.5
Avg.	91.5	95.3	92.3	88.4	99.3	97.6	99
N	100	100	194	194	200	200	200

Table 2: Results of quality assessment, reported in Accuracy (%). Four annotators (A1-A4) evaluated sampled data across three aspects: question compliance (Recognition Q1 and Reasoning Q2), topic appropriateness (Topic Q3 and Subtopic Q4), and clarity (Question Q5, Image Q6, and Image Need Q7). N indicates the number of samples evaluated for each question.

with recognition and reasoning question design guidelines

- **Topic Classification Appropriateness** - compliance with topic and subtopic classification definitions
- **Content Clarity** - question comprehensibility, image clarity, and the necessity of the image for answering the question

As shown in Table 2, all criteria achieved over 85% agreement rate from annotators, demonstrating high consistency in question design and content presentation.

Model	Overall		Recognition		Reasoning	
	w/	w/o	w/	w/o	w/	w/o
GPT-4o	61.7	12.5	73.6	7.7	49.8	17.2
Llama-3.2-90B	51.6	11.1	61.8	7.0	41.4	15.2
InternVL2-76B	64.3	21.9	75.9	17.2	52.6	26.5
Qwen2-VL-72B	75.0	24.8	83.7	18.3	66.2	31.3

Table 3: Performances of VLMs in Normal and Text-only Conditions. The Accuracies (%) evaluated with images (w/) and without images (w/o) are reported.

Furthermore, to validate the necessity of visual information, in addition to the previously mentioned manual inspection of image dependency (Table 2, Q7), we compared four major VLMs' performance with and without images. Table 3 shows that all models performed significantly worse in text-only (w/o) conditions, confirming that our benchmark requires visual reasoning capabilities for accurate answers.

4 Experiments

4.1 Evaluation Strategy

Prompting Approach In our experiments, we design a standardized prompt structure to ensure consistent model evaluation. Figure 3 presents our prompt template used during the evaluation process. To directly assess models' intrinsic instruction-following capabilities, we conduct our evaluation in a zero-shot setting.

Scoring Method To obtain model predictions, we select the option token ("A", "B", "C", or "D") that receives the highest probability among the 20 most probable tokens in the model's output distribution. If none of the option tokens appear in these 20 tokens, the prediction is marked as null and counted as incorrect. We evaluate performance using accuracy as our primary metric, calculated as Accuracy $= \frac{N_{\text{correct}}}{N_{\text{total}}} \times 100\%$, where N_{correct} represents the number of correctly answered questions, and N_{total} represents the total number of questions in our benchmark.

Robust Evaluation Recognizing the sensitivity of language models to the ordering of options in multiple-choice questions (Pezeshkpour and Hruschka, 2023), we adopt the **CircularEval** strategy proposed by (Liu et al., 2024). Details of this approach are provided in Appendix C. This strategy evaluates model responses across four iterations, each applying a circular shift to the answer choices.

[Question content]
有以下幾個選項： (Here are the following options:)
A. <Option A>
B. <Option B>
C. <Option C>
D. <Option D>

請直接使用所提供的選項字母作為答案回答。 (Please answer directly with the option letter provided.)

Figure 3: The Prompt Template for the Zero-shot Setting

A question is considered correctly answered only if the model provides the accurate answer in all iterations, ensuring robustness against option positioning.

4.2 Experimental Setup

Models We evaluate our benchmark using a diverse set of vision-language models, including both open-source and proprietary models. For open-source models, we include: (1) leading multilingual VLMs; and (2) Chinese-based VLMs, which are VLMs that integrate large language models developed in countries where Chinese is the native language. We also include different versions from a proprietary model series. A comprehensive list of the evaluated models and their specifications is provided in Table 9(Appendix D).

Implementation Details Proprietary models are evaluated through OpenAI's API, while open-source models are deployed in containers using the `vLLM` framework (Kwon et al., 2023). This setup maintains API consistency across all evaluations, facilitating fair comparisons. Due to API constraints, we can only access the 20 most probable tokens from the model's output distribution. All open-source models are hosted on DGX-1 V100 GPUs. Our evaluation pipeline is built upon `lmms-eval`[1] with modifications to accommodate our experimental requirements. Detailed implementation information, including chat completion parameters and model deployment configurations, is provided in Appendix D.

4.3 Results

We evaluate eleven VLMs and present their performance in three aspects. Table 4 shows the overall performance and results on two question types: Recognition and Reasoning. We further examine model performance across different topics for Recognition (Table 5) and Reasoning (Table 7). For more detailed analysis, we break down the performance by subtopics; complete results are in Appendix E.

[1]`https://github.com/EvolvingLMMs-Lab/lmms-eval`

Model	Overall	Recognition	Reasoning
Phi3.5-Vision-Instruct	29.95	33.80	26.10
Llama-3.2-11B	33.10	46.80	19.40
Llama-3.2-90B	51.60	61.80	41.40
LLaVA-v1.6-mistral-7B	28.90	33.50	24.30
LLaVA-v1.6-34B	49.50	57.80	41.20
InternVL2-8B	60.45	71.80	49.10
InternVL2-76B	64.25	75.90	52.60
Qwen2-VL-7B	65.35	79.40	51.30
Qwen2-VL-72B	**74.95**	**83.70**	**66.20**
GPT-4o	61.70	73.60	49.80
GPT-4o-mini	50.05	59.80	40.30

Table 4: Performance (in Accuracy, %) Comparison on Overall Performance and Two Question Types: Recognition and Reasoning

5 Analysis

5.1 Recognition and Reasoning Performance

Table 4 shows the performance variations across models in recognition and reasoning tasks related to Taiwan. Among the evaluated models, Qwen2-VL-72B demonstrates the highest overall score (74.95), significantly outperforming other models in both recognition (83.70) and reasoning (66.20). This indicates its robust capability to handle diverse knowledge-intensive tasks. Conversely, smaller models, such as LLaVA-v1.6-mistral-7B and Phi3.5-Vision-Instruct, exhibit lower scores in both categories, suggesting that model size and architectural sophistication are critical for domain-specific generalization.

Generally, model performance tends to scale with size, with larger models typically outperforming smaller ones. However, the results reveal an exception to this trend: Qwen2-VL-7B and InternVL2-8B both outperform larger models such as LLaVA-v1.6-34B and Llama-3.2-90B in both recognition and reasoning tasks. This suggests that, within our benchmark, InternVL2 and Qwen exhibit superior capabilities in both cognitive tasks and Taiwan-specific reasoning, demonstrating a clear advantage over Llama and LLaVA despite their smaller scale.

5.2 Recognition Questions

Recognition questions in the Taiwan Vision Benchmark test models on identifying Taiwan-specific

Model	S&S	Att	Food	Trans	C&A	Pol	Geo	Spo	F&F	His	Ent	DN	ODL
Phi3.5-Vision-Instruct	34.82	22.78	32.56	37.74	35.85	20.00	35.71	45.00	26.37	20.00	31.58	47.92	42.86
Llama-3.2-11B	55.87	35.44	42.79	49.06	33.96	37.50	35.71	65.00	34.07	40.00	55.26	64.58	34.29
Llama-3.2-90B	68.83	46.84	62.79	62.26	62.26	50.00	60.71	65.00	46.15	20.00	71.05	73.96	54.29
LLaVA-v1.6-mistral-7B	35.63	20.25	31.16	50.94	26.42	25.00	21.43	30.00	30.77	20.00	42.11	47.92	28.57
LLaVA-v1.6-34B	57.49	55.70	57.21	67.92	54.72	45.00	60.71	65.00	48.35	20.00	57.89	72.92	54.29
InternVL2-8B	82.59	60.76	65.12	71.70	77.36	67.50	75.00	75.00	62.64	60.00	71.05	72.92	77.14
InternVL2-76B	82.59	68.35	73.49	71.70	84.91	60.00	67.86	**90.00**	63.74	60.00	**84.21**	82.29	77.14
Qwen2-VL-7B	87.45	68.35	76.28	77.36	75.47	82.50	**89.29**	**90.00**	67.03	**80.00**	81.58	79.17	**88.57**
Qwen2-VL-72B	**89.88**	**78.48**	**82.79**	**73.58**	**88.68**	**90.00**	**89.29**	**90.00**	**68.13**	**80.00**	**84.21**	**84.38**	**88.57**
GPT-4o	76.52	72.15	77.21	67.92	73.58	62.50	85.71	85.00	59.34	**80.00**	76.32	77.08	62.86
GPT-4o-mini	68.42	53.16	58.60	60.38	49.06	57.50	60.71	70.00	48.35	60.00	57.89	65.62	48.57

Table 5: Performances of **recognition questions** across different models and topics, including Symbols and Signs (S&S), Attractions (Att), Food, Transportation (Trans), Culture and Arts (C&A), Politics (Pol), Geography (Geo), Sports (Spo), Flora and Fauna (F&F), History (His), Entertainment (Ent), Daily Necessities (DN), and Other Daily Life (ODL). All results are reported in Accuracy (%).

visual elements like local cuisine, transportation, native ecology, and cultural artifacts. These tasks focus on precise object detection without requiring advanced contextual reasoning.

General Patterns and High-Performing Topics Models performed best in visually distinct and simpler categories like *Transportation*, *Symbols and Signs*, and *Sports*. Qwen2-VL-72B excelled, achieving over 89% in *Geography* and *Symbols and Signs*, while InternVL2-76B also performed well, particularly in *Symbols and Signs* (82.59%) and *Daily Necessities* (82.29%). Table 5 highlights Qwen2-VL-72B's dominance and InternVL's strength. Categories like *Food* and *Daily Necessities* further show models' effectiveness in recognizing familiar objects. The high accuracy of Qwen2-VL and InternVL models reflects their robust architectures and multilingual training, enabling strong performance with Traditional Chinese text.

Challenging Topics Across Models Despite overall progress in recognition tasks, certain topics posed significant challenges, particularly those requiring nuanced cultural understanding or visual differentiation. Categories such as *Politics*, *Flora and Fauna*, and *History* consistently recorded lower accuracy, with models like Phi3.5-Vision-Instruct scoring as low as 20% in *Politics*. Table 5 shows a pronounced dip in performance for smaller and less advanced models like LLaVA-v1.6-mistral-7B across complex topics. Text-heavy categories, such as *Politics* and *Culture and Arts*, were particularly difficult for models without some cultural knowledge of Taiwanese culture. These findings emphasize the need for enriched cultural datasets and improved linguistic understanding to enhance performance in these challenging areas.

Comparison of Models The Qwen2-VL models outperformed others in recognition tasks, with the 72B model excelling in Politics (90.00%), Geography (89.29%), and Culture and Arts (88.68%). The smaller 7B version also performed well in visually distinct areas like Symbols and Signs (87.45%). InternVL models were balanced, with the 76B model strong in Symbols and Signs (82.59%) and Daily Necessities (82.29%) but slightly behind Qwen2 in nuanced tasks. GPT models excelled in reasoning-heavy areas like History (80.00%) and Sports (85.00%) but struggled in visual categories, especially smaller versions. LLaVA models, even the larger 34B version, lagged in nuanced areas like Politics (45.00%). Overall, Qwen2-VL led in accuracy, highlighting the importance of model size and training depth.

Model	w/ OCR	w/o OCR
Phi3.5-Vision-Instruct	31.56	34.95
Llama-3.2-11B	47.20	46.60
Llama-3.2-90B	59.59	62.93
LLaVA-v1.6-mistral-7B	23.89	38.43
LLaVA-v1.6-34B	49.26	62.18
InternVL2-8B	84.96	65.05
InternVL2-76B	83.19	72.16
Qwen2-VL-7B	92.63	72.62
Qwen2-VL-72B	93.51	78.67
GPT-4o	75.81	72.47
GPT-4o-mini	63.72	57.79

Table 6: Performances of Recognition Task with and without OCR, reported in Accuracy (%)

OCR and Text Recognition As shown in Table 6 the OCR capabilities of the Phi, Llama, and GPT series models are similar to their performance in general QA tasks, showing no significant differentiation. In contrast, the LLaVA series struggles noticeably with OCR-related questions. Notably,

Model	S&S	Att	Food	Trans	C&A	Pol	Geo	Spo	F&F	His	Ent	DN	ODL
Phi3.5-Vision-Instruct	31.34	24.24	20.79	25.45	30.86	23.64	23.29	39.39	25.35	20.41	27.27	30.77	19.61
Llama-3.2-11B	26.37	15.15	17.33	20.00	20.99	7.27	10.96	36.36	11.27	14.29	34.09	23.08	13.73
Llama-3.2-90B	54.23	30.30	38.61	40.00	39.51	27.27	20.55	51.52	40.85	40.82	45.45	53.85	37.25
LLaVA-v1.6-mistral-7B	23.88	33.33	21.78	25.45	25.93	21.82	17.81	42.42	29.58	22.45	27.27	26.92	15.69
LLaVA-v1.6-34B	48.76	36.36	42.08	43.64	40.74	36.36	26.03	48.48	43.66	36.73	36.36	46.15	31.37
InternVL2-8B	58.21	45.45	45.05	60.00	54.32	45.45	32.88	60.61	33.80	42.86	54.55	57.69	45.10
InternVL2-76B	62.19	33.33	45.05	61.82	58.02	49.09	39.73	54.55	49.30	48.98	63.64	61.54	49.02
Qwen2-VL-7B	65.67	36.36	45.54	56.36	51.85	47.27	39.73	60.61	42.25	42.86	56.82	63.46	39.22
Qwen2-VL-72B	**76.12**	**57.58**	**65.84**	**63.64**	**69.14**	**70.91**	**52.05**	**72.73**	**50.70**	**67.35**	**65.91**	**73.08**	**56.86**
GPT-4o	60.20	42.42	45.54	47.27	53.09	52.73	41.10	51.52	40.85	42.86	59.09	57.69	39.22
GPT-4o-mini	52.74	30.30	37.13	47.27	48.15	30.91	30.14	45.45	29.58	30.61	43.18	42.31	31.37

Table 7: Performances of **reasoning questions** across different models and topics, including Symbols and Signs (S&S), Attractions (Att), Food, Transportation (Trans), Culture and Arts (C&A), Politics (Pol), Geography (Geo), Sports (Spo), Flora and Fauna (F&F), History (His), Entertainment (Ent), Daily Necessities (DN), and Other Daily Life (ODL). All results are reported in Accuracy (%).

the InternVL2 and Qwen models perform better on OCR tasks than on general QA, suggesting a strong specialization. Given that our benchmark primarily consists of Traditional Chinese OCR tasks, we speculate that InternVL2 and Qwen were trained with more extensive Traditional Chinese OCR data compared to other models.

5.3 Reasoning Questions

Reasoning questions required models to interpret visual elements and apply external knowledge, such as culture or history, to answer questions beyond the image content. Unlike Recognition tasks, these questions tested deeper, abstract understanding, posing unique challenges for VLMs.

General Patterns and High-Performing Topics Reasoning tasks revealed significant variation in model performance. Categories like Transportation, Symbols and Signs, and Daily Necessities were strengths for larger models. Qwen2-VL-72B led across the board, achieving top scores in Symbols and Signs (76.12%), Politics (70.91%), and Daily Necessities (73.08%). InternVL2-76B also performed well, excelling in Transportation (61.82%) and Culture and Arts (58.02%). Other models like GPT-4o showed strength in reasoning-intensive topics such as Politics (52.73%), but struggled in more visually complex tasks. Table 7 highlights Qwen2-VL-72B's dominance across reasoning tasks.

Challenging Topics Across Models Topics requiring cultural or linguistic reasoning, such as Politics, Flora and Fauna, and History, were difficult for most models. Smaller models like Phi3.5-Vision-Instruct and Llama-3.2-11B scored poorly in these areas, with accuracy as low as 14.29% in History and 7.24% in Politics, respectively. Even intermediate models like LLaVA-v1.6-34B struggled in nuanced reasoning, achieving only 36.36% in Politics, emphasizing a need for better Taiwanese linguistic and cultural training.

Comparison of Models Qwen2-VL-72B outperformed all others, achieving exceptional accuracy in reasoning categories like Culture and Arts (69.14%), Geography (52.05%), and Politics (70.91%). Its smaller version, Qwen2-VL-7B, maintained competitive scores in areas like Daily Necessities (63.46%) and Symbols and Signs (65.67%). InternVL2-76B offered balanced results across most tasks, while GPT-4o excelled in text-heavy reasoning but fell short in visual topics. Smaller models like LLaVA consistently underperformed, demonstrating the importance of scale and training diversity.

Analysis of Types of Reasoning Questions Model size generally correlates strongly with reasoning ability, a trend also observed within the same model series in Figure 4. However, InternVL2-8B and Qwen2-VL-7B, despite being smaller models, outperform larger models such as LLaVA-34B and Llama-90B in reasoning tasks, an unexpected result. Across our types of reasoning questions, Qwen2-VL-72B consistently demonstrate a deeper understanding of Taiwan-specific content compared to other models.

5.4 Model Analysis and Insights

Analysis of Chinese-based Model In Figure 5, we analyze base models, where "O" represents Chinese-based models and "X" represents non-Chinese-based models. The choice of base model has a significant impact on our TaiwanVQA benchmark. Chinese-based models excel in recognition

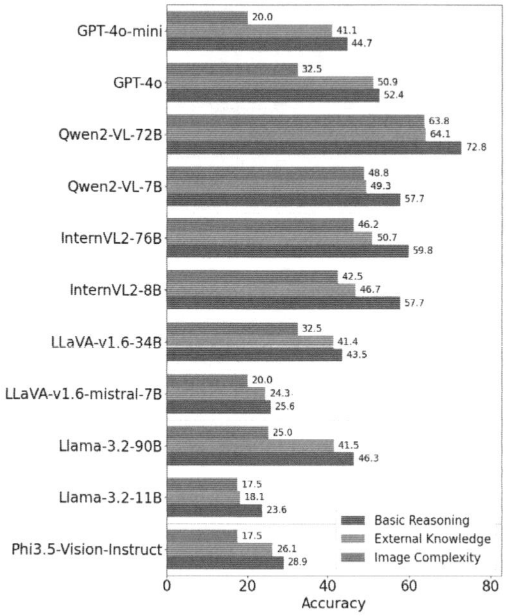

Figure 4: Analysis of Types of Reasoning Questions

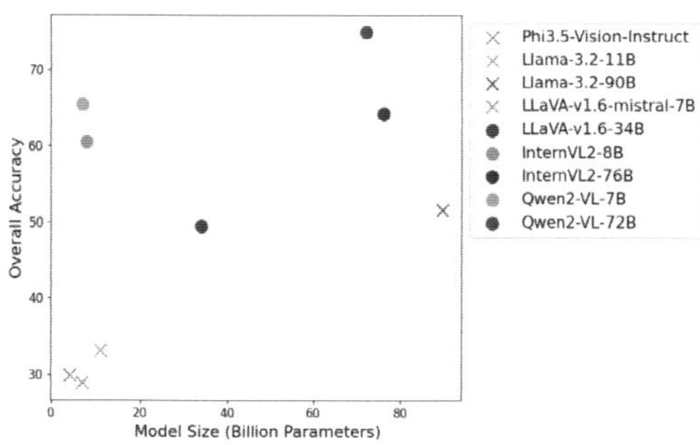

Figure 5: The Impact of Base Model Selection: Comparing Chinese-Based ("O") and Non-Chinese-Based ("X") Models

tasks, while also outperforming in reasoning tasks due to their optimization for Chinese semantic understanding and content-specific pretraining. Notably, InternVL2-8B and Qwen2-VL-7B achieve higher overall scores than Llama-90B, despite their smaller size.

Impact of Model Size on Accuracy The relationship between model size and overall accuracy underscores the significant impact of scale on performance. Larger models, such as Qwen2-VL-72B and InternVL2-76B, consistently achieved the highest overall accuracy, exceeding 70% and 60% accuracy, respectively. In contrast, smaller models like Phi3.5-Vision-Instruct and LLaVA-v1.6-mistral-7B struggled to surpass 30% accuracy, demonstrating a clear limitation in their ability to handle complex tasks. Notably, mid-sized models such as LLaVA-v1.6-34B showed moderate improvements in accuracy (around 50%), indicating that scaling up provides diminishing but still significant returns in accuracy. This trend emphasizes the importance of large-scale architectures and extensive training datasets for achieving state-of-the-art performance in multimodal recognition and reasoning tasks, though some smaller models still demonstrate reasonable accuracy.

6 Conclusion

In this paper, we introduced TaiwanVQA, a novel visual question answering benchmark specifically designed to evaluate the capabilities of VLMs in understanding and reasoning about Taiwan-specific content. TaiwanVQA consists of 1,000 images and 2,000 questions covering a diverse range of topics relevant to Taiwanese daily life and culture, including local cuisine, public signage, tourist attractions, and local flora and fauna. We categorized the questions into recognition and reasoning tasks, further sub-classifying the reasoning questions based on the level of external knowledge required.

Our extensive experiments with state-of-the-art models, including GPT-4 (OpenAI, 2023), revealed significant limitations in current VLMs when dealing with culturally specific content. The results demonstrated that while models perform reasonably well on recognition tasks, their performance on reasoning tasks that require deeper cultural understanding is substantially lower. This highlights the need for more culturally diverse training data and improved model architectures that can better integrate visual and textual information in culturally nuanced contexts.

By providing the first VQA benchmark that focuses on culturally rich content specific to Taiwan, TaiwanVQA fills a critical gap in the evaluation of VLMs. We believe this benchmark will contribute to the development of more inclusive and culturally aware AI models, ultimately facilitating their deployment in diverse real-world scenarios (Nayak et al., 2024).

7 Limitations

While TaiwanVQA makes significant strides in evaluating VLMs on culturally specific content, several limitations exist in our current work. First, due to technical challenges during the experimentation phase, we were unable to successfully infer and evaluate some models. These models are marked with an asterisk (*) or dagger (†) in our experimental settings and results (see Appendix D and E). The inability to include these models may affect the comprehensiveness of our evaluation. In future work, we plan to resolve these technical issues and include a broader range of models in our analysis.

Second, the dataset, though diverse, may not cover all aspects of Taiwanese culture and daily life. Certain niche or less visually represented cultural elements might be underrepresented, potentially limiting the assessment of models' understanding in those areas.

Third, the dataset primarily focuses on visual content accompanied by textual questions in Traditional Chinese. This language-specific focus might make it challenging to generalize the findings to other underrepresented languages and cultures without additional adaptation.

Finally, our current evaluation is conducted in a zero-shot setting without fine-tuning on Taiwan-specific data. While this approach highlights inherent model capabilities, it does not account for improvements that might be achieved through targeted training or domain-specific adaptation (Li et al., 2024a).

Acknowledgments

This work was supported by the National Center for High-performance Computing (NCHC), National Applied Research Laboratories (NARLabs), and the National Science and Technology Council (NSTC) under the project "Taiwan's 113th year endeavoring in the promotion of a trustworthy generative AI large language model and the cultivation of literacy capabilities (Trustworthy AI Dialog Engine, TAIDE)".

References

Mehar Bhatia, Sahithya Ravi, Aditya Chinchure, Eunjeong Hwang, and Vered Shwartz. 2024. From local concepts to universals: Evaluating the multicultural understanding of vision-language models. *arXiv preprint arXiv:2407.00263*.

Olena Burda-Lassen, Aman Chadha, Shashank Goswami, and Vinija Jain. 2024. How culturally aware are vision-language models? *arXiv preprint arXiv:2405.17475*.

Wenliang Dai, Junnan Li, Dongxu Li, Anthony Tiong, Junqi Zhao, Weisheng Wang, Boyang Li, Pascale Fung, and Steven Hoi. 2023. InstructBLIP: Towards general-purpose vision-language models with instruction tuning. In *Thirty-seventh Conference on Neural Information Processing Systems*.

Chaoyou Fu, Peixian Chen, Yunhang Shen, Yulei Qin, Mengdan Zhang, Xu Lin, Jinrui Yang, Xiawu Zheng, Ke Li, Xing Sun, Yunsheng Wu, and Rongrong Ji. 2024. Mme: A comprehensive evaluation benchmark for multimodal large language models. *Preprint*, arXiv:2306.13394.

Daniel Hershcovich, Stella Frank, Heather Lent, Miryam de Lhoneux, Mostafa Abdou, Stephanie Brandl, Emanuele Bugliarello, Laura Cabello Piqueras, Ilias Chalkidis, Ruixiang Cui, Constanza Fierro, Katerina Margatina, Phillip Rust, and Anders Søgaard. 2022. Challenges and strategies in cross-cultural NLP. In *Proceedings of the 60th Annual Meeting of the Association for Computational Linguistics (Volume 1: Long Papers)*, pages 6997–7013, Dublin, Ireland. Association for Computational Linguistics.

Woosuk Kwon, Zhuohan Li, Siyuan Zhuang, Ying Sheng, Lianmin Zheng, Cody Hao Yu, Joseph E. Gonzalez, Hao Zhang, and Ion Stoica. 2023. Efficient memory management for large language model serving with pagedattention. In *Proceedings of the ACM SIGOPS 29th Symposium on Operating Systems Principles*.

Bohao Li, Yuying Ge, Yixiao Ge, Guangzhi Wang, Rui Wang, Ruimao Zhang, and Ying Shan. 2024a. Seed-bench: Benchmarking multimodal large language models. In *Proceedings of the IEEE/CVF Conference on Computer Vision and Pattern Recognition*, pages 13299–13308.

Junnan Li, Dongxu Li, Silvio Savarese, and Steven Hoi. 2023. Blip-2: Bootstrapping language-image pre-training with frozen image encoders and large language models. In *International conference on machine learning*, pages 19730–19742. PMLR.

Wenyan Li, Xinyu Zhang, Jiaang Li, Qiwei Peng, Raphael Tang, Li Zhou, Weijia Zhang, Guimin Hu, Yifei Yuan, Anders Søgaard, et al. 2024b. Foodieqa: A multimodal dataset for fine-grained understanding of chinese food culture. *arXiv preprint arXiv:2406.11030*.

Fangyu Liu, Emanuele Bugliarello, Edoardo Maria Ponti, Siva Reddy, Nigel Collier, and Desmond Elliott. 2021. Visually grounded reasoning across languages and cultures. *arXiv preprint arXiv:2109.13238*.

Yuan Liu, Haodong Duan, Yuanhan Zhang, Bo Li, Songyang Zhang, Wangbo Zhao, Yike Yuan, Jiaqi Wang, Conghui He, Ziwei Liu, Kai Chen, and Dahua Lin. 2024. Mmbench: Is your multi-modal model an all-around player? *Preprint*, arXiv:2307.06281.

Shravan Nayak, Kanishk Jain, Rabiul Awal, Siva Reddy, Sjoerd van Steenkiste, Lisa Anne Hendricks, Karolina Stańczak, and Aishwarya Agrawal. 2024. Benchmarking vision language models for cultural understanding. *arXiv preprint arXiv:2407.10920*.

OpenAI. 2023. Gpt-4 technical report.

Pouya Pezeshkpour and Estevam Hruschka. 2023. Large language models sensitivity to the order of options in multiple-choice questions. *Preprint*, arXiv:2308.11483.

William A Gaviria Rojas, Sudnya Diamos, Keertan Ranjan Kini, David Kanter, Vijay Janapa Reddi, and Cody Coleman. 2022. The dollar street dataset: Images representing the geographic and socioeconomic diversity of the world. In *Thirty-sixth Conference on Neural Information Processing Systems Datasets and Benchmarks Track*.

T. Weyand, A. Araujo, B. Cao, and J. Sim. 2020. Google Landmarks Dataset v2 - A Large-Scale Benchmark for Instance-Level Recognition and Retrieval. In *Proc. CVPR*.

Xiang Yue, Yuansheng Ni, Kai Zhang, Tianyu Zheng, Ruoqi Liu, Ge Zhang, Samuel Stevens, Dongfu Jiang, Weiming Ren, Yuxuan Sun, et al. 2024a. Mmmu: A massive multi-discipline multimodal understanding and reasoning benchmark for expert agi. In *Proceedings of the IEEE/CVF Conference on Computer Vision and Pattern Recognition*, pages 9556–9567.

Xiang Yue, Tianyu Zheng, Yuansheng Ni, Yubo Wang, Kai Zhang, Shengbang Tong, Yuxuan Sun, Ming Yin, Botao Yu, Ge Zhang, et al. 2024b. Mmmu-pro: A more robust multi-discipline multimodal understanding benchmark. *arXiv preprint arXiv:2409.02813*.

Xue Zhang, Xiangyu Shi, Xinyue Lou, Rui Qi, Yufeng Chen, Jinan Xu, and Wenjuan Han. 2024. Transportationgames: Benchmarking transportation knowledge of (multimodal) large language models. *Preprint*, arXiv:2401.04471.

A Annotation Guideline

In this section we demonstrate the detail annotation guideline we asked annotator to do. There are three steps in our annotation step. First, we give annotators an general guideline and asked them to take a picture with Taiwan information. Second, we asked annotator to generate a recognition question. Final, we asked annotator to generate a reasoning question.

A.1 General Guideline

Before the annotators begin annotating data, we first provided them with a general guideline. This guideline asked the annotator follow the rules to write the recognition question and choices, including:

- The primary purpose of data collection: to collect images and questions featuring elements specific to Taiwan.
- Ensuring that the language used in questions reflects common terms and expressions used in Taiwan.
- Ensuring that annotators do not violate any legal issues, such as those related to privacy or copyright.

After reading the overall guideline, the annotator should upload an image containing a Taiwan-specific object.

A.2 Recognition Question

Next, we asked them to generate a recognition question and corresponding multiple-choice answers. To help annotators understand the guidelines, we provide clear examples and detailed explanations, ensuring both the questions and answer choices meet the required conditions. This guideline introduces key concepts of writing a recognition question, including:

- The definition of a recognition question: questions that assess whether the model can identify and name the object in an image without requiring analysis or inference.
- Emphasize that the question should be answerable solely based on all visible text or clearly identifiable objects in the image, and that the designed options do not include these visible texts or identifiable objects as possible answers.
- Ensure that questions cannot be answered without actually viewing the image.
- If there are multiple objects in the image, specify exactly which person or object to identify to avoid overly simplistic questions.
- Include misleading choices to make it harder for the model to select the correct answer, increasing the challenge.
- No length limit for questions and options.

Additionally, we asked annotators to classify whether the recognition question required ORC capability or not.

Once the question is written, annotators are required to categorize the question's topic. The topics definition is shown in Table 8. This helps in further analyzing the questions and ensuring data quality.

A.3 Reasoning Question

After writing a recognition question, annotator should write a reasoning question with the guideline. This guideline introduces key concepts of writing a reasoning question, including:

- The definition of a reasoning question: questions that require not only identifying the object but also understanding additional information, such as quantity, use, location, relative position, physical properties, or price, to provide an answer.
- Ensure that questions cannot be answered without actually viewing the image.
- No length limit for questions and options.

Once the reasoning question is written, we also asked the annotator to classify the question topic, similar to the recognition question. Additionally, we asked them to further label the question by identifying the capabilities required to answer it. The annotator should also indicate whether the question requires information about current events.

Topic	Subtopic	Definition
Symbols and Signs		Recognition and understanding of symbols, like priority seating, restrooms, no smoking, etc.
	Trademarks and Store Signs	Registered trademarks and store signs, such as FamilyMart, Louisa Coffee, YongChing Real Estate, Hua Nan Bank, etc.
	Public Notices and Announcements	Images or text providing information, such as advertisements, banners, usage instructions, and rules.
	Instruction Signs	Signs indicating rules or directions, like no smoking, emergency exit, restrooms, priority seating, parking, turn off devices, etc.
Attractions		Including Taiwan's natural and cultural landscapes.
	Natural Scenery	Includes Taiwan's mountains, coastlines, lakes, etc., such as Alishan, Taroko National Park, etc.
	Cultural Landmarks	Covers Taiwan's historical sites, architectural landmarks, and other non-natural tourist spots, such as Anping Fort in Tainan, Chiang Kai-shek Memorial Hall in Taipei, National Palace Museum, Jiufen Old Street.
Food		Including content related to Taiwan's culinary culture.
	Cuisine and Ingredients	Names of dishes and their ingredients, including distinctive foods, components, and garnishes on plates.
	Dietary Customs and Taboos	Features of Taiwan's daily dietary habits and customs, including combinations and taboos, like breakfast culture, adding cilantro, etc.
	Menus	Judging information based on menu or price list content; images only show text, no actual dishes.
	Cuisine Origin	Judging a dish's origin by time or location, or associating it with the culture that originated it.
Transportation		Including content related to Taiwan's transportation.
	Transit Systems	Includes Taiwan's metro, train, and bus systems, their operations and features.
	Traffic Signs	Covers Taiwan's traffic lights, violation checks, driving tests, etc.
Culture and Arts		Including content related to Taiwan's culture and arts.
	Folklore and Beliefs	All things related to culture and religion, including Taiwan's festivals, customs, and taboos like the Mid-Autumn Festival, Dragon Boat Festival, marriage and funeral traditions, religious buildings and decorations, gods, religious practices, temple culture, folk beliefs like Mazu worship.
	Indigenous Culture	Taiwan's indigenous customs, languages, and arts, such as those of the Amis and Atayal tribes.
	Artistic Activities	Activities like art exhibitions, cultural artifacts, musical instruments, operas, etc.
Politics		Including content related to Taiwan's politics.

Topic	Subtopic	Definition
	Political System	Taiwan's political system and electoral system, such as central and local government bodies, legislative election systems, etc.
	Political Events	Activities like elections and social movements.
	Political Figures and Parties	Contemporary Taiwanese political figures or parties, such as Lai Ching-te, Chu Li-lun, Taiwan People's Party.
Geography		Including content related to Taiwan's geography.
	Natural Geography	Taiwan's landforms and natural features, such as the Central Mountain Range and the eastern coast.
	Human Geography	Taiwan's administrative divisions, place name origins, population distribution, industry distribution, etc.
Sports		Including content related to Taiwan's sports and athletics.
	Sports	Types of sports and sports venues, such as tennis, badminton, baseball fields.
	Athletes	Taiwanese athletes, such as Chuang Chih-yuan, Tai Tzu-ying, Wang Chien-ming.
	Teams and Mascots	Taiwan's professional or amateur teams and mascots, such as the Uni Lions, Rakuten Monkeys, Monkeys Kids, Ryan.
Flora and Fauna		Including Taiwan's common flora and fauna.
	Animals	Common animal species in Taiwan, such as the Taiwan blue magpie and the Formosan landlocked salmon.
	Plants	Common plant species in Taiwan, such as the blackboard tree and large flower impatiens.
History		Covers historical events (e.g., the February 28 Incident, Kaohsiung Incident) and figures who impacted Taiwanese history, such as Chiang Ching-kuo, Lee Teng-hui.
Entertainment		Including content related to Taiwan's entertainment.
	Films and TV Shows	Movies, TV series, related events, and venues.
	Music Industry	Music genres, important music events, music works, and related venues.
	Gaming Industry	Games and industry development.
Daily Necessities		Common items or tools with specific purposes in daily life, requiring identification of the items and their possible uses or purposes.
Other Daily Life		Other content related to the daily lifestyle and habits of Taiwanese people.

Table 8: Definition of Each Topic

B Topic Definition and Classification Prompt

In this section, we show the detail of the definition of the topics and the analysis of it.

B.1 Definition

We classify the questions into 13 topics and 27 subtopics. The definition of the topics and subtopics is shown in Table 8.

B.2 Classification Prompt

In this section, we present the detailed prompt used to instruct GPT-4o to classify question topics.

The system prompt is shown in Figure 6. It includes a role-play request, asking GPT-4o to act as an assistant with a deep understanding of Taiwanese culture. Furthermore, we instruct GPT-4o to respond in a specific format, which includes both the topic and subtopic of the question. Additionally, we emphasize that GPT-4o should avoid selecting subtopics that do not align with the chosen topic.

你是一個專業的主題分類助理，且十分理解台灣的日常生活文化。請根據以下的分類標準，為每個問題選擇最適合的主題類別和子類別。

<Topics Definition>

分類標準：

- 若選擇 "交通標示" 作為子類別，主題必須是 "交通"。
- 若選擇 "文宣與告示" 作為子類別，主題必須是 "標誌標示"。

注意：
1. 部分主題沒有子類別，這種情況下只需提供主題即可。
2. 子類別必須屬於其主題，例如：
主題：[主題名稱]
子類別：[子類別名稱]（若該主題沒有子類別則此行可省略）。
回答格式：
- 主題：[主題名稱]。
- 子類別：[子類別名稱]。

Figure 6: System Prompt for Classifying Question Topics

The user prompt is shown in Figure 7. This section directly includes the question, the options, and the correct answer.

問題：<question>
選項：
A. <option A>
B. <option B>
C. <option C>
D. <option D>
答案：<correct option>

Figure 7: User Prompt for Classifying Question Topics

Original Question:

請問照片拍攝的是以下哪種台灣小吃？ (Which Taiwanese snack is shown in the photo?)
A. 蚵仔煎 (Oyster Omelette)
B. 地瓜球 (Sweet Potato Balls)
C. 牛肉湯 (Beef Soup)
D. 蚵仔麵線 (Oyster Vermicelli)
Answer: D

Four Iterations with Circular Shifts:
1: A. 蚵仔煎 B. 地瓜球 C. 牛肉湯 D. 蚵仔麵線 → D
2: A. 地瓜球 B. 牛肉湯 C. 蚵仔麵線 D. 蚵仔煎 → C
3: A. 牛肉湯 B. 蚵仔麵線 C. 蚵仔煎 D. 地瓜球 → B
4: A. 蚵仔麵線 B. 蚵仔煎 C. 地瓜球 D. 牛肉湯 → A

Figure 8: CircularEval example. A model must correctly track the target answer (Oyster Vermicelli) through all shifted positions to be considered successful.

C Evaluation Strategy

C.1 Robust Evaluation

To ensure robust evaluation of model performance on multiple-choice questions, we implement the CircularEval strategy as illustrated in Figure 8. This approach addresses potential biases in model responses due to option positioning.

Consider an example where the model is asked to identify a Taiwanese snack from an image. The original question is presented with four options (A: Oyster Omelette, B: Sweet Potato Balls, C: Beef Soup, D: Oyster Vermicelli), where the correct answer is "Oyster Vermicelli" (Option D). CircularEval then creates four iterations by circularly shifting these options:

- Original: The correct answer "Oyster Vermicelli" is at position D
- First shift: The answer moves to position C
- Second shift: The answer moves to position B
- Third shift: The answer moves to position A

For a model's prediction to be considered correct, it must accurately track the answer through all

Model	Language Model	Vision Encoder	Size (B)
Phi3.5-Vision-Instruct	Phi-3.5-mini-instruct	CLIP ViT-L/14	4.2
Llama-3.2-11B	Llama-3.1-8B	ViT–H/14	11
Llama-3.2-90B	Llama-3.1-70B	ViT–H/14	90
LLaVA-v1.6-mistral-7B	Mistral-7B	CLIP ViT-L/14	7
LLaVA-v1.6-34B	Nous-Hermes-2-Yi-34B	CLIP ViT-L/14	34
InternVL2-8B	InternLM2.5-7B-Chat	InternViT-300M	8
InternVL2-76B	Hermes-2-Theta-Llama-3-70B	InternViT-6B	76
Qwen2-VL-7B	Qwen2-7B	CLIP ViT-L/14	7
Qwen2-VL-72B	Qwen2-72B	CLIP ViT-L/14	72
GPT-4o	–	–	–
GPT-4o-mini	–	–	–

Table 9: Model specifications of evaluated VLMs. Size is measured in billions of parameters (B).

four positions (D→C→B→A). This methodology ensures that the model's performance is based on genuine understanding rather than position-based biases or patterns.

D Experimental Setup

D.1 Models

We evaluate a diverse set of vision-language models in our experiments, categorized into three groups based on their primary language capabilities and model characteristics.

The first category includes leading **multilingual VLMs**:

- **Phi3.5-Vision-Instruct**: A lightweight model from Microsoft.
- **Llama-based models**: Including Llama-3.2-11B and Llama-3.2-90B.
- **LLaVA-v1.6-mistral-7B**: Designed for multilingual tasks.

The second category comprises **Chinese-based VLMs**:

- **InternVL2 series**: Consisting of InternVL2-8B and InternVL2-76B.
- **Qwen2-VL series**: Including Qwen2-VL-7B and Qwen2-VL-72B.
- **LLaVA-v1.6-34B**: Tailored for Chinese language understanding.

The third category consists of **proprietary models**:

Parameter	Value	Description
logprobs	True	Return log prob. of output tokens
top_logprobs	20	Return top 20 likely tokens
temperature	0	Deterministic sampling

Table 10: Chat completion parameters for model inference.

- **GPT-4o series**: This includes GPT-4o and GPT-4o-mini, proprietary models whose architectural details are not publicly disclosed.

Table 9 presents the specifications of all evaluated models. For open-source models, we detail their language models, vision encoders, and total parameters in billions (B). The size ranges from 4.2B (Phi3.5) to 90B (Llama-3.2-90B) parameters, offering a comprehensive evaluation across different model scales. For proprietary models in the GPT-4o series, these specifications are not publicly available and thus marked with dashes.

D.2 Implementation Details

In this subsection, we present our experimental configurations for both model inference and deployment. Table 10 shows the chat completion parameters used consistently across all evaluations. For serving open-source models, we utilize the `vLLM` framework (Kwon et al., 2023) to evaluate the performance and scalability of the serving infrastructure under different configurations, which are detailed in Table 11.

The evaluated models include a wide range of vision-language models such as **LLaVA**, **Qwen-**

VL, **InternVL**, among others. For each model, key configuration parameters were recorded:

- **Maximum Model Length (`max-model-len`):** The maximum sequence length supported by the model.
- **Tensor Parallel Size (`tensor-parallel-size`):** The number of GPUs allocated for parallel inference.
- **GPU Memory Utilization:** The proportion of GPU memory utilized during serving.
- **Batching Parameters:**
  - **Maximum Number of Batched Tokens:** The maximum number of tokens that can be processed in a single batch.
  - **Maximum Number of Sequences:** The maximum number of sequences processed in parallel.
- **Swap Space:** Indicates whether disk-based swap space is enabled to handle memory overflow scenarios.
- **Worker Configuration (`worker-use-ray`):** Specifies whether Ray-based worker management is employed for distributed serving.

To clarify the model status during the experiments:

- Models currently **in progress** or **pending evaluation** are marked with '†' before their names.
- Models encountering **errors** during serving are marked with '*' before their names.

The `vLLM` framework was used for all experiments. This framework is optimized for high-throughput inference with features such as:

- Token-level pipelining to maximize GPU utilization.
- Tensor-parallel support for efficient multi-GPU inference.
- Dynamic batching for reducing latency and improving throughput.

Table 11 provides a detailed summary of the experiment configurations and results. These settings can serve as a practical reference for deploying vision-language models in research or production environments.

E Experiment Results

Detailed performance results for recognition and reasoning questions across various subtopics are presented in Table 12 and Table 13.

Model	**max-model-len**	**tensor-parallel-size**	**gpu-memory-utilization**	**max-num-batched-tokens**	**max-num-seqs**	**swap-space**	**worker-use-ray**
Llama-3.2-11B	16384	4	0.8	16384	4	1	✓
Llama-3.2-90B	16384	8	0.9	16384	8	-	-
Qwen2-VL-7B-Instruct	16384	4	0.85	16384	8	1	✓
Qwen2-VL-72B-Instruct	16384	8	0.85	16384	8	1	✓
LLaVA-1.6-Mistral-7B	32000	4	-	8192	4	-	✓
*LLaVA-1.6-Vicuna-7B	4096	4	0.9	4096	4	1	✓
*LLaVA-1.6-Vicuna-13B	4096	4	0.9	4096	4	1	✓
LLaVA-1.6-34B	4096	8	0.9	4096	16	1	✓
†LLaVA OneVision 7B	8192	4	0.88	8192	4	1	✓
†LLaVA OneVision 72B	8192	8	0.85	8192	8	1	✓
*Pixtral 12B	8192	4	0.9	8192	4	1	✓
†Molmo-D 7B	4096	4	0.88	4096	4	1	✓
†Molmo 72B	8192	8	0.85	8192	16	1	✓
InternVL2-8B	12288	4	0.85	12288	4	1	✓
†InternVL2-26B	8192	8	0.85	8192	16	1	✓
InternVL2-Llama-3-76B	12288	8	0.85	12288	4	1	✓
†InternVL-Chat-V1-5	4096	8	0.9	4096	8	1	✓
†Mono-InternVL-2B	4096	4	0.70	4096	2	1	-
*cogvlm2-llama3-chinese-chat-19B	4096	4	0.85	4096	4	1	-
*Deepseek-vl-7b-chat	4096	4	0.9	4096	4	1	-
*BLIP-3 (XGen-MM)	4096	4	0.9	4096	8	1	✓
Phi3.5-Vision-Instruct	8192	4	0.9	8192	8	1	✓

Table 11: Configuration and Status of Vision-Language Models in vLLM Serving Framework. The table summarizes the key parameters used for serving various models, including model length, tensor parallelism, GPU utilization, and batching settings. Models marked with '*' encountered errors during the experiments, while models marked with '†' are in progress or pending evaluation.

Model	Symbols & Signs			Attractions		Food			Transport		Culture & Arts			Politics		
	T&S	PN	IS	NS	CL	C&I	Men	CO	TS	TrS	F&B	IC	AA	PS	PE	PFP
Phi3.5-Vision	33.87	29.73	44.90	15.79	25.00	33.51	30.00	0.00	47.06	21.05	34.48	25.00	43.75	33.33	44.44	4.55
Llama-3.2-11B	67.74	36.49	55.10	36.84	35.00	45.55	20.00	25.00	61.76	26.32	27.59	25.00	50.00	66.67	55.56	18.18
Llama-3.2-90B	71.77	62.16	71.43	36.84	50.00	63.87	55.00	50.00	67.65	52.63	55.17	50.00	81.25	88.89	66.67	27.27
LLaVA-v1.6-m-7B	30.65	31.08	55.10	15.79	21.67	31.41	35.00	0.00	55.88	42.11	27.59	0.00	37.50	55.56	44.44	4.55
LLaVA-v1.6-34B	52.42	58.11	69.39	57.89	55.00	60.73	35.00	0.00	73.53	57.89	51.72	25.00	75.00	55.56	55.56	36.36
InternVL2-8B	84.68	81.08	79.59	63.16	60.00	65.97	55.00	75.00	76.47	63.16	72.41	75.00	87.50	88.89	88.89	50.00
InternVL2-76B	87.90	75.68	79.59	57.89	71.67	76.44	45.00	75.00	79.41	57.89	79.31	87.50	93.75	88.89	88.89	36.36
Qwen2-VL-7B	93.55	82.43	79.59	57.89	71.67	75.39	85.00	75.00	85.29	63.16	75.86	50.00	87.50	100.00	88.89	72.73
Qwen2-VL-72B	92.74	85.14	89.80	68.42	81.67	83.77	75.00	75.00	82.35	57.89	93.10	75.00	87.50	100.00	100.00	81.82
GPT-4o	87.90	58.11	75.51	68.42	73.33	81.68	35.00	75.00	76.47	52.63	65.52	87.50	81.25	88.89	88.89	40.91
GPT-4o-mini	72.58	62.16	67.35	63.16	50.00	61.78	30.00	50.00	70.59	42.11	37.93	50.00	68.75	88.89	66.67	40.91

Model	Geography		Sports			F&F		His	Entertainment			DN	ODL
	NG	HG	SAV	Ath	T&M	Ani	Pla	His	FTS	Mus	Gam	DN	ODL
Phi3.5-Vision	50.00	16.67	60.00	25.00	33.33	29.17	23.26	20.00	35.00	50.00	16.67	47.92	42.86
Llama-3.2-11B	37.50	33.33	50.00	75.00	83.33	33.33	34.88	40.00	55.00	66.67	50.00	64.58	34.29
Llama-3.2-90B	68.75	50.00	70.00	25.00	83.33	50.00	41.86	20.00	80.00	50.00	66.67	73.96	54.29
LLaVA-v1.6-m-7B	37.50	0.00	20.00	0.00	66.67	31.25	30.23	20.00	55.00	33.33	25.00	47.92	28.57
LLaVA-v1.6-34B	75.00	41.67	70.00	0.00	100.00	45.83	51.16	20.00	60.00	66.67	50.00	72.92	54.29
InternVL2-8B	81.25	66.67	60.00	100.00	83.33	64.58	60.47	60.00	80.00	83.33	50.00	72.92	77.14
InternVL2-76B	68.75	66.67	80.00	100.00	100.00	70.83	55.81	60.00	90.00	83.33	75.00	82.29	77.14
Qwen2-VL-7B	87.50	91.67	80.00	100.00	100.00	64.58	69.77	80.00	85.00	66.67	83.33	79.17	88.57
Qwen2-VL-72B	87.50	91.67	80.00	100.00	100.00	62.50	74.42	80.00	90.00	66.67	83.33	84.38	88.57
GPT-4o	87.50	83.33	70.00	100.00	100.00	56.25	62.79	80.00	75.00	66.67	83.33	77.08	62.86
GPT-4o-mini	62.50	58.33	50.00	75.00	100.00	47.92	48.84	60.00	50.00	66.67	66.67	65.62	48.57

Table 12: Subtopic Performance of Recognition Questions (Accuracy, %).
Subtopics: T&S=Trademarks & Store Signs, PN=Public Notices & Announcements, IS=Instruction Signs, NS=Natural Scenery, CL=Cultural Landmarks, C&I=Cuisine & Ingredients, Men=Menus, CO=Cuisine Origin, TS=Transit Systems, TrS=Traffic Signs, F&B=Folklore & Beliefs, IC=Indigenous Culture, AA=Artistic Activities, PS=Political System , PE=Political Events, PFP=Political Figures & Parties, NG=Natural Geography, HG=Human Geography, SAV=Sports Activities & Venues, Ath=Athletes, T&M=Teams & Mascots, Ani=Animals, Pla=Plants, His=History, FTS=Films & TV Shows, Mus=Music, Gam=Gaming, DN=Daily Necessities, ODL=Other Daily Life.

Model	Symbols & Signs			Attractions		Food				Transport		Culture & Arts		
	T&S	PN	IS	NS	CL	C&I	DCT	Men	CO	TS	TrS	F&B	IC	AA
Phi3.5-Vision	30.00	26.74	42.22	33.33	16.67	21.59	17.78	24.32	18.75	28.57	20.00	39.53	23.08	16.67
Llama-3.2-11B	24.29	18.60	44.44	20.00	11.11	14.77	24.44	16.22	15.62	25.71	10.00	27.91	15.38	8.33
Llama-3.2-90B	52.86	46.51	71.11	20.00	38.89	40.91	48.89	21.62	37.50	45.71	30.00	44.19	23.08	58.33
LLaVA-v1.6-m-7B	27.14	16.28	33.33	33.33	33.33	19.32	33.33	16.22	18.75	25.71	25.00	30.23	15.38	33.33
LLaVA-v1.6-34B	47.14	46.51	55.56	33.33	38.89	44.32	53.33	16.22	50.00	45.71	40.00	44.19	34.62	41.67
InternVL2-8B	54.29	59.30	62.22	46.67	44.44	42.05	51.11	43.24	46.88	62.86	55.00	65.12	42.31	41.67
InternVL2-76B	61.43	60.47	66.67	26.67	38.89	48.86	42.22	37.84	46.88	68.57	50.00	65.12	42.31	66.67
Qwen2-VL-7B	68.57	61.63	68.89	33.33	38.89	47.73	46.67	40.54	43.75	60.00	50.00	55.81	42.31	58.33
Qwen2-VL-72B	74.29	76.74	77.78	53.33	61.11	72.73	57.78	56.76	68.75	68.57	55.00	79.07	53.85	66.67
GPT-4o	61.43	58.14	62.22	46.67	38.89	53.41	55.56	21.62	37.50	51.43	40.00	55.81	42.31	66.67
GPT-4o-mini	55.71	44.19	64.44	26.67	33.33	39.77	46.67	21.62	34.38	42.86	55.00	51.16	38.46	58.33

Model	Politics			Geography		Sports			F&F		His	Entertainment			DN	ODL
	PS	PE	PFP	NG	HG	SA&V	Ath	T&M	Ani	Pla	His	F&TS	Mus	Gam	DN	ODL
Phi3.5-Vision	15.38	61.54	10.34	33.33	19.23	55.56	25.00	18.18	23.68	30.30	20.41	20.00	50.00	33.33	30.77	19.61
Llama-3.2-11B	7.69	23.08	0.00	9.52	11.54	50.00	25.00	18.18	15.79	6.06	14.29	24.00	50.00	46.67	23.08	13.73
Llama-3.2-90B	30.77	46.15	17.24	38.10	13.46	72.22	50.00	18.18	44.74	36.36	40.82	44.00	50.00	46.67	53.85	37.25
LLaVA-v1.6-m-7B	30.77	38.46	10.34	23.81	15.38	61.11	50.00	9.09	28.95	30.30	22.45	24.00	50.00	26.67	26.92	15.69
LLaVA-v1.6-34B	30.77	61.54	27.59	38.10	21.15	66.67	25.00	27.27	44.74	42.42	36.73	24.00	50.00	53.33	46.15	31.37
InternVL2-8B	53.85	76.92	27.59	28.57	34.62	83.33	75.00	18.18	31.58	36.36	42.86	48.00	75.00	60.00	57.69	45.10
InternVL2-76B	69.23	76.92	27.59	47.62	36.54	72.22	50.00	27.27	57.89	39.39	48.98	60.00	50.00	73.33	61.54	49.02
Qwen2-VL-7B	69.23	69.23	27.59	38.10	40.38	77.78	75.00	27.27	39.47	45.45	42.86	48.00	50.00	73.33	63.46	39.22
Qwen2-VL-72B	92.31	76.92	58.62	47.62	53.85	83.33	100.00	45.45	55.26	45.45	67.35	60.00	50.00	80.00	73.08	56.86
GPT-4o	69.23	76.92	34.48	52.38	36.54	77.78	25.00	18.18	52.63	27.27	42.86	56.00	75.00	60.00	57.69	39.22
GPT-4o-mini	53.85	61.54	6.90	23.81	32.69	55.56	50.00	27.27	34.21	24.24	30.61	36.00	50.00	53.33	42.31	31.37

Table 13: Subtopic Performance of Reasoning Questions (Accuracy, %).
Subtopics: T&S=Trademarks & Store Signs, PN=Public Notices & Announcements, IS=Instruction Signs, NS=Natural Scenery, CL=Cultural Landmarks, C&I=Cuisine & Ingredients, DCT=Dietary Customs & Taboos, Men=Menus, CO=Cuisine Origin, TS=Transit Systems, TrS=Traffic Signs, F&B=Folklore & Beliefs, IC=Indigenous Culture, AA=Artistic Activities, PS=Political System, PE=Political Events, PFP=Political Figures & Parties, NG=Natural Geography, HG=Human Geography, SA&V=Sports Activities & Venues, Ath=Athletes, T&M=Teams & Mascots, Ani=Animals, Pla=Plants, His=History, F&TS=Films & TV Shows, Mus=Music, Gam=Gaming, DN=Daily Necessities, ODL=Other Daily Life.

Guiding Vision-Language Model Selection for Visual Question-Answering Across Tasks, Domains, and Knowledge Types

Neelabh Sinha[1], **Vinija Jain**[2*], **Aman Chadha**[3†]
[1]Georgia Institute of Technology [2]Meta AI [3]Amazon GenAI
nsinha68@gatech.edu, hi@vinija.ai, hi@aman.ai

Abstract

Visual Question-Answering (VQA) has become key to user experience, particularly after improved generalization capabilities of Vision-Language Models (VLMs). But evaluating VLMs for an application requirement using a standardized framework in practical settings is still challenging. This paper aims to solve that using an end-to-end framework. We present `VQA360` – a novel dataset derived from established VQA benchmarks, annotated with task types, application domains, and knowledge types, for a comprehensive evaluation. We also introduce `GoEval`, a multimodal evaluation metric developed using GPT-4o, achieving a correlation factor of 56.71% with human judgments. Our experiments with state-of-the-art VLMs reveal that no single model excels universally, thus, making a right choice a key design decision. Proprietary models such as Gemini-1.5-Pro and GPT-4o-mini generally outperform others, but open-source models like InternVL-2-8B and CogVLM-2-Llama-3-19B also demonstrate competitive strengths, while providing additional advantages. Our framework can also be extended to other tasks[1].

1 Introduction

Visual Question Answering (VQA) (Antol et al., 2015) is the task of answering a question q about an image $\mathcal{I}$ correctly. This field has been faced with constant challenges in terms of the nature of the problem. For example, the question q can be about the image directly (Goyal et al., 2017a; Zhu et al., 2016; Goyal et al., 2017b), or outside the scope of the image with external knowledge (Marino et al., 2019; Schwenk et al., 2022). The images $\mathcal{I}$ can be a photograph, a mathematical chart (Masry et al., 2022; Li and Tajbakhsh, 2023), a document screenshot (Mathew et al., 2021), or more.

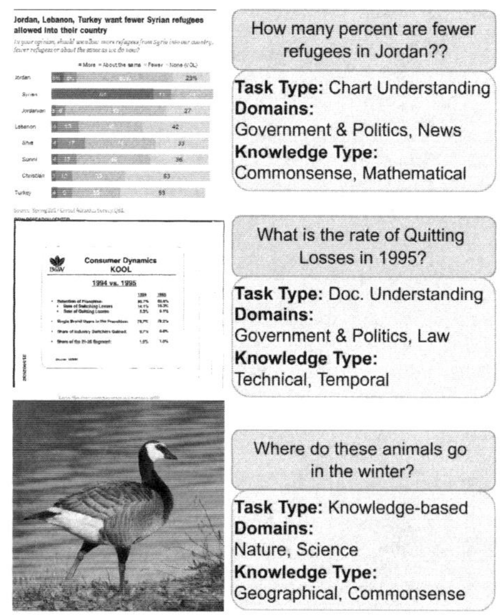

Figure 1: Examples of `VQA360` tasks and their labels for task types, application domains, and knowledge type in our dataset.

Dedicated methods (Zhu et al., 2016; Goyal et al., 2017b; Kafle and Kanan, 2017) have long existed to solve different challenges in VQA. But, with the advancement of Vision-Language models (VLMs) (Chen et al., 2023; Bai et al., 2023; Team et al., 2024; OpenAI et al., 2024; Liu et al., 2023a) in multimodal research, several applications have started adapting them due to their versatility. This is because after pre-training (Lin et al., 2024; Wei et al., 2024) on vast multimodal datasets (Chen et al., 2015; Thomee et al., 2016; Changpinyo et al., 2021; Masry et al., 2022; Mathew et al., 2021; Marino et al., 2019), VLMs can effectively generalize across various types of images, and can also incorporate external knowledge beyond the image.

But which VLM to utilize for a given VQA-based requirement? The complexity of this stems

*Work does not relate to position at Meta.
†Work does not relate to position at Amazon.
[1]Code and dataset can be found in the following link: https://github.com/neelabhsinha/vlm-selection-tasks-domains-knowledge-type.

Proceedings of the First Workshop of Evaluation of Multi-Modal Generation, pages 76–94
January 20, 2025.

from two directions - new VLMs being proposed and the diverse nature of tasks in VQA. New VLMs come up every month now (Liu et al., 2023a, 2024; Bai et al., 2023; team, 2024; Chen et al., 2023, 2024; Wang et al., 2023; Hong et al., 2024), and they differ in their architecture, training data, training strategy, size, etc., possessing different capabilites. In addition, users often face technical and business constraints in terms of compute, memory, cost of inference, data, and regulatory risks, which can favor specific VLMs over others. Second, tasks may vary from types such as Chart Question-Answering (Masry et al., 2022) or Document Understanding (Mathew et al., 2021), to application domains such as Science, or Sports, and the type of knowledge required, like Geographical Information, Mathematical Reasoning, and beyond. For an application that can fall into one or more such categories, how do you identify the best suited VLM? How to compare them meaningfully? These are gaps in existing literature. Technical reports of VLMs provide benchmarks and comparison, but they are very theoretical and limited.

To bridge the gap in evaluating VLMs on VQA, we propose an end-to-end framework that provides a standardized paradigm for evaluating vision-language models (VLMs) across three key aspects: *task type*, *application domain*, and *knowledge type*. Existing datasets like VQAv2 (Goyal et al., 2017a), OK-VQA (Marino et al., 2019), and ChartQA (Masry et al., 2022) offer task instances for training and evaluation but lack labels for other practical aspects. Our framework addresses this by developing and sharing a dataset `VQA360` derived from the above benchmarks, where tasks are also labeled with their application domains and the knowledge types required for successful completion, as illustrated in Figure 1, allowing for a evaluation 360° in practical settings. Each task can have multiple tags for all these aspects. In addition, traditional NLP evaluation metrics have been shown to be poorly correlated with human judgments for generative models (Kamalloo et al., 2023; Liu et al., 2023b), an issue that extends to VLM. To address this, we introduce `GoEval`, a multimodal evaluation metric leveraging GPT-4o (OpenAI et al., 2024), which demonstrates superior alignment with human judgment compared to existing metrics. Together, they complement each other to provide an end-to-end, completely multimodal evaluation framework. Our framework evaluates 10 variations of 8 VLMs, accommodating diverse requirements such as open-source, resource-efficient, or privacy-compliant models.

In summary, our aim is to address the following **research questions (RQs)**: **(1)** How to compare VLMs for different types of VQA tasks in practical settings? **(2)** How to evaluate those VLM outputs closely with human judgments? **(3)** As per current SOTA, which VLM is suited for which application, depending on various external constraints?

Our **key contributions** are as follows:

(i) We release `VQA360` - a dataset of VQA tasks with three labeled aspects: *task types*, *application domains*, and *knowledge type*, enabling comparison based on different practical requirements.

(ii) We propose `GoEval`, which is a multimodal evaluation metric based on GPT-4o (OpenAI et al., 2024), and aligns more closely with human judgments for visual question-answering.

(iii) We analyze 10 variants of 8 state-of-the-art VLMs of different sizes and families, using our framework to compare their performance.

(iv) Using our analysis, we make recommendations on the best-suited VLMs for a given application requirement under different constraints.

2 `VQA360`: A Practical Evaluation Dataset

In this section, we discuss our dataset creation steps we followed in detail, which we propose to utilize for evaluating VLMs for VQA.

2.1 Source Datasets

To be able to evaluate VLMs in a wide variety of QA tasks, `VQA360` is created from five standard datasets - VQAv2 (Goyal et al., 2017a), OK-VQA (Marino et al., 2019), A-OKVQA (Schwenk et al., 2022), ChartQA (Masry et al., 2022) and DocumentVQA (Mathew et al., 2021). VQAv2 is an extensive VQA benchmark, while OK-VQA and A-OKVQA are used primarily for knowledge-based VQA, where the answer to the question does not lie within the scope of the image. ChartQA and DocumentVQA are taken to evaluate the performance of VLMs on questions based on mathematical graphs and charts, and documents, respectively. From the test split of each dataset $\mathcal{D}_{test}$, we take $\max(|\mathcal{D}_{test}|, 1145)$ task instances, randomly sampled without replacement. 1145 was used as it is the minimum size of test set among the five datasets. Thus, our final experimental set contains 5725 task instances, with equal contributions from each dataset.

Aspect	Considered Tags
Application Domains	Anthropology, Formal logic, Economics, History, Law, Government and Politics, Linguistics, Computer Science, Mathematics, Science, Books, Fiction, Movies, News, Reviews, Justice, Professions, Public Places, Knowledge Base, Nature, Nutrition and Food, Social Media, Sports
Knowledge Types	Commonsense Knowledge, Visual Knowledge, Cultural Knowledge, Geographical Knowledge, Temporal Knowledge, Social Knowledge, Scientific Knowledge, Technical Knowledge, Mathematical Knowledge, Literary Knowledge, Other

Table 1: Application domains and knowledge types considered to label all the task instances.

2.2 Instance Tags

Using the dataset mentioned above only allows us to differentiate based on task types. But there are more ways in which a practical application can be classified. To enable that, we also classify `VQA360` in two more aspects - application domains, and knowledge types. This is inspired from a recent work (Sinha et al., 2024), but adapted to suit this task. The application domain is the field a task belongs to, such as history, science, sports, etc., and the knowledge type is a specific type of knowledge required, such as geographic, common sense, etc.

Our initial set of tags is crafted manually, with an aim to achieve a broad spectrum of application domains and reasoning types. They are specified in Table 1, and cover a wide range of domains and knowledge types. We tag each of our task instances in the dataset with one or more application domains and knowledge types using the method described in Figure 2 and discussed in the following.

2.3 Generating Instance Tags

For creating the tags for task types, we map ChartQA to 'Chart Understanding', DocumentVQA to 'Document Understanding', A-OKVQA and OKVQA to 'Knowledge-based Visual Question-Answering' and VQAv2 to 'Visual Question-Answering'.

For application domains and knowledge types, we use `gpt-3.5-turbo` (Brown et al., 2020; OpenAI, 2023). To correctly generate instance tags, we require key features of the image and question, and also need to eliminate less useful information from the image to avoid confusions. To achieve this, following a recent work (Fu et al., 2023), we generate captions of images from VIT-GPT2[2], and object tags from the Azure Computer Vision API. Using these two as the descriptors of the image and the question, we prompt `gpt-3.5-turbo` to get the application domains and knowledge type. The prompt used for this task is given in Table 7 in Appendix A.

After this, we post-process the tags by removing entries that do not belong to any of the entries in Table 1. If all tags are removed for a task instance, we add "Other" by default. Finally, we manually go through each of the labels and ensure that they are correctly tagged and replace any erroneous tag. The final set contains questions, images, candidate answers, task type, application domains, and knowledge type of all 5725 candidates.

From the instance tags, we remove the tags for which number of instances are less than 300 from our analyses. Please note, we do not remove the task instances entirely, as they may contain other tags included in the study, but just not consider those tags in reporting our results in Section 4 due to less number of instances. This gives a final set of 5 task types, 14 application domains, and 9 knowledge types, which are shown in Figure 3. We also report statistis of `VQA360` in Table 2.

Statistic (per instance)	Mean	Std.	Max
Caption Length	46.56	8.84	96
Object Tags	13.01	7.83	59
Application Domains	1.7	0.68	7
Knowledge Type	2.19	0.83	9

Table 2: Average, std. and maximum of length of caption and count of object tags in generated image descriptors, and number of application domains and knowledge types per instance. This clarifies that significant number of task instances have multiple application domains and knowledge type tags.

`VQA360` allows extended analysis of diverse VQA tasks and allows looking into performance of VLMs from entirely new perspectives. Further, the creation methodology can also be extended for enriching other datasets and creating benchmarks for evaluating VLMs in different settings.

We use `VQA360` for rest of the analysis, and also release it publicly (linked in footnote of Page 1), for the research community to utilize in future research.

[2]https://huggingface.co/nlpconnect/vit-gpt2-image-captioning

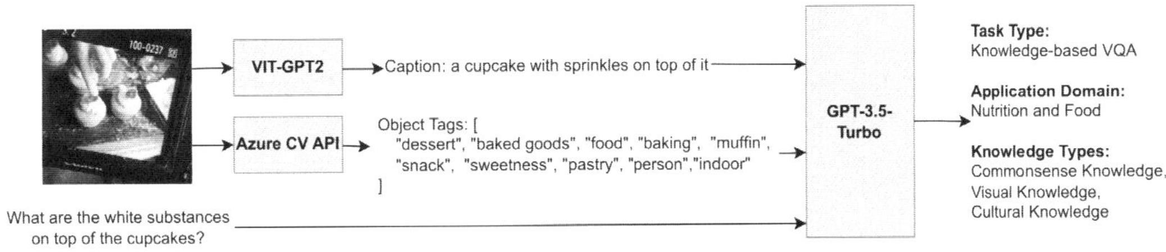

Figure 2: An example with steps taken to generate the instance tags for application domains and knowledge type (task type is mapped directly from the dataset the image is taken).

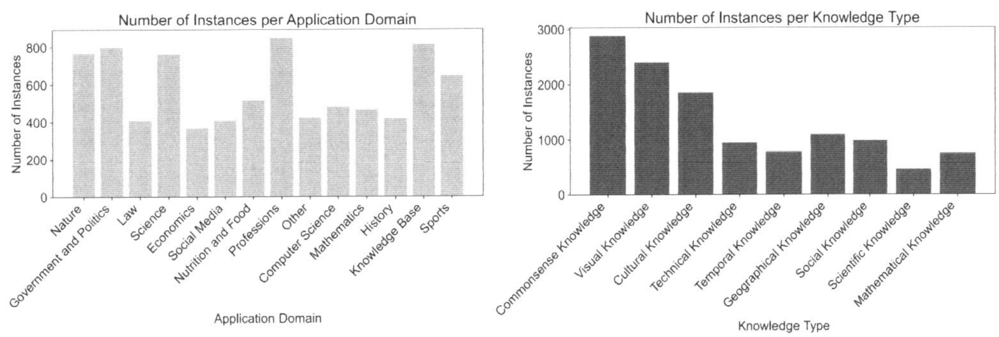

Figure 3: Number of task instances per application domain (left) and knowledge type (right) after generating the instance tags using GPT-3.5-Turbo. All categories are represented by approx 400 instances, which is sufficient for a representative analysis. Categories with < 300 instances are filtered out, and a task instance can be tagged to multiple categories of a single aspect.

Although it contains instances of existing benchmarks, it is a one-stop benchmark for an extended evaluation with labels for task types, application domains, and knowledge types. We also provide object tags and captions.

3 `GoEval`: A VQA Evaluation Metric

Evaluating QA using lexical matching has significant limitations, particularly when correct answers don't match with set of gold answers (Kamalloo et al., 2023). A recent work (Kamalloo et al., 2023) evaluated traditional VQA metrics against GPT-based evaluation for open-domain QA, and found it to be more aligned with human judgments.

Another alternative is to evaluate using NLG metrics such as ROUGE (Lin, 2004), METEOR (Banerjee and Lavie, 2005), and then use a threshold to determine correct/wrong. However, they also suffer from similar limitations, as evaluated from previous work (Liu et al., 2023b). A probable solution is to use BERTScore (Zhang et al., 2019), which compares texts in embedding space, focusing more on semantic similarity.

These metrics may be promising, but they are not equipped to handle multimodal settings. To fill this gap, we propose `GoEval` - a multimodal metric based on GPT-4o, which can be used to evaluate VQA. Similar to existing works (Kamalloo et al., 2023; Liu et al., 2023b), we create a prompt, and ask GPT-4o if the generated answer is correct. However, to incorporate the vision modality in making judgments, we also use the image. We use zero-shot evaluation with prompting, using both GPT-4o and GPT-4o-mini, to compare and contrast performance v/s cost trade-offs.

Formally, we pick a prompt function $\mathcal{P}$ from the first row of Table 8 of the Appendix A, and generate a prompt $p = \mathcal{P}(q, r, c)$ based on question q, the reference answer set r and the candidate response c. Using this prompt and the image, we prompt GPT-4o (OpenAI et al., 2024; OpenAI, 2024) to ask if it is correct. We also compare our prompt against two other ways – without using the image, and without reference answers. This is to understand which technique shows highest correlation with human judgments. We don't compare with traditional methods, as it is already done in the above discussed works (Kamalloo et al., 2023; Liu et al., 2023b), and our method without using the image is similar to what is used in (Kamalloo et al., 2023).

3.1 Validating GoEval

To validate GoEval, we first generate outputs on our experimental dataset using Gemini-1.5-Pro (Team et al., 2024), a state-of-the-art VLM. Then, we manually evaluate all the answers on the validation set, marking 0 for incorrect answer and 1 for correct answer. These are the results of human evaluation.

We compare BERTScore precision, recall, F1-score, and six variants of GoEval using GPT-4o and GPT-4o mini (OpenAI et al., 2024), with and without reference answers, and with and without using images with human evaluations in terms of accuracy and Kendall Tau. The exact prompts that we use are outlined in Table 8 of Appendix A. When we don't use the image, we also alter the template text by a little to not ask model to refer the image. The results are detailed in Table 3.

Method	Acc (%)	τ
BERTScore-p	1.30	36.21
BERTScore-r	1.30	12.68
BERTScore-f1	1.30	28.50
GoEval (-R, -I)	49.91	16.17
GoEval-mini (-R, -I)	52.70	10.84
GoEval (-R)	71.43	35.94
GoEval-mini (-R)	64.01	24.37
GoEval	78.48	52.43
GoEval-mini	**80.33**	**56.71**

Table 3: Comparison of different evaluation methods: Accuracy (Acc.) and correlation (τ for Kendall's Tau) of evaluation metrics with human judgement. -R indicates absence of reference answers, -I indicates absence of image from the request. GoEval with all components (reference answers, image) performs the best.

From the results, we can see that GoEval with reference answer and image provides the best alignment with human judgment. Without using the image (-R, -I), the performance proves to be very weak, depicting that existing metrics that do not utilize the image will perform poorly on VQA. We believe this is because image context is crucial for VQA, and in the absence of it, the model isn't able to reason well whether the provided answer is correct or not. Moreover, the differences between models are largely influenced by the amount of information. For example, performance of GoEval and GoEval-mini with image but without reference only has a difference of $\Delta\tau = 11$, but as soon as the reference answers are added, τ increases by 20 units. This is because the reference answers serve as an extra guidance in addition of the image to determine the correctness of the candidate answer, making the model perform better.

In summary, GoEval shows high accuracy and Kendall's Tau correlation with human evaluation, and GoEval-mini marginally outperforms GoEval. This complements VQA360 to provide an end-to-end cohesive framework for VLM evaluation in entirely multimodal settings.

4 Comparative Evaluation of VLMs

We evaluate state-of-the-art (SOTA) VLMs in practical settings using our framework using GoEval-mini, since it demonstrated maximum correlation with human judgments, and is more cost-efficient.

For VLMs, we use InternVL-2 1B and 8B (Chen et al., 2023, 2024), PaliGemma-3B (Beyer* et al., 2024), Qwen-2-VL 2B and 7B (Bai et al., 2023; team, 2024), LlaVa-1.6-Mistral-7B (Liu et al., 2024), CogVLM2-Llama-3-19B (Wang et al., 2023; Hong et al., 2024), Gemini-1.5 Flash and Pro (Team et al., 2024), and GPT-4o-Mini (OpenAI et al., 2024). The rationale behind choosing these models is to have sufficient diversity to allow users to choose the appropriate VLM based on other constraints.

All models except Gemini-1.5 and GPT-4o are open sourced, which gives freedom to customize the models as desired, and host it in-house. It takes away the privacy and regulatory risk of sending data to a third-party, and reduces operational and opportunity cost factor, as these APIs are costly with rate limits. In-house hosting allows a relatively fixed cost. We have taken smaller models in the 1B-3B range which can be used in resource-constrained environments and on-device AI.

For all open-source models, we use the HuggingFace implementation with the image and question in a prompt recommended by the model card, since we want to evaluate all scenarios uniformly. We use Gemini APIs[3] OpenAI API[4] for Gemini and GPT-4o-mini. The results are discussed in the following subsections. More details of the artifacts used are given in Table 5 of the Appendix A.1.

4.1 Correlation Between VLM Outputs

Our first hypothesis was that all VLMs do not perform similarly with all task instances. They have their own strengths and weaknesses. To establish that, we evaluated the correlation between the out-

[3]https://ai.google.dev/gemini-api/docs
[4]https://platform.openai.com/docs/overview

puts of different models for all tasks and document the results in Figure 4.

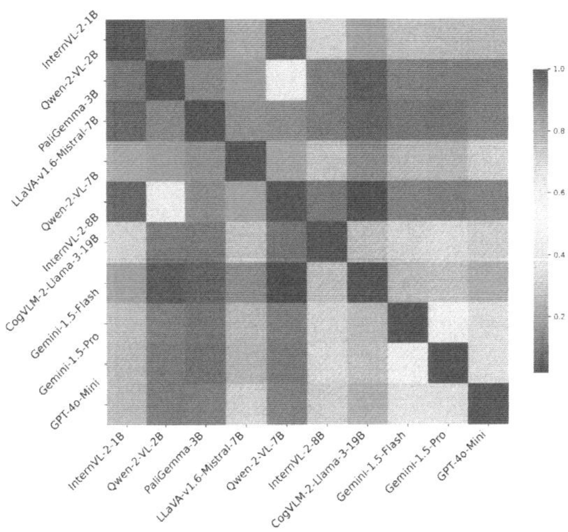

Figure 4: Correlation of GoEval-mini values between performance of different VLMs for all task instances. The low correlation values for outputs between all models indicate different VLMs perform differently with task instances.

From the figure, most of the correlations are low. This shows that the performance difference between VLMs is not just in terms of a global statistic, but also differs for individual task instances. Thus, some VLMs that might be great in a subset of tasks may be poor in another subset.

The highest correlation is observed between Gemini-1.5 Flash and Pro, followed by Qwen-2-VL 2B and 7B, and InternVL-2-1B and 8B. Since they are from the same family, they might have similar training data, training strategy, and architecture. Some open-source VLMs also exhibit higher correlations (light blue) with Gemini and GPT, though these correlations remain relatively low.

Since task types, application domains, and knowledge types are key factors in which tasks can be differentiated in practical settings, we move to analyzing the performance on those factors.

4.2 Evaluation on Task Types

We evaluated VLMs on four different task types: chart understanding using ChartQA dataset (Masry et al., 2022), Document Understanding using DocVQA dataset (Mathew et al., 2021), knowledge-based VQA using A-OKVQA (Schwenk et al., 2022) and OK-VQA (Marino et al., 2019), and general VQA using VQAv2 (Goyal et al., 2017a). The performance of VLMs across these is summarized in Table 4.

From the table, the closed models, which are believed to be SOTA, outperform the smaller, open-sourced models. This is expected considering that those models are larger. Within them, we identify that Gemini-1.5-Pro performs significantly better than GPT-4o-mini when extracting information from an image is key, like interpreting documents and charts. On the other hand, where knowledge and comprehension are critical, GPT-4o-mini outperforms Gemini-1.5-Pro. If processing cost is a factor, Gemini-1.5-Flash can be chosen with approximately 7-10% performance loss.

Among open-source models, InternVL-2 shows promising results with both 1B and 8B models given their size, and can be chosen if open-source models are needed. CogVLM-2-Llama-3-19B also competes closely with Gemini-1.5-Flash in Chart and Document understanding tasks. Llava-1.6-Mistral-7B performs acceptable in knowledge-based VQA and VQA, but the performance degrades drastically in the other two categories, where visual comprehension is critical, exposing its limitations in that area. Qwen-2-VL variants and PaliGemma-3B surprisingly prove to be weak in all tasks.

4.3 Evaluation on Application Domains

We evaluated the VLMs in all application domains that had more than 300 task instances, and the results are shown in Figure 5.

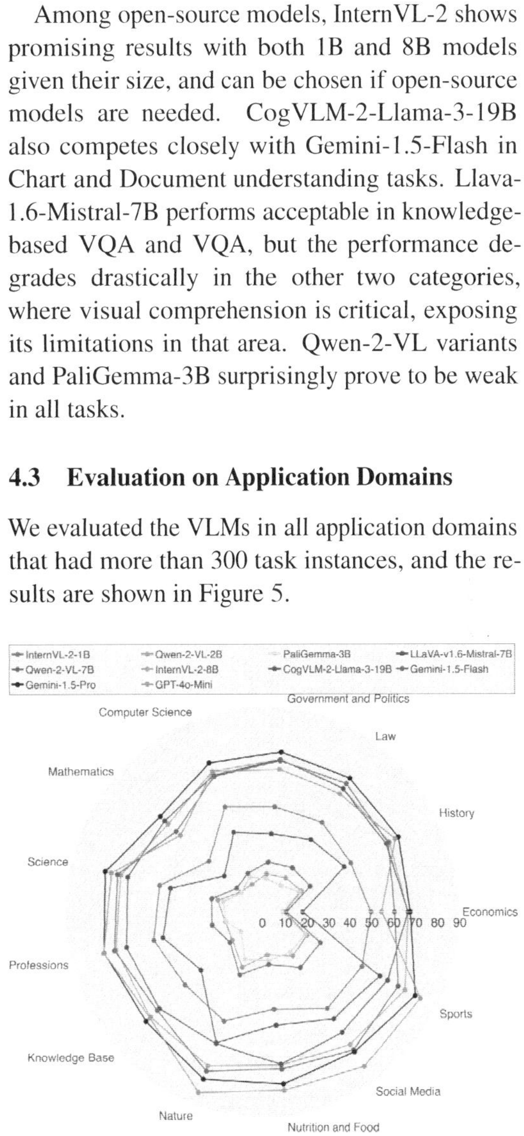

Figure 5: Mean GoEval-mini scores for different application domains for all VLMs. Gemini-1.5-Pro and GPT-4o-mini are the best performing closed models, with CogVLM-2-LlaMa-3-19B and InternVL-2-8B performing the best amongst open models.

Task Type	Intern-VL-2-1B	Qwen-2-VL-2B	Pali-Gemma-3B	LLaVA-1.6-Mistral-7B	Qwen-2-VL-7B	Intern-VL-2-8B	Cog-VLM-2-Llama-3-19B	Gemini-1.5-Flash	Gemini-1.5-Pro	GPT-4o-Mini
Chart U.	46.81	12.31	12.84	22.88	14.06	65.68	67.34	62.17	**67.66**	60.36
Document U.	45.68	15.81	12.49	30.07	20.00	65.76	68.17	64.36	**70.53**	54.68
KBQA	45.41	19.83	19.22	58.65	26.94	71.43	62.77	70.66	77.31	**84.04**
VQA	55.81	26.29	23.58	57.64	29.52	68.65	57.18	69.11	73.25	**77.74**

Table 4: Mean GoEval-mini scores for different task types for all VLMs. **Bold** numbers indicate best results. Gemini-1.5-Pro performs better in chart and document understanding, while GPT-4o-mini performs better in the other two (U. = Understanding, KBQA = Knowledge-based VQA).

If the VLMs were similar in all application domains, their result would be perfectly circular. However, we see that most of the VLM performance graphs have aberrations in multiple categories, highlighting variance in strengths. In most cases, the weakness of one of the few VLMs is compensated for by the strength of others. So, choosing a VLM wisely according to the application need can help mitigate weaknesses.

Among the closed models, GPT-4o-mini proves to be the best in four categories - Nature, Nutrition and Food, Social Media and Sports, and Gemini-1.5-Pro proves to be the best in all other categories. GPT-4o-mini doesn't even remain second best in some categories like Mathematics, Economics, Law, and is outperformed by many open-sourced models here. Gemini-1.5-Flash remains strong with a performance deficit compared to Pro, but in Social Media tasks, it almost matches Pro. Therefore, while the appropriate model should be selected based on requirements, the Gemini-1.5-Pro generally looks to be the best overall choice.

In the open-source model category, InternVL-2-8B and CogVLM-2-Llama-3-19B are the best possible choices. CogVLM-2-Llama-3-19B generally performs well in more academic topics like Mathematics, Computer Science, law, Government and Politics, but suffers a lot of performance degradation in more social topics like Nature, Nutrition and Food, Social Media, Sports. InternVL-2-8B also shows similar traits, but the difference is relatively less. For academic topics, these models even outperform some of the closed models. Llava-1.6-Mistral-7B is one model that shows exactly opposite trait than this, being limited in academic topics as compared to social topics. Qwen-2 variants and PaliGemma show weak results in all domains, like in task types. InternVL-2-1B remains the best choice if a small model is required, with decent results using 1B parameters.

4.4 Evaluation on Knowledge Types

Similar to application domains, we evaluate all VLMs on all knowledge types where number of task instances is greater than 300. We demonstrate the results using a similar radar chart in Figure 6.

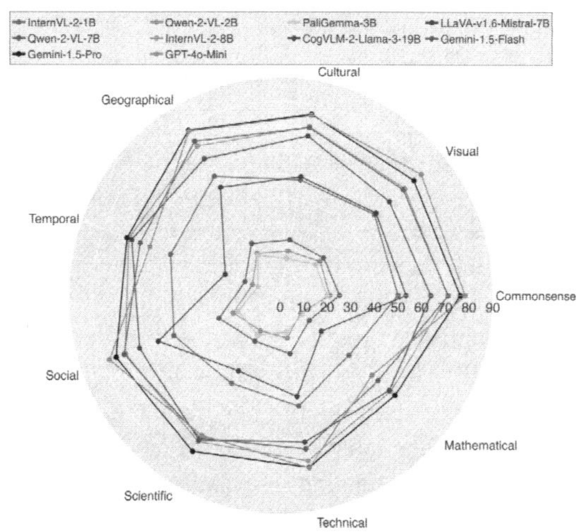

Figure 6: Mean GoEval-mini scores for different knowledge types for all VLMs. Gemini-1.5-Pro and GPT-4o-mini perform the best in most knowledge types, while InternVL-2 models also demonstrate competitive performance based on their size.

In the closed models category, the SOTA performance is again shared by Gemini-1.5-Pro and GPT-4o-mini. But unlike in application domains, GPT-4o-mini competes more strongly with Gemini-1.5-Pro on several knowledge types. Visual, Social and Commonsense knowledge is where the advantage of GPT-4o-mini over Gemini-1.5-Pro is maximum, again depicting its strength in social knowledge types. It is still considerably weak in temporal, scientific, and mathematical knowledge, falling behind even some of the small open-source models. Gemini-1.5-Pro will still be the best overall choice, but different models can be selected based on the results obtained for specific knowledge types. Gemini-1.5-Flash again follows similar trend, with slight performance difference from Pro.

Comparing open-source models, InternVL-2-8B and CogVLM-2-Llama-3-8B are the best choices here as well, but here we can see that InternVL-2-8B outperforms the latter in all knowledge types. InternVL-2-1B continues to be the best overall choice if small models are required, and the Qwen-2 variants and PaliGemma continue to be the least effective. Therefore, InternVL-2-8B is the best overall choice for open source models.

4.5 Overall Analysis and Recommendations

In subsections 4.2, 4.3 and 4.4, we evaluated all vision-language models under three different aspects of task types, application domains and knowledge types. We also discussed their strengths and weaknesses in those categories and recommended different VLMs to use under different requirements. In this section, we will take a higher level look at everything together.

We identified that Gemini-1.5-Pro and GPT-4o-mini are different. In general, GPT-4o-mini is weaker in analytical tasks, like tasks of Mathematics or Economics domain, or scientific or mathematical knowledge types. It not only falls behind Gemini-1.5-Pro in these tasks, but also behind open models like InternVL-2-8B or CogVLM-2-Llama-3-19B. However, it is strong is social and topical tasks like Nature, Sports, Nutrition and Food domains. Gemini-1.5-Pro proves strong more generally, but is expensive. It is either the best, or comes close second or third best. Therefore, if cost is a significant factor, Gemini-1.5-Flash can be considered as a decent alternative at a performance deficit of around 7-10%.

InternVL-2-8B and CogVLM-2-Llama-3-19B are strong open-source models. Due to size differences, resource availability also contributes to deciding which model to use. CogVLM-2-Llama-3-19B is better at more academic tasks, that belong to domains like History, Law, Computer Science, etc., or knowledge types like Temporal, Scientific or Mathematical Knowledge. InternVL-2-8B is a more general capable model that demonstrates more suitability in broader application requirements. In some cases, it outperforms GPT-4o-mini as well. Possessing superior performance in addition to other advantages of open-sourced model makes it a strong choice. It can also be aligned for downstream tasks to improve performance.

Among small models suited for on-device AI, resource-efficient environments, InternVL-2-1B proves is strongest overall, significantly outperforming models like Qwen2-VL-2B and PaliGemma-3B in all categories.

The Qwen-2-VL variants and PaliGemma-3B did not prove fit for use in our experimental settings, being very weak on all categories. LlaVa-1.6-Mistral-7B also performs average, similar to InternVL-2-1B, but is weak in all aspects compared to InternVL-2-8B, a similar-sized model.

Since Gemini-1.5-Pro was the most successful model, we demonstrate some of the qualitative examples using that model in Table 9 in the Appendix A. Finally, Tables 10 and 11 of the Appendix A contain quantitative results on all application domains and knowledge types, respectively, including the categories that were excluded from the study of the main paper.

5 Conclusion

In this paper, we propose a comprehensive framework for evaluating Vision-Language Models (VLMs) across diverse visual question-answering (VQA) tasks, addressing specific application requirements. Our framework introduces a novel evaluation paradigm that classifies VQA tasks along three dimensions: *task types*, *application domains*, and *knowledge types*. To support this, we release `VQA360`, a dataset annotated across 4 task types, 22 application domains, and 15 knowledge types, derived from established VQA benchmarks. We also present `GoEval`, a new evaluation metric to complement it, leveraging GPT-4o to integrate visual and textual information, achieving a 56.71% correlation with human judgments and outperforming traditional metrics.

Through experiments with 10 state-of-the-art VLMs, we observe significant performance variation across categories, with no single model proving universally optimal. Proprietary models like Gemini-1.5-Pro and GPT-4o-mini achieve the highest overall performance, while open-source models such as InternVL-2-8B and CogVLM-2-Llama-3-19B excel in specific scenarios. Our findings provide actionable insights for task-specific VLM selection, and establishes a evaluation framework that can be extended to other vision-language tasks, fostering progress in multimodal research.

References

Stanislaw Antol, Aishwarya Agrawal, Jiasen Lu, Margaret Mitchell, Dhruv Batra, C. Lawrence Zitnick, and Devi Parikh. 2015. Vqa: Visual question answering. In *Proceedings of the IEEE International Conference on Computer Vision (ICCV)*.

Jinze Bai, Shuai Bai, Shusheng Yang, Shijie Wang, Sinan Tan, Peng Wang, Junyang Lin, Chang Zhou, and Jingren Zhou. 2023. Qwen-vl: A versatile vision-language model for understanding, localization, text reading, and beyond. *arXiv preprint arXiv:2308.12966*.

Satanjeev Banerjee and Alon Lavie. 2005. Meteor: An automatic metric for mt evaluation with improved correlation with human judgments. In *Proceedings of the acl workshop on intrinsic and extrinsic evaluation measures for machine translation and/or summarization*, pages 65–72.

Lucas Beyer*, Andreas Steiner*, André Susano Pinto*, Alexander Kolesnikov*, Xiao Wang*, Daniel Salz, Maxim Neumann, Ibrahim Alabdulmohsin, Michael Tschannen, Emanuele Bugliarello, Thomas Unterthiner, Daniel Keysers, Skanda Koppula, Fangyu Liu, Adam Grycner, Alexey Gritsenko, Neil Houlsby, Manoj Kumar, Keran Rong, Julian Eisenschlos, Rishabh Kabra, Matthias Bauer, Matko Bošnjak, Xi Chen, Matthias Minderer, Paul Voigtlaender, Ioana Bica, Ivana Balazevic, Joan Puigcerver, Pinelopi Papalampidi, Olivier Henaff, Xi Xiong, Radu Soricut, Jeremiah Harmsen, and Xiaohua Zhai*. 2024. PaliGemma: A versatile 3B VLM for transfer. *arXiv preprint arXiv:2407.07726*.

Tom B. Brown, Benjamin Mann, Nick Ryder, Melanie Subbiah, Jared Kaplan, Prafulla Dhariwal, Arvind Neelakantan, Pranav Shyam, Girish Sastry, Amanda Askell, Sandhini Agarwal, Ariel Herbert-Voss, Gretchen Krueger, Tom Henighan, Rewon Child, Aditya Ramesh, Daniel M. Ziegler, Jeffrey Wu, Clemens Winter, Christopher Hesse, Mark Chen, Eric Sigler, Mateusz Litwin, Scott Gray, Benjamin Chess, Jack Clark, Christopher Berner, Sam McCandlish, Alec Radford, Ilya Sutskever, and Dario Amodei. 2020. Language models are few-shot learners. In *Advances in Neural Information Processing Systems*, volume 33, pages 1877–1901.

Soravit Changpinyo, Piyush Sharma, Nan Ding, and Radu Soricut. 2021. Conceptual 12m: Pushing web-scale image-text pre-training to recognize long-tail visual concepts. In *Proceedings of the IEEE/CVF Conference on Computer Vision and Pattern Recognition (CVPR)*, pages 3558–3568.

Xinlei Chen, Hao Fang, Tsung-Yi Lin, Ramakrishna Vedantam, Saurabh Gupta, Piotr Dollar, and C. Lawrence Zitnick. 2015. Microsoft coco captions: Data collection and evaluation server. *Preprint*, arXiv:1504.00325.

Zhe Chen, Weiyun Wang, Hao Tian, Shenglong Ye, Zhangwei Gao, Erfei Cui, Wenwen Tong, Kongzhi Hu, Jiapeng Luo, Zheng Ma, et al. 2024. How far are we to gpt-4v? closing the gap to commercial multimodal models with open-source suites. *arXiv preprint arXiv:2404.16821*.

Zhe Chen, Jiannan Wu, Wenhai Wang, Weijie Su, Guo Chen, Sen Xing, Muyan Zhong, Qinglong Zhang, Xizhou Zhu, Lewei Lu, Bin Li, Ping Luo, Tong Lu, Yu Qiao, and Jifeng Dai. 2023. Internvl: Scaling up vision foundation models and aligning for generic visual-linguistic tasks. *arXiv preprint arXiv:2312.14238*.

Tri Dao. 2023. Flashattention-2: Faster attention with better parallelism and work partitioning. *Preprint*, arXiv:2307.08691.

Xingyu Fu, Sheng Zhang, Gukyeong Kwon, Pramuditha Perera, Henghui Zhu, Yuhao Zhang, Alexander Hanbo Li, William Yang Wang, Zhiguo Wang, Vittorio Castelli, Patrick Ng, Dan Roth, and Bing Xiang. 2023. Generate then select: Open-ended visual question answering guided by world knowledge. In *Findings of the Association for Computational Linguistics: ACL 2023*, pages 2333–2346, Toronto, Canada. Association for Computational Linguistics.

Yash Goyal, Tejas Khot, Douglas Summers-Stay, Dhruv Batra, and Devi Parikh. 2017a. Making the v in vqa matter: Elevating the role of image understanding in visual question answering. In *Proceedings of the IEEE Conference on Computer Vision and Pattern Recognition (CVPR)*.

Yash Goyal, Tejas Khot, Douglas Summers-Stay, Dhruv Batra, and Devi Parikh. 2017b. Making the v in vqa matter: Elevating the role of image understanding in visual question answering. In *Proceedings of the IEEE Conference on Computer Vision and Pattern Recognition (CVPR)*.

Wenyi Hong, Weihan Wang, Ming Ding, Wenmeng Yu, Qingsong Lv, Yan Wang, Yean Cheng, Shiyu Huang, Junhui Ji, Zhao Xue, et al. 2024. Cogvlm2: Visual language models for image and video understanding. *Preprint*, arXiv:2408.16500.

Kushal Kafle and Christopher Kanan. 2017. An analysis of visual question answering algorithms. *Preprint*, arXiv:1703.09684.

Ehsan Kamalloo, Nouha Dziri, Charles Clarke, and Davood Rafiei. 2023. Evaluating open-domain question answering in the era of large language models. In *Proceedings of the 61st Annual Meeting of the Association for Computational Linguistics (Volume 1: Long Papers)*, pages 5591–5606, Toronto, Canada. Association for Computational Linguistics.

Shengzhi Li and Nima Tajbakhsh. 2023. Scigraphqa: A large-scale synthetic multi-turn question-answering dataset for scientific graphs. *Preprint*, arXiv:2308.03349.

Chin-Yew Lin. 2004. Rouge: A package for automatic evaluation of summaries. In *Text summarization branches out*, pages 74–81.

Ji Lin, Hongxu Yin, Wei Ping, Pavlo Molchanov, Mohammad Shoeybi, and Song Han. 2024. Vila: On pre-training for visual language models. In *Proceedings of the IEEE/CVF Conference on Computer Vision and Pattern Recognition (CVPR)*, pages 26689–26699.

Haotian Liu, Chunyuan Li, Yuheng Li, and Yong Jae Lee. 2024. Improved baselines with visual instruction tuning. *Preprint*, arXiv:2310.03744.

Haotian Liu, Chunyuan Li, Qingyang Wu, and Yong Jae Lee. 2023a. Visual instruction tuning. *Preprint*, arXiv:2304.08485.

Yang Liu, Dan Iter, Yichong Xu, Shuohang Wang, Ruochen Xu, and Chenguang Zhu. 2023b. G-eval: NLG evaluation using gpt-4 with better human alignment. In *Proceedings of the 2023 Conference on Empirical Methods in Natural Language Processing*, pages 2511–2522, Singapore. Association for Computational Linguistics.

Kenneth Marino, Mohammad Rastegari, Ali Farhadi, and Roozbeh Mottaghi. 2019. Ok-vqa: A visual question answering benchmark requiring external knowledge. In *Conference on Computer Vision and Pattern Recognition (CVPR)*.

Ahmed Masry, Xuan Long Do, Jia Qing Tan, Shafiq Joty, and Enamul Hoque. 2022. ChartQA: A benchmark for question answering about charts with visual and logical reasoning. In *Findings of the Association for Computational Linguistics: ACL 2022*, pages 2263–2279, Dublin, Ireland. Association for Computational Linguistics.

Manoj Mathew, Shijian Lu, Antonio Torralba, and Dimosthenis Karatzas. 2021. Document visual question answering (docvqa). In *Proceedings of the IEEE/CVF Winter Conference on Applications of Computer Vision (WACV)*, pages 2200–2209.

OpenAI. 2023. Gpt-3.5 turbo. OpenAI API. Available from OpenAI: `https://platform.openai.com/docs/models/gpt-3.5-turbo`.

OpenAI. 2024. Gpt-4o: Large language model. Accessed: 2024-09-06.

OpenAI, Josh Achiam, Steven Adler, Sandhini Agarwal, Lama Ahmad, Ilge Akkaya, Florencia Leoni Aleman, Diogo Almeida, Janko Altenschmidt, Sam Altman, Shyamal Anadkat, Red Avila, Igor Babuschkin, Suchir Balaji, Valerie Balcom, Paul Baltescu, Haiming Bao, Mohammad Bavarian, Jeff Belgum, Irwan Bello, Jake Berdine, Gabriel Bernadett-Shapiro, Christopher Berner, Lenny Bogdonoff, Oleg Boiko, Madelaine Boyd, Anna-Luisa Brakman, Greg Brockman, Tim Brooks, Miles Brundage, Kevin Button, Trevor Cai, Rosie Campbell, Andrew Cann, Brittany Carey, Chelsea Carlson, Rory Carmichael, Brooke Chan, Che Chang, Fotis Chantzis, Derek Chen, Sully Chen, Ruby Chen, Jason Chen, Mark Chen, Ben Chess, Chester Cho, Casey Chu, Hyung Won Chung, Dave Cummings, Jeremiah Currier, Yunxing Dai, Cory Decareaux, Thomas Degry, Noah Deutsch, Damien Deville, Arka Dhar, David Dohan, Steve Dowling, Sheila Dunning, Adrien Ecoffet, Atty Eleti, Tyna Eloundou, David Farhi, Liam Fedus, Niko Felix, Simón Posada Fishman, Juston Forte, Isabella Fulford, Leo Gao, Elie Georges, Christian Gibson, Vik Goel, Tarun Gogineni, Gabriel Goh, Rapha Gontijo-Lopes, Jonathan Gordon, Morgan Grafstein, Scott Gray, Ryan Greene, Joshua Gross, Shixiang Shane Gu, Yufei Guo, Chris Hallacy, Jesse Han, Jeff Harris, Yuchen He, Mike Heaton, Johannes Heidecke, Chris Hesse, Alan Hickey, Wade Hickey, Peter Hoeschele, Brandon Houghton, Kenny Hsu, Shengli Hu, Xin Hu, Joost Huizinga, Shantanu Jain, Shawn Jain, Joanne Jang, Angela Jiang, Roger Jiang, Haozhun Jin, Denny Jin, Shino Jomoto, Billie Jonn, Heewoo Jun, Tomer Kaftan, Łukasz Kaiser, Ali Kamali, Ingmar Kanitscheider, Nitish Shirish Keskar, Tabarak Khan, Logan Kilpatrick, Jong Wook Kim, Christina Kim, Yongjik Kim, Jan Hendrik Kirchner, Jamie Kiros, Matt Knight, Daniel Kokotajlo, Łukasz Kondraciuk, Andrew Kondrich, Aris Konstantinidis, Kyle Kosic, Gretchen Krueger, Vishal Kuo, Michael Lampe, Ikai Lan, Teddy Lee, Jan Leike, Jade Leung, Daniel Levy, Chak Ming Li, Rachel Lim, Molly Lin, Stephanie Lin, Mateusz Litwin, Theresa Lopez, Ryan Lowe, Patricia Lue, Anna Makanju, Kim Malfacini, Sam Manning, Todor Markov, Yaniv Markovski, Bianca Martin, Katie Mayer, Andrew Mayne, Bob McGrew, Scott Mayer McKinney, Christine McLeavey, Paul McMillan, Jake McNeil, David Medina, Aalok Mehta, Jacob Menick, Luke Metz, Andrey Mishchenko, Pamela Mishkin, Vinnie Monaco, Evan Morikawa, Daniel Mossing, Tong Mu, Mira Murati, Oleg Murk, David Mély, Ashvin Nair, Reiichiro Nakano, Rajeev Nayak, Arvind Neelakantan, Richard Ngo, Hyeonwoo Noh, Long Ouyang, Cullen O'Keefe, Jakub Pachocki, Alex Paino, Joe Palermo, Ashley Pantuliano, Giambattista Parascandolo, Joel Parish, Emy Parparita, Alex Passos, Mikhail Pavlov, Andrew Peng, Adam Perelman, Filipe de Avila Belbute Peres, Michael Petrov, Henrique Ponde de Oliveira Pinto, Michael, Pokorny, Michelle Pokrass, Vitchyr H. Pong, Tolly Powell, Alethea Power, Boris Power, Elizabeth Proehl, Raul Puri, Alec Radford, Jack Rae, Aditya Ramesh, Cameron Raymond, Francis Real, Kendra Rimbach, Carl Ross, Bob Rotsted, Henri Roussez, Nick Ryder, Mario Saltarelli, Ted Sanders, Shibani Santurkar, Girish Sastry, Heather Schmidt, David Schnurr, John Schulman, Daniel Selsam, Kyla Sheppard, Toki Sherbakov, Jessica Shieh, Sarah Shoker, Pranav Shyam, Szymon Sidor, Eric Sigler, Maddie Simens, Jordan Sitkin, Katarina Slama, Ian Sohl, Benjamin Sokolowsky, Yang Song, Natalie Staudacher, Felipe Petroski Such, Natalie Summers, Ilya Sutskever, Jie Tang, Nikolas Tezak, Madeleine B. Thompson, Phil Tillet, Amin Tootoonchian, Elizabeth Tseng, Preston Tuggle, Nick Turley, Jerry Tworek, Juan Felipe Cerón Uribe, Andrea Vallone, Arun Vijayvergiya, Chelsea Voss, Carroll Wainwright, Justin Jay Wang, Alvin Wang, Ben Wang, Jonathan Ward, Jason Wei, CJ Weinmann, Akila Welihinda, Peter Welinder, Jiayi Weng, Lilian Weng, Matt Wiethoff, Dave Willner,

Clemens Winter, Samuel Wolrich, Hannah Wong, Lauren Workman, Sherwin Wu, Jeff Wu, Michael Wu, Kai Xiao, Tao Xu, Sarah Yoo, Kevin Yu, Qiming Yuan, Wojciech Zaremba, Rowan Zellers, Chong Zhang, Marvin Zhang, Shengjia Zhao, Tianhao Zheng, Juntang Zhuang, William Zhuk, and Barret Zoph. 2024. Gpt-4 technical report. *Preprint*, arXiv:2303.08774.

Dustin Schwenk, Apoorv Khandelwal, Christopher Clark, Kenneth Marino, and Roozbeh Mottaghi. 2022. A-okvqa: A benchmark for visual question answering using world knowledge. *Preprint*, arXiv:2206.01718.

Neelabh Sinha, Vinija Jain, and Aman Chadha. 2024. Are small language models ready to compete with large language models for practical applications? *Preprint*, arXiv:2406.11402.

Gemini Team, Petko Georgiev, Ving Ian Lei, Ryan Burnell, Libin Bai, Anmol Gulati, Garrett Tanzer, Damien Vincent, Zhufeng Pan, Shibo Wang, Soroosh Mariooryad, Yifan Ding, Xinyang Geng, Fred Alcober, Roy Frostig, Mark Omernick, Lexi Walker, Cosmin Paduraru, Christina Sorokin, Andrea Tacchetti, Colin Gaffney, Samira Daruki, Olcan Sercinoglu, Zach Gleicher, Juliette Love, Paul Voigtlaender, Rohan Jain, Gabriela Surita, Kareem Mohamed, Rory Blevins, Junwhan Ahn, Tao Zhu, Kornraphop Kawintiranon, Orhan Firat, Yiming Gu, Yujing Zhang, Matthew Rahtz, Manaal Faruqui, Natalie Clay, Justin Gilmer, JD Co-Reyes, Ivo Penchev, Rui Zhu, Nobuyuki Morioka, Kevin Hui, Krishna Haridasan, Victor Campos, Mahdis Mahdieh, Mandy Guo, Samer Hassan, Kevin Kilgour, Arpi Vezer, Heng-Tze Cheng, Raoul de Liedekerke, Siddharth Goyal, Paul Barham, DJ Strouse, Seb Noury, Jonas Adler, Mukund Sundararajan, Sharad Vikram, Dmitry Lepikhin, Michela Paganini, Xavier Garcia, Fan Yang, Dasha Valter, Maja Trebacz, Kiran Vodrahalli, Chulayuth Asawaroengchai, Roman Ring, Norbert Kalb, Livio Baldini Soares, Siddhartha Brahma, David Steiner, Tianhe Yu, Fabian Mentzer, Antoine He, Lucas Gonzalez, Bibo Xu, Raphael Lopez Kaufman, Laurent El Shafey, Junhyuk Oh, Tom Hennigan, George van den Driessche, Seth Odoom, Mario Lucic, Becca Roelofs, Sid Lall, Amit Marathe, Betty Chan, Santiago Ontanon, Luheng He, Denis Teplyashin, Jonathan Lai, Phil Crone, Bogdan Damoc, Lewis Ho, Sebastian Riedel, Karel Lenc, Chih-Kuan Yeh, Aakanksha Chowdhery, Yang Xu, Mehran Kazemi, Ehsan Amid, Anastasia Petrushkina, Kevin Swersky, Ali Khodaei, Gowoon Chen, Chris Larkin, Mario Pinto, Geng Yan, Adria Puigdomenech Badia, Piyush Patil, Steven Hansen, Dave Orr, Sebastien M. R. Arnold, Jordan Grimstad, Andrew Dai, Sholto Douglas, Rishika Sinha, Vikas Yadav, Xi Chen, Elena Gribovskaya, Jacob Austin, Jeffrey Zhao, Kaushal Patel, Paul Komarek, Sophia Austin, Sebastian Borgeaud, Linda Friso, Abhimanyu Goyal, Ben Caine, Kris Cao, Da-Woon Chung, Matthew Lamm, Gabe Barth-Maron, Thais Kagohara, Kate Olszewska, Mia Chen, Kaushik Shivakumar, Rishabh Agarwal, Harshal Godhia, Ravi Rajwar, Javier Snaider, Xerxes Dotiwalla, Yuan Liu, Aditya Barua, Victor Ungureanu, Yuan Zhang, Bat-Orgil Batsaikhan, Mateo Wirth, James Qin, Ivo Danihelka, Tulsee Doshi, Martin Chadwick, Jilin Chen, Sanil Jain, Quoc Le, Arjun Kar, Madhu Gurumurthy, Cheng Li, Ruoxin Sang, Fangyu Liu, Lampros Lamprou, Rich Munoz, Nathan Lintz, Harsh Mehta, Heidi Howard, Malcolm Reynolds, Lora Aroyo, Quan Wang, Lorenzo Blanco, Albin Cassirer, Jordan Griffith, Dipanjan Das, Stephan Lee, Jakub Sygnowski, Zach Fisher, James Besley, Richard Powell, Zafarali Ahmed, Dominik Paulus, David Reitter, Zalan Borsos, Rishabh Joshi, Aedan Pope, Steven Hand, Vittorio Selo, Vihan Jain, Nikhil Sethi, Megha Goel, Takaki Makino, Rhys May, Zhen Yang, Johan Schalkwyk, Christina Butterfield, Anja Hauth, Alex Goldin, Will Hawkins, Evan Senter, Sergey Brin, Oliver Woodman, Marvin Ritter, Eric Noland, Minh Giang, Vijay Bolina, Lisa Lee, Tim Blyth, Ian Mackinnon, Machel Reid, Obaid Sarvana, David Silver, Alexander Chen, Lily Wang, Loren Maggiore, Oscar Chang, Nithya Attaluri, Gregory Thornton, Chung-Cheng Chiu, Oskar Bunyan, Nir Levine, Timothy Chung, Evgenii Eltyshev, Xiance Si, Timothy Lillicrap, Demetra Brady, Vaibhav Aggarwal, Boxi Wu, Yuanzhong Xu, Ross McIlroy, Kartikeya Badola, Paramjit Sandhu, Erica Moreira, Wojciech Stokowiec, Ross Hemsley, Dong Li, Alex Tudor, Pranav Shyam, Elahe Rahimtoroghi, Salem Haykal, Pablo Sprechmann, Xiang Zhou, Diana Mincu, Yujia Li, Ravi Addanki, Kalpesh Krishna, Xiao Wu, Alexandre Frechette, Matan Eyal, Allan Dafoe, Dave Lacey, Jay Whang, Thi Avrahami, Ye Zhang, Emanuel Taropa, Hanzhao Lin, Daniel Toyama, Eliza Rutherford, Motoki Sano, HyunJeong Choe, Alex Tomala, Chalence Safranek-Shrader, Nora Kassner, Mantas Pajarskas, Matt Harvey, Sean Sechrist, Meire Fortunato, Christina Lyu, Gamaleldin Elsayed, Chenkai Kuang, James Lottes, Eric Chu, Chao Jia, Chih-Wei Chen, Peter Humphreys, Kate Baumli, Connie Tao, Rajkumar Samuel, Cicero Nogueira dos Santos, Anders Andreassen, Nemanja Rakićević, Dominik Grewe, Aviral Kumar, Stephanie Winkler, Jonathan Caton, Andrew Brock, Sid Dalmia, Hannah Sheahan, Iain Barr, Yingjie Miao, Paul Natsev, Jacob Devlin, Feryal Behbahani, Flavien Prost, Yanhua Sun, Artiom Myaskovsky, Thanumalayan Sankaranarayana Pillai, Dan Hurt, Angeliki Lazaridou, Xi Xiong, Ce Zheng, Fabio Pardo, Xiaowei Li, Dan Horgan, Joe Stanton, Moran Ambar, Fei Xia, Alejandro Lince, Mingqiu Wang, Basil Mustafa, Albert Webson, Hyo Lee, Rohan Anil, Martin Wicke, Timothy Dozat, Abhishek Sinha, Enrique Piqueras, Elahe Dabir, Shyam Upadhyay, Anudhyan Boral, Lisa Anne Hendricks, Corey Fry, Josip Djolonga, Yi Su, Jake Walker, Jane Labanowski, Ronny Huang, Vedant Misra, Jeremy Chen, RJ Skerry-Ryan, Avi Singh, Shruti Rijhwani, Dian Yu, Alex Castro-Ros, Beer Changpinyo, Romina Datta, Sumit Bagri, Arnar Mar Hrafnkelsson, Marcello Maggioni, Daniel Zheng, Yury Sulsky, Shaobo Hou, Tom Le Paine, Antoine Yang, Jason Riesa, Dominika Rogozinska, Dror Marcus, Dalia El Badawy, Qiao Zhang, Luyu Wang, Helen Miller, Jeremy Greer, Lars Lowe Sjos, Azade Nova, Heiga Zen, Rahma Chaabouni, Mihaela Rosca, Jiepu

Jiang, Charlie Chen, Ruibo Liu, Tara Sainath, Maxim Krikun, Alex Polozov, Jean-Baptiste Lespiau, Josh Newlan, Zeyncep Cankara, Soo Kwak, Yunhan Xu, Phil Chen, Andy Coenen, Clemens Meyer, Katerina Tsihlas, Ada Ma, Juraj Gottweis, Jinwei Xing, Chenjie Gu, Jin Miao, Christian Frank, Zeynep Cankara, Sanjay Ganapathy, Ishita Dasgupta, Steph Hughes-Fitt, Heng Chen, David Reid, Keran Rong, Hongmin Fan, Joost van Amersfoort, Vincent Zhuang, Aaron Cohen, Shixiang Shane Gu, Anhad Mohananey, Anastasija Ilic, Taylor Tobin, John Wieting, Anna Bortsova, Phoebe Thacker, Emma Wang, Emily Caveness, Justin Chiu, Eren Sezener, Alex Kaskasoli, Steven Baker, Katie Millican, Mohamed Elhawaty, Kostas Aisopos, Carl Lebsack, Nathan Byrd, Hanjun Dai, Wenhao Jia, Matthew Wiethoff, Elnaz Davoodi, Albert Weston, Lakshman Yagati, Arun Ahuja, Isabel Gao, Golan Pundak, Susan Zhang, Michael Azzam, Khe Chai Sim, Sergi Caelles, James Keeling, Abhanshu Sharma, Andy Swing, YaGuang Li, Chenxi Liu, Carrie Grimes Bostock, Yamini Bansal, Zachary Nado, Ankesh Anand, Josh Lipschultz, Abhijit Karmarkar, Lev Proleev, Abe Ittycheriah, Soheil Hassas Yeganeh, George Polovets, Aleksandra Faust, Jiao Sun, Alban Rrustemi, Pen Li, Rakesh Shivanna, Jeremiah Liu, Chris Welty, Federico Lebron, Anirudh Baddepudi, Sebastian Krause, Emilio Parisotto, Radu Soricut, Zheng Xu, Dawn Bloxwich, Melvin Johnson, Behnam Neyshabur, Justin Mao-Jones, Renshen Wang, Vinay Ramasesh, Zaheer Abbas, Arthur Guez, Constant Segal, Duc Dung Nguyen, James Svensson, Le Hou, Sarah York, Kieran Milan, Sophie Bridgers, Wiktor Gworek, Marco Tagliasacchi, James Lee-Thorp, Michael Chang, Alexey Guseynov, Ale Jakse Hartman, Michael Kwong, Ruizhe Zhao, Sheleem Kashem, Elizabeth Cole, Antoine Miech, Richard Tanburn, Mary Phuong, Filip Pavetic, Sebastien Cevey, Ramona Comanescu, Richard Ives, Sherry Yang, Cosmo Du, Bo Li, Zizhao Zhang, Mariko Iinuma, Clara Huiyi Hu, Aurko Roy, Shaan Bijwadia, Zhenkai Zhu, Danilo Martins, Rachel Saputro, Anita Gergely, Steven Zheng, Dawei Jia, Ioannis Antonoglou, Adam Sadovsky, Shane Gu, Yingying Bi, Alek Andreev, Sina Samangooei, Mina Khan, Tomas Kocisky, Angelos Filos, Chintu Kumar, Colton Bishop, Adams Yu, Sarah Hodkinson, Sid Mittal, Premal Shah, Alexandre Moufarek, Yong Cheng, Adam Bloniarz, Jaehoon Lee, Pedram Pejman, Paul Michel, Stephen Spencer, Vladimir Feinberg, Xuehan Xiong, Nikolay Savinov, Charlotte Smith, Siamak Shakeri, Dustin Tran, Mary Chesus, Bernd Bohnet, George Tucker, Tamara von Glehn, Carrie Muir, Yiran Mao, Hideto Kazawa, Ambrose Slone, Kedar Soparkar, Disha Shrivastava, James Cobon-Kerr, Michael Sharman, Jay Pavagadhi, Carlos Araya, Karolis Misiunas, Nimesh Ghelani, Michael Laskin, David Barker, Qiujia Li, Anton Briukhov, Neil Houlsby, Mia Glaese, Balaji Lakshminarayanan, Nathan Schucher, Yunhao Tang, Eli Collins, Hyeontaek Lim, Fangxiaoyu Feng, Adria Recasens, Guangda Lai, Alberto Magni, Nicola De Cao, Aditya Siddhant, Zoe Ashwood, Jordi Orbay, Mostafa Dehghani, Jenny Brennan, Yifan He, Kelvin Xu, Yang Gao, Carl Saroufim, James Molloy, Xinyi Wu, Seb Arnold, Solomon Chang, Julian Schrittwieser, Elena Buchatskaya, Soroush Radpour, Martin Polacek, Skye Giordano, Ankur Bapna, Simon Tokumine, Vincent Hellendoorn, Thibault Sottiaux, Sarah Cogan, Aliaksei Severyn, Mohammad Saleh, Shantanu Thakoor, Laurent Shefey, Siyuan Qiao, Meenu Gaba, Shuo yiin Chang, Craig Swanson, Biao Zhang, Benjamin Lee, Paul Kishan Rubenstein, Gan Song, Tom Kwiatkowski, Anna Koop, Ajay Kannan, David Kao, Parker Schuh, Axel Stjerngren, Golnaz Ghiasi, Gena Gibson, Luke Vilnis, Ye Yuan, Felipe Tiengo Ferreira, Aishwarya Kamath, Ted Klimenko, Ken Franko, Kefan Xiao, Indro Bhattacharya, Miteyan Patel, Rui Wang, Alex Morris, Robin Strudel, Vivek Sharma, Peter Choy, Sayed Hadi Hashemi, Jessica Landon, Mara Finkelstein, Priya Jhakra, Justin Frye, Megan Barnes, Matthew Mauger, Dennis Daun, Khuslen Baatarsukh, Matthew Tung, Wael Farhan, Henryk Michalewski, Fabio Viola, Felix de Chaumont Quitry, Charline Le Lan, Tom Hudson, Qingze Wang, Felix Fischer, Ivy Zheng, Elspeth White, Anca Dragan, Jean baptiste Alayrac, Eric Ni, Alexander Pritzel, Adam Iwanicki, Michael Isard, Anna Bulanova, Lukas Zilka, Ethan Dyer, Devendra Sachan, Srivatsan Srinivasan, Hannah Muckenhirn, Honglong Cai, Amol Mandhane, Mukarram Tariq, Jack W. Rae, Gary Wang, Kareem Ayoub, Nicholas FitzGerald, Yao Zhao, Woohyun Han, Chris Alberti, Dan Garrette, Kashyap Krishnakumar, Mai Gimenez, Anselm Levskaya, Daniel Sohn, Josip Matak, Inaki Iturrate, Michael B. Chang, Jackie Xiang, Yuan Cao, Nishant Ranka, Geoff Brown, Adrian Hutter, Vahab Mirrokni, Nanxin Chen, Kaisheng Yao, Zoltan Egyed, Francois Galilee, Tyler Liechty, Praveen Kallakuri, Evan Palmer, Sanjay Ghemawat, Jasmine Liu, David Tao, Chloe Thornton, Tim Green, Mimi Jasarevic, Sharon Lin, Victor Cotruta, Yi-Xuan Tan, Noah Fiedel, Hongkun Yu, Ed Chi, Alexander Neitz, Jens Heitkaemper, Anu Sinha, Denny Zhou, Yi Sun, Charbel Kaed, Brice Hulse, Swaroop Mishra, Maria Georgaki, Sneha Kudugunta, Clement Farabet, Izhak Shafran, Daniel Vlasic, Anton Tsitsulin, Rajagopal Ananthanarayanan, Alen Carin, Guolong Su, Pei Sun, Shashank V, Gabriel Carvajal, Josef Broder, Iulia Comsa, Alena Repina, William Wong, Warren Weilun Chen, Peter Hawkins, Egor Filonov, Lucia Loher, Christoph Hirnschall, Weiyi Wang, Jingchen Ye, Andrea Burns, Hardie Cate, Diana Gage Wright, Federico Piccinini, Lei Zhang, Chu-Cheng Lin, Ionel Gog, Yana Kulizhskaya, Ashwin Sreevatsa, Shuang Song, Luis C. Cobo, Anand Iyer, Chetan Tekur, Guillermo Garrido, Zhuyun Xiao, Rupert Kemp, Huaixiu Steven Zheng, Hui Li, Ananth Agarwal, Christel Ngani, Kati Goshvadi, Rebeca Santamaria-Fernandez, Wojciech Fica, Xinyun Chen, Chris Gorgolewski, Sean Sun, Roopal Garg, Xinyu Ye, S. M. Ali Eslami, Nan Hua, Jon Simon, Pratik Joshi, Yelin Kim, Ian Tenney, Sahitya Potluri, Lam Nguyen Thiet, Quan Yuan, Florian Luisier, Alexandra Chronopoulou, Salvatore Scellato, Praveen Srinivasan, Minmin Chen, Vinod Koverkathu, Valentin Dalibard, Yaming Xu, Brennan Saeta, Keith Anderson, Thibault Sellam, Nick Fernando, Fantine Huot, Junehyuk Jung, Mani

Varadarajan, Michael Quinn, Amit Raul, Maigo Le, Ruslan Habalov, Jon Clark, Komal Jalan, Kalesha Bullard, Achintya Singhal, Thang Luong, Boyu Wang, Sujeevan Rajayogam, Julian Eisenschlos, Johnson Jia, Daniel Finchelstein, Alex Yakubovich, Daniel Balle, Michael Fink, Sameer Agarwal, Jing Li, Dj Dvijotham, Shalini Pal, Kai Kang, Jaclyn Konzelmann, Jennifer Beattie, Olivier Dousse, Diane Wu, Remi Crocker, Chen Elkind, Siddhartha Reddy Jonnalagadda, Jong Lee, Dan Holtmann-Rice, Krystal Kallarackal, Rosanne Liu, Denis Vnukov, Neera Vats, Luca Invernizzi, Mohsen Jafari, Huanjie Zhou, Lilly Taylor, Jennifer Prendki, Marcus Wu, Tom Eccles, Tianqi Liu, Kavya Kopparapu, Francoise Beaufays, Christof Angermueller, Andreea Marzoca, Shourya Sarcar, Hilal Dib, Jeff Stanway, Frank Perbet, Nejc Trdin, Rachel Sterneck, Andrey Khorlin, Dinghua Li, Xihui Wu, Sonam Goenka, David Madras, Sasha Goldshtein, Willi Gierke, Tong Zhou, Yaxin Liu, Yannie Liang, Anais White, Yunjie Li, Shreya Singh, Sanaz Bahargam, Mark Epstein, Sujoy Basu, Li Lao, Adnan Ozturel, Carl Crous, Alex Zhai, Han Lu, Zora Tung, Neeraj Gaur, Alanna Walton, Lucas Dixon, Ming Zhang, Amir Globerson, Grant Uy, Andrew Bolt, Olivia Wiles, Milad Nasr, Ilia Shumailov, Marco Selvi, Francesco Piccinno, Ricardo Aguilar, Sara McCarthy, Misha Khalman, Mrinal Shukla, Vlado Galic, John Carpenter, Kevin Villela, Haibin Zhang, Harry Richardson, James Martens, Matko Bosnjak, Shreyas Rammohan Belle, Jeff Seibert, Mahmoud Alnahlawi, Brian McWilliams, Sankalp Singh, Annie Louis, Wen Ding, Dan Popovici, Lenin Simicich, Laura Knight, Pulkit Mehta, Nishesh Gupta, Chongyang Shi, Saaber Fatehi, Jovana Mitrovic, Alex Grills, Joseph Pagadora, Dessie Petrova, Danielle Eisenbud, Zhishuai Zhang, Damion Yates, Bhavishya Mittal, Nilesh Tripuraneni, Yannis Assael, Thomas Brovelli, Prateek Jain, Mihajlo Velimirovic, Canfer Akbulut, Jiaqi Mu, Wolfgang Macherey, Ravin Kumar, Jun Xu, Haroon Qureshi, Gheorghe Comanici, Jeremy Wiesner, Zhitao Gong, Anton Ruddock, Matthias Bauer, Nick Felt, Anirudh GP, Anurag Arnab, Dustin Zelle, Jonas Rothfuss, Bill Rosgen, Ashish Shenoy, Bryan Seybold, Xinjian Li, Jayaram Mudigonda, Goker Erdogan, Jiawei Xia, Jiri Simsa, Andrea Michi, Yi Yao, Christopher Yew, Steven Kan, Isaac Caswell, Carey Radebaugh, Andre Elisseeff, Pedro Valenzuela, Kay McKinney, Kim Paterson, Albert Cui, Eri Latorre-Chimoto, Solomon Kim, William Zeng, Ken Durden, Priya Ponnapalli, Tiberiu Sosea, Christopher A. Choquette-Choo, James Manyika, Brona Robenek, Harsha Vashisht, Sebastien Pereira, Hoi Lam, Marko Velic, Denese Owusu-Afriyie, Katherine Lee, Tolga Bolukbasi, Alicia Parrish, Shawn Lu, Jane Park, Balaji Venkatraman, Alice Talbert, Lambert Rosique, Yuchung Cheng, Andrei Sozanschi, Adam Paszke, Praveen Kumar, Jessica Austin, Lu Li, Khalid Salama, Wooyeol Kim, Nandita Dukkipati, Anthony Baryshnikov, Christos Kaplanis, Xiang-Hai Sheng, Yuri Chervonyi, Caglar Unlu, Diego de Las Casas, Harry Askham, Kathryn Tunyasuvunakool, Felix Gimeno, Siim Poder, Chester Kwak, Matt Miecnikowski, Vahab Mirrokni, Alek Dimitriev, Aaron Parisi, Dangyi Liu, Tomy Tsai, Toby Shevlane, Christina Kouridi, Drew Garmon, Adrian Goedeckemeyer, Adam R. Brown, Anitha Vijayakumar, Ali Elqursh, Sadegh Jazayeri, Jin Huang, Sara Mc Carthy, Jay Hoover, Lucy Kim, Sandeep Kumar, Wei Chen, Courtney Biles, Garrett Bingham, Evan Rosen, Lisa Wang, Qijun Tan, David Engel, Francesco Pongetti, Dario de Cesare, Dongseong Hwang, Lily Yu, Jennifer Pullman, Srini Narayanan, Kyle Levin, Siddharth Gopal, Megan Li, Asaf Aharoni, Trieu Trinh, Jessica Lo, Norman Casagrande, Roopali Vij, Loic Matthey, Bramandia Ramadhana, Austin Matthews, CJ Carey, Matthew Johnson, Kremena Goranova, Rohin Shah, Shereen Ashraf, Kingshuk Dasgupta, Rasmus Larsen, Yicheng Wang, Manish Reddy Vuyyuru, Chong Jiang, Joana Ijazi, Kazuki Osawa, Celine Smith, Ramya Sree Boppana, Taylan Bilal, Yuma Koizumi, Ying Xu, Yasemin Altun, Nir Shabat, Ben Bariach, Alex Korchemniy, Kiam Choo, Olaf Ronneberger, Chimezie Iwuanyanwu, Shubin Zhao, David Soergel, Cho-Jui Hsieh, Irene Cai, Shariq Iqbal, Martin Sundermeyer, Zhe Chen, Elie Bursztein, Chaitanya Malaviya, Fadi Biadsy, Prakash Shroff, Inderjit Dhillon, Tejasi Latkar, Chris Dyer, Hannah Forbes, Massimo Nicosia, Vitaly Nikolaev, Somer Greene, Marin Georgiev, Pidong Wang, Nina Martin, Hanie Sedghi, John Zhang, Praseem Banzal, Doug Fritz, Vikram Rao, Xuezhi Wang, Jiageng Zhang, Viorica Patraucean, Dayou Du, Igor Mordatch, Ivan Jurin, Lewis Liu, Ayush Dubey, Abhi Mohan, Janek Nowakowski, Vlad-Doru Ion, Nan Wei, Reiko Tojo, Maria Abi Raad, Drew A. Hudson, Vaishakh Keshava, Shubham Agrawal, Kevin Ramirez, Zhichun Wu, Hoang Nguyen, Ji Liu, Madhavi Sewak, Bryce Petrini, DongHyun Choi, Ivan Philips, Ziyue Wang, Ioana Bica, Ankush Garg, Jarek Wilkiewicz, Priyanka Agrawal, Xiaowei Li, Danhao Guo, Emily Xue, Naseer Shaik, Andrew Leach, Sadh MNM Khan, Julia Wiesinger, Sammy Jerome, Abhishek Chakladar, Alek Wenjiao Wang, Tina Ornduff, Folake Abu, Alireza Ghaffarkhah, Marcus Wainwright, Mario Cortes, Frederick Liu, Joshua Maynez, Andreas Terzis, Pouya Samangouei, Riham Mansour, Tomasz Kępa, François-Xavier Aubet, Anton Algymr, Dan Banica, Agoston Weisz, Andras Orban, Alexandre Senges, Ewa Andrejczuk, Mark Geller, Niccolo Dal Santo, Valentin Anklin, Majd Al Merey, Martin Baeuml, Trevor Strohman, Junwen Bai, Slav Petrov, Yonghui Wu, Demis Hassabis, Koray Kavukcuoglu, Jeffrey Dean, and Oriol Vinyals. 2024. Gemini 1.5: Unlocking multimodal understanding across millions of tokens of context. *Preprint*, arXiv:2403.05530.

Qwen team. 2024. Qwen2-vl.

Bart Thomee, David A. Shamma, Gerald Friedland, Benjamin Elizalde, Karl Ni, Douglas Poland, Damian Borth, and Li-Jia Li. 2016. Yfcc100m: the new data in multimedia research. *Communications of the ACM*, 59(2):64–73.

Weihan Wang, Qingsong Lv, Wenmeng Yu, Wenyi Hong, Ji Qi, Yan Wang, Junhui Ji, Zhuoyi Yang,

Lei Zhao, Xixuan Song, Jiazheng Xu, Bin Xu, Juanzi Li, Yuxiao Dong, Ming Ding, and Jie Tang. 2023. Cogvlm: Visual expert for pretrained language models. *Preprint*, arXiv:2311.03079.

Zihao Wei, Zixuan Pan, and Andrew Owens. 2024. Efficient vision-language pre-training by cluster masking. In *Proceedings of the IEEE/CVF Conference on Computer Vision and Pattern Recognition (CVPR)*, pages 26815–26825.

Tianyi Zhang, Varsha Kishore, Felix Wu, Kilian Q Weinberger, and Yoav Artzi. 2019. Bertscore: Evaluating text generation with bert. *arXiv preprint arXiv:1904.09675*.

Yuke Zhu, Oliver Groth, Michael Bernstein, and Li Fei-Fei. 2016. Visual7w: Grounded question answering in images. In *Proceedings of the IEEE Conference on Computer Vision and Pattern Recognition (CVPR)*.

A Appendix

In this appendix, we provide additional details and results related to our work. The implementation details can be found in Section A.1. Table 7 provides prompts designed to classify tasks by domain (e.g., "Anthropology," "Computer Science") and by the type of knowledge required (e.g., "Commonsense Knowledge," "Visual Knowledge"). Table 8 presents the prompts used in `GoEval` to verify whether a candidate answer is correct, with or without reference answers, both for visual and text-only evaluation. Additionally, Table 9 details some qualitative examples using the best overall model that we found - Gemini-1.5-Pro. Finally, Tables 10 and 11 contain quantitative results on all application domains and knowledge types, respectively, including the categories that were excluded from the study of the main paper.

A.1 Implementation Details

In this subsection, we will discuss more details around implementation. Table 5 contains all the model cards, which contain exact details of how we implemented all the VLMs, and the recommended prompt templates that we used in our evaluation.

For all the models, we prepend the question with a static text saying 'Only answer the below question. Do not provide any additional information. In addition, we resize all images to 448×448 before sending them through the model. This is the input to every model. For decoding the output, we use Greedy sampling, since fluency is not a key factor in VQA as long as the answers are correct. We use $max\_new\_tokens = 2048$ for all models.

Artifact	**Link**
VQAv2	Dataset Card
OK-VQA	Dataset Card
A-OKVQA	Dataset Card
ChartQA	Dataset Card
DocumentVQA	Dataset Card
InternVL-2-1B	Model Card
Qwen-2-VL-2B	Model Card
PaliGemma-3B	Model Card
Qwen-2-VL-7B	Model Card
LLaVA-v1.6-Mistral-7B	Model Card
InternVL-2-8B	Model Card
CogVLM-2-Llama-3-19B	Model Card
Gemini-1.5-Flash	Model Card
Gemini-1.5-Pro	Model Card
GPT-4o-Mini	Model Card
BERTScore	Doc (used using Roberta Large)

Table 5: Details of artifacts used with artifact links.

The implementation of executing all models and our evaluation metric can be found in the Code provided. We also provide the implementation of captions and object tags that can be used if this framework is being adapted to other tasks. All the configuration parameters and hardware used are detailed in Table 6.

Configuration Parameter	Specification
Number of GPUs	1, 2 for CogVLM-2
GPU Model	Nvidia A40
GPU Memory Capacity	48 GB
Batch Size	8
Image Resolution	448 × 448 (224 for PaliGemma)
Maximum New Tokens	2048

Table 6: Hardware and model configuration details used in the experiments, highlighting specialized settings for certain models.

We also use 4-bit quantization and Flash Attention 2 (Dao, 2023) wherever supported for memory and execution efficiency.

A.2 Using this Work to Select VLM

The prerequisite to using this work is to lay down the problem statement and its scope along with other system parameters that should include, but should not be limited to resource availability, data availability, system constraints, resource or data processing budget, acceptable performance bounds, etc.

Start with finding the task type, application domain and reasoning type closest to your requirement from Table 4, 10 and 11. Next, from your design constraints, identify some sets of VLMs acceptable for your solution. For example, if using on-device AI, you might only be able to use either small VLMs, or closed model accessible by APIs, depending on your acceptable performance bounds, and regulatory aspects of being able to share data across, having the inference budget for using APIs, and so on. Refer to Section 4 for a more detailed discussion around which models will fit which needs. Between those, check the performance of the subset of categories and subset of models, and choose the best model.

These models provide a comparison on a uniform foundation so that a comparative analysis can be done. These models can further be customized as desired for best outputs as per other design parameters and needs.

Aspect	Prompt to Extract Tags
Prompt to Extract Application Domains	Following are source application domains: Anthropology, Books, Computer Science, Economics, Fiction, Formal logic, Government and Politics, History, Justice, Knowledge Base, Law, Linguistics, Movies, Mathematics, Nature, News, Nutrition and Food, Professions, Public Places, Reviews, Science, Social Media, Sports. There is an image which can be described as: {caption}. The image has the following objects: {object_tags}. A user is asking the following question on the image: {question}, What type of application domain does this task belong to? Choose one or many alternatives from the above options. Return output as list of strings as JSON Object. Example: {{'application_domain': ['domain_a', 'domain_b']}}
Prompt to Extract Knowledge Type	Following are the names and explanation of types of knowledge: Commonsense Knowledge: Knowledge about the world that humans learn from their everyday experiences (e.g., many donuts being made in a cart implies they are for sale rather than for personal consumption). Visual Knowledge: Knowledge of concepts represented visually (e.g., muted color palettes are associated with the 1950s). Cultural Knowledge: Understanding cultural references, norms, and practices (e.g., knowing that a red envelope is associated with good luck in Chinese culture). Temporal Knowledge: Awareness of historical events, timelines, and changes over time (e.g., recognizing a specific style of clothing as being from the 1980s). Geographical Knowledge: Information about locations, landmarks, and regional characteristics (e.g., identifying a famous monument like the Eiffel Tower in Paris). Social Knowledge: Understanding social interactions, relationships, and behaviors (e.g., recognizing that a handshake is a form of greeting). Scientific Knowledge: Knowledge from various scientific domains like physics, biology, chemistry, astronomy, etc. (e.g., understanding that certain plants are poisonous). Technical Knowledge: Familiarity with technology, machinery, and tools (e.g., identifying parts of a computer or types of construction equipment). Mathematical Knowledge: Basic mathematical concepts and their applications (e.g., understanding geometric shapes or calculating areas). Literary Knowledge: Awareness of literature, authors, and genres (e.g., recognizing characters from classic novels). There is an image which can be described as: {caption}. The image has the following objects: {object_tags}. A user is asking the following question on the image: {question}. What type of knowledge is required to answer the question? Choose one or many alternatives from the above options. Return output as list of strings as JSON Object. Example: {{'knowledge_type': ['knowledge_a', 'knowledge_b']}}

Table 7: Prompts used to generate domain and knowledge type tags using the question, image caption and object tags.

Prompt	Reference	Image
Question: {question} Reference Answers: {reference} Candidate Answer: {candidate} Consider Reference Answers to be multiple answers provided for the given question in context with the above image. If there are multiple answers, they are separated by semi-colon(;). Based on the image, is the candidate answer a correct answer for the given question? Answer only 'yes' if the candidate answer is correct or only 'no' if it is not.	✓	✓
Question: {question} Candidate Answer: {candidate} Based on the image, is the candidate answer a correct answer for the given question? Answer only 'yes' if the candidate answer is correct or only 'no' if it is not.	×	✓
Question: {question} Reference Answers: {reference} Candidate Answer: {candidate} Consider Reference Answers to be multiple answers provided for the given question in context. If there are multiple answers, they are separated by semi-colon(;). Based on the context, is the candidate answer a correct answer for the given question? Answer only 'yes' if the candidate answer is correct or only 'no' if it is not.	✓	×
Question: {question} Candidate Answer: {candidate} Based on the context, is the candidate answer a correct answer for the given question? Answer only 'yes' if the candidate answer is correct or only 'no' if it is not.	×	×

Table 8: Prompts used with GoEval in different settings. (✓) represents included, (×) represents excluded.

Image	**Question**	**Labels**	**Response**	**Human Evaluated Label**	`GoEval-mini`
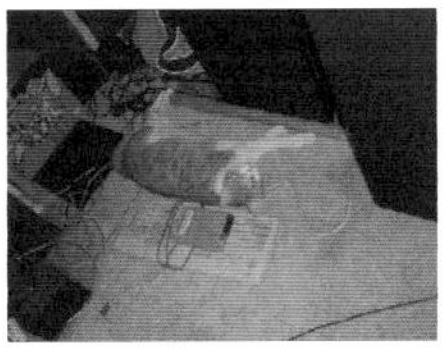	The cat is doing what?	laying down, sleeping, laying down, laying, sleeping, resting, laying, laying, laying down, resting	Lying down	✓	✓
	What number is closest to the number of people that are pushing the bus?	eight, eight, eight, ten, twelve, nine, twenty, ten, nine, 15	10	×	✓
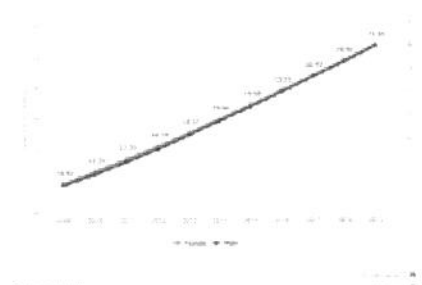	Is there any difference between the male and female values?	No	No	✓	×
	What is the name of the company mentioned in logo?	golden tobacco limited, Golden Tobacco Limited	The logo	×	×
	What is the message written on?	sign, sign, metal sign, stop sign, signs, street sign, sign, metal sign, street sign	A sign	✓	✓

Table 9: Some qualitative examples with Gemini-1.5-Pro. (✓) represents correct answer, saying that response correctly answers the question, (×) represents incorrect answer.

Domain	Intern-VL-2-1B	Qwen-2-VL-2B	Pali-Gemma-3B	LLaVA-v1.6-Mistral-7B	Qwen-2-VL-7B	Intern-VL-2-8B	Cog-VLM-2-Llama-3-19B	Gemini-1.5-Flash	Gemini-1.5-Pro	GPT-4o-Mini
Anthropology	46.47	20.33	16.60	60.58	21.99	73.86	63.18	71.91	74.69	**82.16**
Books	55.56	21.37	10.68	40.60	20.94	70.51	66.23	63.79	**72.22**	66.95
Computer Science	48.96	12.86	16.18	37.14	18.05	65.77	63.83	63.29	**69.65**	65.61
Economics	49.73	9.73	8.92	17.84	10.54	66.49	66.58	60.39	**67.57**	54.47
Fiction	53.70	22.22	24.07	61.11	29.63	81.48	57.41	62.96	70.37	**83.33**
Formal logic	31.96	23.71	14.43	37.50	22.68	56.70	50.00	58.33	**63.92**	58.76
Government and Politics	46.11	16.71	14.57	34.30	21.86	66.96	66.96	66.45	**70.28**	62.72
History	45.80	19.42	18.47	42.21	23.98	65.47	63.86	64.88	**70.19**	68.56
Justice	41.07	23.21	10.71	46.43	32.14	66.07	62.50	64.81	**73.21**	71.43
Knowledge Base	47.91	18.60	13.05	38.30	20.20	68.97	63.44	64.76	**71.78**	69.40
Law	47.29	17.98	14.04	38.18	23.40	65.27	65.17	67.92	**70.79**	62.34
Linguistics	48.00	17.78	20.89	44.89	21.33	67.56	58.04	63.64	75.00	**79.46**
Mathematics	33.33	13.12	12.69	23.71	15.70	57.85	60.00	52.99	**62.80**	50.44
Movies	53.80	22.78	20.89	51.90	32.91	69.62	63.29	66.24	76.58	**78.06**
Nature	50.98	25.92	22.22	61.05	29.41	71.99	61.50	74.34	78.14	**84.32**
News	54.59	17.84	11.35	31.89	17.84	68.11	68.51	70.79	**71.74**	62.78
Nutrition and Food	42.83	18.99	21.55	49.81	23.26	67.44	67.05	69.22	75.73	**78.56**
Other	48.46	19.39	23.64	52.96	24.35	68.32	58.91	67.46	71.63	**78.10**
Professions	51.53	17.88	17.55	47.18	24.35	69.65	64.62	70.24	75.03	**75.15**
Public Places	54.48	18.34	21.72	60.34	24.83	77.59	66.55	75.00	82.35	**82.41**
Reviews	52.86	18.57	23.19	50.00	24.29	64.29	60.00	69.12	70.00	**72.46**
Science	48.75	21.42	18.79	43.63	24.31	67.28	63.94	68.78	**74.34**	71.56
Social Media	51.34	23.47	21.52	56.72	29.58	70.42	63.88	73.27	**74.26**	82.06
Sports	51.55	22.33	21.36	60.53	29.26	73.53	64.50	69.98	78.79	**81.46**

Table 10: Mean GoEval-mini for various application domains across multiple VLMs. The best result in each domain is represented in **BOLD**. Note, this also includes the domains that were excluded from main paper's analysis because of having less than 300 task instances.

Knowledge Type	Intern-VL-2-1B	Qwen-2-VL-2B	Pali-Gemma-3B	LLaVA-v1.6-Mistral-7B	Qwen-2-VL-7B	Intern-VL-2-8B	Cog-VLM-2-Llama-3-19B	Gemini-1.5-Flash	Gemini-1.5-Pro	GPT-4o mini
Commonsense	49.95	21.10	19.88	53.33	25.25	71.06	63.91	71.24	76.32	**78.41**
Cultural	48.36	18.70	15.57	49.65	23.26	70.54	66.70	70.21	**75.77**	75.31
Geographical	56.58	19.95	19.20	51.37	24.77	71.00	64.98	73.28	**78.50**	78.12
Literary	44.25	17.42	13.24	41.46	20.91	68.64	71.58	67.97	**73.78**	66.78
Mathematical	38.13	11.33	12.40	22.93	16.13	61.20	60.51	54.30	**63.67**	50.88
Other	41.82	13.64	20.00	45.45	16.36	62.73	57.27	63.30	67.59	**76.85**
Scientific	41.72	16.78	18.98	35.76	21.63	69.54	68.81	67.87	**74.22**	66.59
Social	48.12	21.49	19.23	55.04	27.87	70.09	63.57	70.63	74.24	**77.20**
Technical	46.15	17.74	15.31	42.13	24.29	69.17	61.32	64.19	71.87	**72.10**
Temporal	49.62	12.69	10.14	25.13	16.15	68.72	67.31	63.42	**69.45**	58.95
Visual	52.03	21.97	19.54	52.92	24.13	68.67	60.27	67.87	73.81	**77.82**

Table 11: Mean GoEval-mini for all knowledge types across multiple VLMs. The best result in each knowledge type is represented in **BOLD**. Note, this also includes the knowledge types that were excluded from main paper's analysis because of having less than 300 task instances.

Author Index

Bai, Yuyu, 24
Bali, Shayan, 52

Chadha, Aman, 76
Chien-Hua, Chen, 57

Eetemadi, Sauleh, 10

Farsi, Farhan, 52

Hsieh, Hsin-Yi, 57
Huang, Hen-Hsen, 57

Jain, Vinija, 76

Li, JinJin, 40
Lin, Hung-Ju, 57
Lin, Shuo-Yueh, 57
Liu, Oliver, 40
Liu, Shang Wei, 57

Ma, Lan, 40
Meng, Chang Chih, 57
Mirzaei, Motahhare, 10
Momtazi, Saeedeh, 52

Pezzelle, Sandro, 24
Pirhadi, Mohammad Javad, 10

Raja, Sana Javaid, 1

Sabouri, Sadra, 52
Shariati Motlagh, Shahriar, 52
Shoaib, Aqsa, 1
Sinha, Neelabh, 76
Sun, Tao, 40

Wu, I-Chen, 57

Zafar, Adeel, 1

Association for Computational Linguistics
209 N. Eighth Street
Stroudsburg, Pennsylvania 18360

ISBN 979-8-3313-1365-4

9 798331 313654

CURRAN ASSOCIATES INC.
proceedings
.com